THE SERMON ON THE MOUNT
AND ITS JEWISH SETTING

ISSN 0575-0741

CAHIERS DE LA REVUE BIBLIQUE

60

THE SERMON ON THE MOUNT AND ITS JEWISH SETTING

edited by

Hans-Jürgen BECKER

and

Serge RUZER

PARIS
J. GABALDA et Cie Éditeurs
Rue Pierre et Marie Curie, 18
—
2005

ISBN : 2-85021-165-5
ISSN : 0575-0741

CONTENTS

Introduction   v-ix

Part One

Jörg FREY
The Character and Background of Matt 5:25-26: On the Value
    of Qumran Literature in New Testament Interpretation   3-39

Hermann LICHTENBERGER
Makarisms in Matthew 5:3ff. in Their Jewish Context   40-56

Hans-Jürgen BECKER
Matthew, the Rabbis and Billerbeck
    on the Kingdom of Heaven   57-69

Berndt SCHALLER
The Character and Function of the Antitheses in Matt 5:21-48
    in the Light of Rabbinical Exegetic Disputes   70-88

Serge RUZER
Antitheses in Matthew 5: Midrashic Aspects of
    Exegetical Techniques   89-116

Menahem KISTER
Words and Formulae in the Gospels in the Light of
    Hebrew and Aramaic Sources   117-147

Part Two

Serge RUZER and Mila GINSBURSKAYA
Matt 6:1-18: Collation of Two Avenues
   to God's Forgiveness   151-177

   APPENDIX: Sources   178-242

Index of Ancient Sources   245-259

Contributors   261-263

INTRODUCTION

This volume had its beginnings in the summer of 1999, when a group of scholars from Israel, Germany and the United States met in Jerusalem to exchange ideas on the New Testament's relationship to other ancient Jewish sources and discuss the requirements for an updated systematic assessment of the issue. In the course of these discussions, the *Kommentar zum Neuen Testament aus Talmud und Midrasch* by H. L. Strack and P. Billerbeck was a constant point of reference. There was complete agreement that, notwithstanding the great achievements of the *Kommentar* in its own time, research over the past few decades has not only widened our perspective on ancient Judaism, owing to the availability of new sources, but also changed our way of analyzing and evaluating the texts, to such an extent that methodological reflections beyond Billerbeck were obviously required to attain a defensible basis for comparative study. The predominant research fields of the participants in our first colloquium pointed to two main avenues to achieving a better interpretation of the New Testament: the texts from Qumran and rabbinic literature. Both are bodies of texts highly relevant to an adequate understanding of the New Testament's Jewish setting, though one may say that since the discoveries in the Judean Desert scholars have become more reluctant to use rabbinic materials in studying earliest Christianity. At a time when the rabbinic tradition, with all its limitations, was the main source of our knowledge with regard to Palestinian Jewry in the late Second Temple period, those interested in the Jewish setting of the New Testament had little choice but to study the often anachronistic evidence of rabbinic literature. Now that we have at our disposal scrolls that were actually read – possibly widely read – in the Land of Israel in the first century CE, rabbinic literature is more easily neglected. But even if the relevant Qumran texts precede the development of early Christianity, the methodological problems in using them for New Testament interpretation are hardly less daunting than those pertaining to the rabbinic texts. In both cases, the eclectic consideration of isolated passages without a comprehensive evaluation of the respective literatures and without a clarification of the hermeneutical approach will not do justice to either of the corpora in question. The participants in the Jerusalem discussions felt there was a need for a systematic, even if selective, attempt to define and apply some essential guidelines for relating New Testament texts to other Jewish sources in a responsible way.

That first meeting in the summer of 1999 inspired the beginning (in 2000) of a project entitled *A Jerusalem Companion to the New Testament from Jewish Sources*, to be principally conducted by two research teams, one from the Hebrew University of Jerusalem and the other from the University of Göttingen. Financial support was generously provided by the Land Niedersachsen and by the Robert Bosch Stiftung. The work on this project has gone in two major directions. The first may be described as reflection on and clarification of methodological problems – such as the search for a meaningful definition of "Jewish setting," or the core problem of the relevance (or irrelevance) of rabbinic materials for New Testament studies. These problems continued to be elaborated upon, inter alia, at two international colloquia convened for that purpose in Jerusalem in 2000 and 2002 and in the course of additional meetings on a smaller scale held both in Israel and in Germany. The other direction of the project has been the work on selected New Testament issues, aiming to present some preliminary results in the format of topic-oriented commentary units. This thematically oriented approach reflects a basic assumption that in light of the multifaceted nature of late Second Temple Judaism, more general matters of concern and patterns of religious discourse rather than specific pronouncements or opinions would represent the common ground.

INTRODUCTION

A considerable number of papers, reflecting methodological concerns or aiming directly at the interpretation of New Testament texts in the light of other Jewish sources, were presented at the two Jerusalem colloquia. We are grateful to the colleagues who contributed to the project by presenting their studies and reflections: Gary Anderson (Harvard-Notre Dame), Hans Dieter Betz (Chicago), Randall Buth (Jerusalem), Jörg Frey (Munich), John Gager (Princeton), Petra Heldt and Menahem Hirshman (Jerusalem), Hermann Lichtenberger (Tübingen), Malcolm Lowe, Emmanuelle Main, Frederic Manns and Doron Mendels (Jerusalem), Gerbern S. Oegema (Tübingen), David Satran (Jerusalem), Berndt Schaller (Göttingen), Daniel Schwartz, Shaul Shaked and Daniel Stökl Ben Ezra (Jerusalem), Justin Taylor (Jerusalem-Rome) and Florian Wilk (Göttingen). Our special thanks go to Guy G. Stroumsa (Jerusalem), who from the start supported us in both word and deed.

This volume presents but a portion of the work on the project. We decided it should focus on a particular cluster of traditions; thus these are selected papers dealing with the Sermon on the Mount. Part One includes five studies suggesting updated reassessments of the question of the New Testament's Jewish setting with regard to individual sayings (Jörg Frey, Hermann Lichtenberger), a general topic (Hans-Jürgen Becker), and exegetical patterns (Berndt Schaller, Serge Ruzer) attested in the Sermon. The *status quaestionis* as well as pertinent methodological problems are discussed. In the studies by Frey and Lichtenberger, "contextualization" is achieved in light of the Qumran texts, apocryphal and pseudepigraphic literature and available historical data. While Frey leaves the rabbinic sources out of consideration, for Lichtenberger they provide an indication of the later reappearance, *mutatis mutandis*, of the patterns under discussion. Becker emphasizes the necessity of analyzing the Matthean text and the rabbinic evidence separately, each in their own right and context. Yet he holds that when this job is done, the resulting knowledge of tendencies and matters of concern in rabbinic sources may lead to a deeper understanding of Matthew's redactional work. Schaller and Ruzer, in different ways, try to discern elements of rabbinic tradition that even in this age of extreme caution may still reasonably be used for illuminating the New Testament Jewish milieu. The sixth study, by Menahem Kister, was not conducted as part of the deliberations on the methodological foundations of the project and is less obliged to them, and it pertains only partially to the Sermon on the Mount. Yet we are glad to include it in this volume, since it aims at reconstructing the possible Hebrew *Vorlage* of New Testament traditions – undoubtedly a tentative but "classical" way of dealing with their original setting.

In Part Two some results of the work, done by the research team associated with the Hebrew University Center for the Study of Christianity, are presented in the format of a condensed, topic-oriented commentary ("companion unit"). Its distinguishing features are the shortened bibliographical references, dictated by the need for brevity, and the extensive sources section. The authors, Serge Ruzer and Mila Ginsburskaya, concentrate on the basic patterns and problems of religious thought underlying Matthew 6:1-18, with a distinctive emphasis on "mapping" the pericope as early witness to more general trends that have their origins in the Second Temple period but are attested in their fully developed forms only later in rabbinic literature. New Testament materials are seen here as "missing links" in the long trajectories of ancient Jewish thought. The discussion is designed with two main groups of addressees in mind: New Testament students who wish to view religious and literary phenomena of earliest Christianity in their appropriate Jewish framework, and students of late Second Temple or rabbinic literature who wish to widen their outlook through consideration of relevant New Testament evidence.

The authors of this volume used different standards of references to the sources and transliteration of Hebrew words and names. Although we strived to introduce a certain degree of uniformity, we did not interfere with explicit personal idiosyncrasies and preferences. The authors are responsible for content, form, and style of their articles.

Finally, we wish to express our appreciation of the contributions made by Shmuel Ben-Or, Mila Ginsburskaya and Ulrike Kämpf – in both research and practical assistance. We also wish to thank Evelyn Katrak for her sensitive and diligent English editing of the volume and Sergey Minov, who prepared the book for print.

Göttingen and Jerusalem, October 2004

Hans-Jürgen Becker
Serge Ruzer

PART ONE

Jörg FREY

THE CHARACTER AND BACKGROUND OF MATT 5:25-26:
ON THE VALUE OF QUMRAN LITERATURE IN NEW TESTAMENT
INTERPRETATION *

A new, comprehensive collection of parallels to and explanations of the New Testament from Jewish sources is a major challenge for scholarship on the history of religions. The work should be able to replace the work of Strack–Billerbeck,[1] with its wealth of information, because in spite of its merits Billerbeck's collection is not only outdated but also controversial on account of its persistent theological or ideological bias against the piety of rabbinic Judaism.[2] Of course, Billerbeck's huge work has provided many

---

* Paper delivered in July 2000 at the Jerusalem conference and in March 2003 at the Reformed Theological Faculty of the University of Potchefstroom (South Africa). I am greatly indebted to Nadine Kessler and Dr. Jutta Leonhardt-Balzer (Munich) for several suggestions regarding content and language.

[1] H. L. STRACK and P. BILLERBECK, *Kommentar zum Neuen Testament aus Talmud und Midrasch*, 5 vols. (Munich: Beck, 1926-28).

[2] Billerbeck's own view is inspired by traditional Lutheran theology and by the earlier interpretation of rabbinic Judaism by Ferdinand WEBER. So he often fails to appreciate the intention or the context of the texts he quotes. This is noticeable chiefly in the explanations and articles in vols. 4/1-4/2 – for example, in the passage on the soteriological "system" of the Synagogue

exegetes unable to read rabbinic sources with a wealth of texts from all parts of talmudic and midrashic literature. But in view of more recent research, that unclassified collection of texts is objectionable because it ignores the chronological distinctions established in more recent critical scholarship. In historical interpretation, neither the New Testament nor the Talmud and Midrashim can be read as a unity or a coherent "system" of thought. The historical and tradition-historical analysis of rabbinic texts poses numerous problems; yet an attempt must be made to distinguish between earlier and later strata in the traditions.[3] In the search for Jewish parallels that might explain the teachings of Jesus and his followers in the first century CE, traditions originating in the fifth or sixth century may be worthless or even completely misleading. So, from the mass of texts provided by Billerbeck (and other compendia), only traditions deriving from the early period of rabbinic Judaism, or even from pre-rabbinic traditions, can be used as valid parallels to the New Testament.

Furthermore, Billerbeck's sourcebook is by no means sufficient, since Judaism in New Testament times is not equivalent to

---

(vol. 4/1, 3-33) and on the teachings on reward (vol. 4/1, 484-500). See also now F. AVEMARIE, *Tora und Leben. Untersuchungen zur Heilsbedeutung der Tora in der frühen rabbinischen Literatur*, TSAJ 55 (Tübingen: Mohr Siebeck, 1996), 12-19 (on Weber and Billerbeck). Avemarie's magisterial monograph shows how views have changed since Billerbeck. Even though he is also a Lutheran theologian, his thorough analysis of the tannaitic sources draws a completely different picture of early rabbinic soteriology.

[3] See G. STEMBERGER, *Einleitung in Talmud und Midrasch*, 8th ed. (Munich: Beck, 1992); and the introduction in P. SCHÄFER, *Studien zur Geschichte und Theologie des rabbinischen Judentums*, AGJU 15 (Leiden: E. J. Brill, 1978), 1-8. For rabbinic soteriology, see the work by AVEMARIE (above, n. 2). For the traditions on miracles and miracle workers, see the most recent study by M. BECKER, *Wunder und Wundertäter im frührabbinischen Judentum. Studien zum Phänomen und seiner Überlieferung im Horizont von Magie und Dämonismus*, WUNT II/144 (Tübingen: Mohr Siebeck, 2002).

rabbinic Judaism. Only as an exception does Billerbeck refer to some non-rabbinic sources – for example, from the *Book of Jubilees* or *4 Ezra* – but these references seem to be quite accidental. Parallels from Hellenistic Judaism that are quite important for the interpretation of many New Testament authors are completely omitted. However, the most obvious shortcoming of Billerbeck's work is that the texts from Qumran and the other sites near the Dead Sea were not able to be included, given that the Dead Sea Scrolls were found only in 1947 and thereafter.[4]

In any attempt to adduce parallels to New Testament texts from Jewish sources, the relevance of the texts from the Qumran library cannot be underestimated. Many premature hypotheses on the relationship between the Qumran community and early Christian groups have been proposed, most of which must be dismissed in the light of sober scholarship.[5] Nevertheless, the discovery and release of the Dead Sea Scrolls has dramatically changed the situation, since the texts from the Qumran library provide a new set of sources for the understanding of Palestinian Judaism at the turn of the era. Before the Qumran finds, practically no Hebrew or Aramaic documents from Palestinian Judaism from the time before 70 CE existed. Scholars would take their views from the Gospels, the Maccabean literature, the various Pseudepigrapha, the writings of Josephus and Philo, and especially from later rabbinic sources.

---

[4] But even the Damascus Document, which was found in the Cairo Geniza and edited in 1910, was not included in Billerbeck's collection; see the index to his work: H. L. STRACK and P. BILLERBECK, *Kommentar zum Neuen Testament aus Talmud und Midrasch 5-6: Rabbinischer Index. Verzeichnis der Schriftgelehrten. Geographisches Register*, J. JEREMIAS (ed.) (Munich: Beck, 1963).

[5] See the critical discussion of different hypotheses in J. FREY, "Die Bedeutung der Qumranfunde für das Verständnis des Neuen Testaments," in M. FIEGER, K. SCHMID and P. SCHWAGMEIER (eds.), *Qumran – Die Schriftrollen vom Toten Meer. Vorträge des St. Galler Qumran-Symposiums vom 2./3. Juli 1999*, NTOA 47 (Freiburg/Göttingen: Universitätsverlag/Vandenhoeck & Ruprecht, 2001), 129-208, esp. 133-52.

Influenced by the rabbinic view, some scholars spoke of a "normative type" of Palestinian Judaism as the background of Jesus and early Christianity.[6] In view of the documents from Qumran, this view has changed completely. We now have a mass of non-biblical texts originating between the third century BCE and the first century CE written not merely by a small "sectarian" group but representing a rich diversity of theological traditions. It is therefore possible to interpret Jesus and early Christianity not just against the foil of a single "normative" type of Judaism, but within a wider range of traditions and discussions of their Jewish contemporaries. And many ideas and terms in the New Testament previously classified as non-Jewish, Hellenistic, syncretistic or even Gnostic can now be explained from the multitude of Jewish traditions evidenced in the Qumran library.[7]

This paper is intended to be a case study of the value of the Qumran texts for interpreting the New Testament. As a test case, I will take a small, often neglected piece of the Sermon on the Mount: the saying on reconciliation before the judgment in Matt 5:25-26, which is now embedded in the first antithesis, Matt 5:21-26. At first glance, the passage appears to be "a strange saying which is

---

[6] Thus, for example, G. F. MOORE, *Judaism in the First Centuries of the Christian Era: The Age of the Tannaim*, 3 vols. (Cambridge, Mass.: Harvard University Press, 1927-30), vol. 1, 125, and vol. 3, v-vii. Despite the differences between Moore and Billerbeck, the two scholars largely agree in their view that rabbinic Judaism provides an adequate picture of "mainstream" Judaism in Jesus' times.

[7] The Pauline antithesis between "flesh" and "spirit," for example, was earlier explained largely on the basis of Hellenism or Hellenistic Judaism; but it has closer parallels not only in some Qumran "sectarian" texts such as the *Hodayot* and the final psalm in 1QS XI but also in some of the recently published sapiential texts from Qumran. See J. FREY, "Die paulinische Antithese von Fleisch und Geist und die palästinisch-jüdische Weisheitstradition," *ZNW* 90 (1999), 45-77; idem, "The Notion of 'Flesh' in 4QInstruction and the Background of Pauline Usage," in D. FALK, F. GARCÍA MARTÍNEZ and E. SCHULLER (eds.), *Sapiential, Poetical and Liturgical Texts: Proceedings of the 3rd Meeting of the IOQS, Oslo 1998,* STJD 35 (Leiden: Brill, 2000), 197-226.

not easily explained."⁸ In the light of some "new" sapiential parallels from the Qumran library, I will try to describe the sociohistorical background of the passage that can be seen in the problem of debts and the need for their quick repayment. The Matthean version – but perhaps also the parallel in Luke, which goes back to the Sayings Source – draws on some piece of sapiential advice concerning debts, sureties and the danger of debt imprisonment. It should be assumed that such problems were of considerable importance for many people in first-century Palestine, in the time of Jesus and in the period of the early Christian community.

1. THE MATT 5:25-26 "COURT SCENE" IN ITS MATTHEAN CONTEXT

In scholarly commentaries on Matthew or the Sermon on the Mount, the two applications or illustrations of the first antithesis, Matt 5:23-24 and 25-26, are often commented on only very briefly.⁹ But this relatively minor interest seems unjustified: Even if the

---

[8] S. VAN TILBORG, *The Sermon on the Mount as an Ideological Intervention* (Assen/Maastricht/Wolfeboro: van Gorcum, 1986), 56.

[9] See the very brief comments in W. GRUNDMANN, *Das Evangelium nach Matthäus*, THKNT 1 (Berlin: Evangelische Verlagsanstalt, 1968), 157-58; E. SCHWEIZER, *Das Evangelium nach Matthäus*, NTD 1 (Göttingen: Vandenhoeck & Ruprecht, 1976), 72-73; U. LUZ, *Das Evangelium nach Matthäus. 1. Teilband Matthäus 1–7*, EKK 1,1 (Zurich: Benziger, 1985), 259-60 (see now the completely revised 5th edition [Düsseldorf/Zürich: Benziger, and Neukirchen-Vluyn: Neukirchener, 2002], 345-46, with an extended and slightly modified interpretation); J. GNILKA, *Das Matthäusevangelium*, Part 1, HTKNT 1,1 (Freiburg/Basel/Vienna: Herder, 1986), 155-57; G. STRECKER, *Die Bergpredigt. Ein exegetischer Kommentar* (Göttingen: Vandenhoeck & Ruprecht, 1984), 70-72; D. A. HAGNER, *Matthew 1–13*, WBC 33A (Dallas: Word, 1993), 117-18. The verses are totally neglected in H. FRANKEMÖLLE, *Matthäus Kommentar*, vol. 1 (Düsseldorf: Patmos, 1994). A more thorough commentary is given only in E. LOHMEYER and W. SCHMAUCH, *Das Evangelium des Matthäus*, KEK (Sonderband/Göttingen: Vandenhoeck & Ruprecht, 1956), 121-25; H. WEDER, *Die 'Rede der Reden'. Eine Auslegung der Bergpredigt heute* (Zurich: Theologischer Verlag, 1985), 108-11; W. D. DA-

two short cases might be later additions to the original antithesis in Matt 5:21-22, the Synoptic parallels[10] show that they must have been taken from an older tradition. In the present context, "they were not chosen without reason."[11] They illustrate the commandment against uncontrolled anger (Matt 5:22) and affirm the necessity for reconciliation. The illustration is given from two different real-life situations concerning matters of cult (Matt 5:23-24) and court (Matt 5:25-26), as shown by the compositional structure of the first antithesis, "on murder" (Matt 5:21-26):[12]

A	**Antithesis**	**vv. 21-22**
A1	Traditional teaching (command / punishment)	v. 21
A2	Jesus' teaching	v. 22
	First assertion (infraction / punishment)	v. 22a
	Second assertion (infraction / punishment)	v. 22b
	Third assertion (infraction / punishment)	v. 22c
B	**Two Illustrations**	**vv. 23-26**
B1	First illustration	vv. 23-24
	Situation (conditional)	v. 23
	Action commanded (imperative)	v. 24
B2	Second illustration	vv. 25-26
	Action commanded (imperative)	v. 25a
	Result of disobedience (negative final clause)	v. 25b
	Concluding announcement (threatening)	v. 26

VIES and D. C. ALLISON, *The Gospel according to Saint Matthew*, vol. 1, ICC (Edinburgh: T. & T. Clark, 1988), 516-21; H. D. BETZ, *The Sermon on the Mount*, Hermeneia (Minneapolis: Augsburg Fortress, 1995), 222-30. BILLERBECK (above, n. 1), vol. 1, 288-94, gives some explanations on synagogal courts and on different types of coins. Notably, he recognizes that the case addresses financial affairs: "Vermögensrechtliche Streitsachen" (289).

[10] See Luke 12:57-59 (on Matt 5:25-26) and Mark 11:25 (on Matt 5:23-24).
[11] BETZ, *Sermon* (above, n. 9), 222.
[12] See DAVIES and ALLISON, *Gospel* (above, n. 9), 509-10.

As the table shows, the passage consists of an antithesis (vv. 21-22) in which Jesus quotes a traditional commandment and then gives his own contrasting teaching in a triadic form. The antithesis is followed by two sayings (vv. 23-24 and 25-26), which form a kind of appendix. These sayings are not formally paralleled but are related semantically to each other and to the preceding antithesis.

In the antithesis, the traditional commandment οὐ φονεύσεις (You shall not murder) (Exod 20:15; Deut 5:18) and the reference to the due punishment (being liable to κρίσις)[13] are contrasted with the teaching of Jesus, which goes beyond the commandment of the law and demands an end to anger and hateful speech in general. In contrast to the traditional teaching, the teaching of Jesus in v. 22 has a triadic structure: three subsequent assertions pronounce the punishment due for the preceding kind of infraction. They were often thought to form a climactic structure; but this view is based neither on the three infractions mentioned (being angry, saying ῥακά and saying μωρέ)[14] nor on the series of punishments (κρίσις, συνέδριον, γέεννα) as a whole, but only on the last punishment mentioned, the judgment in the fiery hell.[15] Consequently, there is no real climax within v. 22. It is more appropriate to state that the second and third assertions form an explication of the first one.[16] The mention of the fiery hell (see Matt 18:9) in the last assertion underlines the severity of the infractions and, on the other hand, the necessity to replace anger and hatred by reconciliation. So it also prepares for the imperatives demanding reconciliation in the subsequent scenes.

---

[13] This term is open to a broad range of meanings: trial, penalty, judgment, legal proceedings, judicial sentence or the court; see DAVIES and ALLISON, *Gospel* (above, n. 9), 511. See also the discussion by S. Ruzer in this volume.

[14] ῥακά and μωρέ are "practically indistinguishable" (DAVIES and ALLISON, *Gospel* [above, n. 9], 514); they do not form a climax. See LUZ, *Evangelium 1* (above, n. 9), 252.

[15] The first punishment mentioned, ἔνοχος ἔσται τῇ κρίσει, just repeats v. 21, and only if it is understood in the sense of "local court" is it a lower court than the συνέδριον. More probably the term has the same meaning as in v. 21, where nothing suggests that it refers only to a local court.

[16] LUZ, *Evangelium 1* (above, n. 9), 253.

In contrast to vv. 21-22, which address the hearers in the second person plural and are then followed by three general conditional structures in the third person singular (πᾶς ὁ ..., ὃς δ' ἂν ...), the two illustrations address their hearers in the second person singular and with imperative forms. The two scenes differ in their narrative structure. Vv. 23-24 are wholly structured by a conditional clause. The protasis with ἐάν + present subjunctive (ἐὰν ... προσφέρῃς ... κἀκεῖ μνησθῇς ...) is continued in the apodosis in imperative forms (ἄφες ... ὕπαγε πρῶτον διαλλάγηθι ... καὶ τότε ἐλθὼν πρόσφερε ...). So a possible situation is narrated, and a command is given about how to act in this case. The hearers or readers have to change their priorities: "Leave your gift ... and go, be reconciled first ..., and then offer your gift." The priority of reconciliation over sacrifice, then, is strongly expressed.

The second scene in vv. 25-26 is structured differently. There is no narrative description of the situation at the beginning. Instead, the scene begins with an imperative form (ἴσθι εὐνοῶν τῷ ἀντιδίκῳ σου), and only at the end of the scene does it become clear that the situation is a court trial on financial matters. The structure of the scene is as follows: imperative (with a temporal complement) + negative final clause (μήποτε ...: describing the consequences of disobedience) + concluding announcement (with the opening formula ἀμὴν λέγω σοι).

Despite the different structure of the two scenes, there are several links between them: Both are shaped by the second person singular, and both contain a command regarding reconciliation or "making friends" with one's brother or opponent. They both illustrate that anger should be replaced by reconciliation. Moreover, the final threatening expression "you will never get out from there ..." (v. 26) may remind the reader of the mention of the γέεννα τοῦ πυρός in v. 22c.[17] The scenes are thus also linked with the preceding antithesis.

The final announcement in v. 26 has caused interpreters to understand the whole saying as a parable on the Last Judgment.[18]

---

[17] See DAVIES and ALLISON, *Gospel* (above, n. 9), 521.
[18] See, for example, R. BULTMANN, *Die Geschichte der synoptischen Tradition*,

However, this interpretation gives rise to numerous problems. To mention only two of them: If the trial is basically a metaphor for the impending judgment, who is the opponent with whom the hearer or reader has to make friends "on the way"? Is it a human being, who is likely to accuse his fellow man at the Last Judgment?[19] Is the opponent God himself,[20] or, if he is the judge, is the accuser another heavenly figure, perhaps the devil?[21] Even if exegetes infer that it is not permissible to allegorize a simple parable,[22] the question remains open and provides an argument against the interpretation of the scene as a mere parable of the Parousia. Another problem is even more compelling: Should anyone get out of the fiery hell by repaying his last quarter-penny? If this idea is thought to be impossible, then why does v. 26 speak in such concrete terms? Or is the meaning that the saying should be understood in a real-life, not a parabolic, sense?

2. INTERPRETING THE SCENE IN MATTHEW AND LUKE

The parabolic and eschatological interpretation of Matt 5:25-26 was mainly inspired by the Synoptic parallel in Luke 12:58-59, where the scene on the court trial is embedded in the context of

---

2nd ed., FRLANT 29 (Göttingen: Vandenhoeck & Ruprecht, 1931), 185, on Luke 12:57-59: "ein aus einem Bildwort entwickeltes Gleichnis"; J. JEREMIAS, *Die Gleichnisse Jesu* 9th ed. (Göttingen: Vandenhoeck & Ruprecht, 1977), 40: "Krisisgleichnis"; WEDER, *Rede* (above, n. 9), 109.

[19] J. SCHNIEWIND, *Das Evangelium nach Matthäus*, NTD 2 (Göttingen: Vandenhoeck & Ruprecht, 1936), 61.

[20] S. SCHULZ, *Q – Die Spruchquelle der Evangelisten* (Zurich: Theologischer Verlag, 1972), 423-24.

[21] E. KLOSTERMANN, *Das Lukasevangelium*, 2nd ed., HNT 3 (Tübingen: Mohr Siebeck, 1929), 141.

[22] From a rigorously critical viewpoint this question might be rejected by pointing out that every "pure" parable has only one point of comparison. But such scholarly "orthodoxy" seems inappropriate to many of the parables. See, for example, on recent developments in parable research, K. ERLEMANN, *Gleichnisauslegung*, UTB 2003 (Tübingen/Basel: Francke, 1999).

other eschatological parables (Luke 12:35-48) and sayings – for example, on the impending division within houses and families (12:51-53) or discerning the time (12:54-56). For this reason, Joachim Jeremias claimed that the saying is an eschatological parable of the κρίσις (Krisisgleichnis).[23] Of course he observes that Matthew uses the scene as an instruction for everyday life; but in his view, Luke has preserved its original setting, whereas Matthew attests to a shift of emphasis from eschatology to exhortation.[24] So he comments on the Matthean version that the motivation of the instruction "sounds dangerously commonplace."[25] This remark reveals that Jeremias' reconstruction depends largely on his overall picture of the (strongly eschatological) teaching of Jesus and the interpretative (de-eschatologizing) tendencies in early Christianity. The more eschatological version, then, is likely to be authentic, whereas commonplace instructions are suspected of originating in the de-eschatologizing and moralizing tendencies of the early Church. And, of course, an eschatological motivation for the advice is theologically legitimate, whereas a piece of advice from everyday life or even a merely casuistic instruction would be less valuable, even "dangerous."[26]

---

[23] JEREMIAS, *Gleichnisse* (above, n. 18), 40: "Es kann kein Zweifel darüber bestehen, daß Lukas recht hat: wir haben ein eschatologisches Gleichnis vor uns, ein Krisisgleichnis." Interestingly, the classification is even adopted by Klaus Berger: see H. D. PREUSS and K. BERGER, *Bibelkunde des Alten und Neuen Testaments*, vol. 2, UTB 972 (Heidelberg/Wiesbaden: Quelle & Mayer, 1980), 251 (on Matt 5:25-26). In K. BERGER, *Formgeschichte des Neuen Testaments* ([Heidelberg: Quelle & Mayer, 1984], 57), Luke 12:57-59 is characterized as "Gleichnis-Diskurs."

[24] JEREMIAS, *Gleichnisse* (above, n.18), 40. See also W. D. DAVIES, *The Setting of the Sermon on the Mount* (Cambridge: Cambridge University Press, 1963), 384.

[25] JEREMIAS, *Gleichnisse* (above, n. 18), 40: "daß die Motivierung dieser Weisung gefährlich alltäglich klingt."

[26] See also A. SCHLATTER, *Der Evangelist Matthäus*, 7th ed. (Stuttgart: Calwer, 1982), 174, who considers the prudential interpretation of Matt 5:25f. but infers: "In dieser Fassung sinkt aber der Spruch, weil er sich der Kasuistik

The predominant view is disputed by, among others, Joseph Fitzmyer, who criticizes "the tendency of modern commentators to allegorize the would-be parable ... and interpret Jesus' words in terms of a greater Lucan context."[27] Fitzmyer not only points to the traces of Lucan redaction in Luke 12:58-59; he also states that "the Matthean setting is really more apt" for these verses.[28] So he can say that the episode "is a piece of prudential advice, stemming from Jesus, which has lost its specific reference and is best interpreted even here as no more than that."[29]

Fitzmyer's view of the Lucan version is important also for interpreting the scene in Matthew. He can show that the context in Luke does not demand a parabolic understanding. Although some eschatological passages precede the verses (such as the parable 12:35-48 and the sayings 12:49-50, 51-53 and 54-56), their semantic connection with Luke 12:58-59 remains uncertain.[30] The preceding verse, Luke 12:57, is likely to be a redactional transition[31] intended to connect vv. 54-56 with vv. 58-59 and to introduce vv. 58-59. In contrast to these verses, which are phrased in the second person singular, in v. 57 the second person plural is used. It is unlikely therefore that v. 57 served as the original introduction to vv. 58-59 in the Lucan tradition.[32] Instead, it is more plausible that

---

nähert, unter die vorangehenden und die folgenden Sätze hinab, die nicht Einzelheiten ordnen, sondern das ganze Verhalten der Jünger vom inwendigen Vorgang aus reinigen."

[27] J. A. FITZMYER, *The Gospel according to Luke X–XXIV*, AncB 28A (New York: Doubleday, 1985), 1002.

[28] Ibid., 1001.

[29] Ibid., 1002.

[30] Fitzmyer even thinks that the topic is "completely unrelated" (ibid., 1001).

[31] See already BULTMANN, *Geschichte* (above, n. 18), 95 and 185-86; SCHULZ, *Q* (above, n. 20), 421; J. JEREMIAS, *Die Sprache des Lukasevangeliums*, KEK Sonderband (Göttingen: Vandenhoeck & Ruprecht, 1980), 224; J. NOLLAND, *Luke 1:1 – 24:53*, 3 vols., WBC 35A-C (Dallas: Word, 1989-1993), vol. 2, 714.

[32] This is D. L. BOCK's argument, *Luke 9:51 – 24:53*, Baker Exegetical Commentary on the New Testament 3B (Grand Rapids, Mich.: Baker, 1998), 1198. A different view has been put forward by H. SCHÜRMANN, "Sprachli-

Luke himself created the link with a specific address to his readers, who are called upon to judge for themselves what τὸ δίκαιον (the right thing) is. Luke himself, then, seems to point to the ethical consequences for his readers as a result of their insight concerning the "time" (v. 56). Does this mean that Luke himself understood the saying in vv. 58-59 in predominantly ethical terms?[33]

Regarding the subsequent passage, Luke 13:1-5, we can see that there is also a redactional link in v. 1.[34] Vv. 1-5 then comment on an incident from history, the murder of certain Galilean pilgrims by Pilate. This incident is interpreted in eschatological terms (see 13:3-5) and conditioned by a short parable on the coming judgment (13:6-9). Both passages are drawn from Luke's own tradition, not from the Sayings Source, and because Luke 13:1 is a redactional transition shaped by Luke himself, the passage cannot provide a firm basis for the understanding of Luke 12:58-59. At most, we can say that Luke has put the two verses into a context with some eschatological elements. But since Luke 12:57 and 13:1 are redactional transitions, the pre-Lucan meaning of Luke 12:58-59 cannot be discerned from Luke's context.

The context in Luke does not provide a compelling argument to understand Luke 12:58-59 (or Matt 5:25-26) as a parable of the Parousia. The question is, then, whether such an argument can be drawn from the probable pre-Lucan context.

Usually, Matt 5:25-26 and Luke 12:58-59 are attributed to the Sayings Source (Q).[35] However, due to the remarkable differences

---

che Reminiszenzen an abgeänderte Bestandteile der Redenquelle im Lukas- und Matthäusevangelium," in idem, *Traditionsgeschichtliche Untersuchungen* (Düsseldorf: Patmos, 1968), 111-26, esp. 116; he is supported by C. P. MÄRZ, "Lk 12,54b-56 par Mt 16,2b.3 und die Akoluthie der Redenquelle," *SNTU* 11 (1986), 83-96, esp. 87.

[33] See F. BOVON, *Das Evangelium nach Lukas. 2. Teilband: Lukas 9,51– 14,53*, EKK 3,2 (Zurich/Düsseldorf: Benziger and Neukirchen/Vluyn: Neukirchener Verlag, 1996), 361-62.

[34] On the redactional elements in v. 1, see JEREMIAS, *Sprache* (above, n. 31), 226-28.

[35] See most recently J. M. ROBINSON, P. HOFFMANN and J. S. KLOPPENBORG (eds.), *The Critical Edition of Q* (Leuven: Peeters, 2000), 394-99; P. SELLEW,

between the Lucan and Matthean versions, not all interpreters accept the view that the two parallel passages both depend on Q. Most recently, two commentators, François Bovon and Darrell L. Bock, have suggested that only the passage in Matthew comes from the Sayings Source, whereas the Lucan version was transmitted by Luke's own tradition (Sondergut).[36]

It is not the purpose of this paper to enter into the complicated discussion on the shape and development of the Sayings Source. For the present purpose I would like to presuppose that the source existed, possibly in two different versions (Q^{Lk} and Q^{Mt}). Even though we can never preclude that the influence of other written or oral traditions could have shaped one or other version, we can take the Q-hypothesis as a starting hypothesis and then see how far we get with these assumptions.

The first problem, however, is the text sequence in Q. Most interpreters assume that Luke has largely maintained the text sequence he found in his sources.[37] Only such a presupposition can provide a basis for reconstructing the text sequence in Q. However, there can be no certainty in such assumptions, since there are also passages for which scholars have suggested that Matthew might have maintained the Q order more adequately than Luke.[38] Most of the interpreters who accept that Luke 12:58-59 comes from the Sayings Source assume that Luke 12:49-59 draws on a text sequence in the source (then called Q 12:49-59).[39] But questions

---

"Reconstruction of Q 12:33-59," in *Society of Biblical Literature, Seminar Papers*, vol. 26 (Atlanta, Ga.: Scholars Press, 1987), 645-68, esp. 661-62. On the discussion in detail, see J. M. ROBINSON, S. CARRUTH and A. GARSKY (eds.), *Q 12:49–59*, Documenta Q (Leuven: Peeters, 1997).

[36] See BOVON, *Evangelium* (above, n. 33), 348; BOCK, *Luke* (above, n. 32), 1190 and 1198-99. According to BOCK, not only vv. 58-59 come from Luke's tradition but also v. 57.

[37] See J. M. ROBINSON, "The Sequence of Q: The Lament over Jerusalem," in R. HOPPE and U. BUSSE (eds.), *Von Jesus zum Christus: Christologische Studien. Festgabe für Paul Hoffmann zum 65. Geburtstag*, BZNW 93 (Berlin/New York: de Gruyter, 1998), 225-60, esp. 226.

[38] Ibid., 227-32.

[39] See *Edition* (above, n. 35), 376-99; or, for example, C.-P. März, "Feuer auf

remain regarding the verses not paralleled in Matthew (Luke 12:50, 52, 57) and the text sequence. If Luke 12:57 is a redactional link inserted by Luke to introduce the traditional vv. 58-59, we cannot ascertain how the episode on the court trial was connected with the sayings on knowing the time in pre-Lucan tradition. Was the "bridge" between vv. 54-56 and vv. 58-59 formed by a slightly different transition,[40] or was there no transition at all? Or were vv. 58-59 taken from another context in the Sayings Source,[41] or even – as is sometimes assumed – from another source? These problems cannot be discussed here, but the questions show how uncertain are all the considerations regarding the text sequence and shape, not to mention the development and redactional history of the Sayings Source.[42] For the present purpose it must suffice to state that even the context in Q cannot provide a compelling argument for assuming that Luke 12:58-59 originally was an eschatological parable. Rather, the Lucan introduction in Luke 12:57 might have caused exegetes to understand the scene as a parable of the impending κρίσις or the Parousia.[43]

---

die Erde zu werfen, bin ich gekommen... Zum Verständnis und zur Entstehung von Lk 12,49," in *A cause de l'Evangile. Études sur les Synoptiques et les Actes offertes au J. Dupont*, LeDiv 123 (Paris: Cerf, 1985), 479-511, esp. 500; A. KIRK, *The Composition of the Sayings Source: Genre, Synchrony, and Wisdom Redaction in Q*, NTSup 91 (Leiden/Boston/Cologne: Brill, 1998), 238-41.

[40] For an attempt to interpret Luke 12:54-59 as a coherent unit within the Sayings Source, see H. SCHÜRMANN, "Sprachliche Reminiszenzen" (above, n. 32), p. 116f.; he wants to reconstruct an original connection between διακρίνειν (in Luke 12:54-56*; cf. Matt 16:3) and κρίνειν (in Luke 12:57). But for this argument, he has to assume that Luke changed from διακρίνειν to δοκιμάζειν. So the reconstruction remains quite implausible.

[41] Interestingly, the International Q Project leaves this possibility open; see *Edition* (above, n. 35), 394 n. 1.

[42] I remain therefore quite skeptical regarding the numerous attempts to determine not only the content and wording of the Sayings Source but also its possible stages of development. They are too hypothetical to allow of firm conclusions.

[43] See LUZ, *Evangelium* 1 (above, n. 9), 252.

3. The original form: A prudential advice, not a parable

In view of the above mentioned problems, it might be almost impossible to reconstruct an original text from the two preserved versions.[44] Of course, such an enterprise could provide only a hypothetical "virtual" text. Even so, a comparison of the versions may help us glean some information on the structure and function of the text in the earlier tradition.

Matt 5:25f.	*Luke 12:58f.*
ἴσθι εὐνοῶν τῷ ἀντιδίκῳ σου ταχύ,	ὡς γὰρ ὑπάγεις μετὰ τοῦ ἀντιδίκου σου ἐπ' ἄρχοντά
ἕως ὅτου εἶ μετ' αὐτοῦ ἐν τῇ ὁδῷ,	ἐν τῇ ὁδῷ δὸς ἐργασίαν ἀπηλλάχθαι ἀπ' αὐτοῦ,
μήποτέ σε παραδῷ ὁ ἀντίδικος τῷ κριτῇ καὶ ὁ κριτὴς τῷ ὑπηρέτῃ	μήποτε κατασύρῃ σε πρὸς τὸν κριτήν καὶ ὁ κριτής σε παραδώσει τῷ πράκτορι,
καὶ εἰς φυλακὴν βληθήσῃ·	καὶ ὁ πράκτωρ σε βαλεῖ εἰς φυλακήν.
ἀμὴν λέγω σοι,	λέγω σοι,
οὐ μὴ ἐξέλθῃς ἐκεῖθεν,	οὐ μὴ ἐξέλθῃς ἐκεῖθεν,
ἕως ἂν ἀποδῷς τὸν ἔσχατον κοδράντην.	ἕως καὶ τὸ ἔσχατον λεπτὸν ἀποδῷς.

---

[44] H. T. Wrege, *Die Überlieferungsgeschichte der Bergpredigt*, WUNT 9 (Tübingen: Mohr Siebeck, 1968), 61-64, rejects the reconstruction of a common written source. See also ibid., 62: "Von einer gemeinsamen, schriftlichen Vorlage findet sich hier keine Spur"; ibid., 63: "das Gleichnis ... ist demnach in zwei von einander unabhängigen Fassungen umgelaufen." See, in addition, Bovon, *Evangelium* (above, n. 33), 349; R. Piper, *Wisdom in the Q*

The synopsis shows that there are many differences, not only in the wording but also in the word order or sentence structure. There are more words in common in the second and third part of the scene than at the beginning, where the correspondence is limited to the term ἀντίδικος + pronoun and to the phrase ἐν τῇ ὁδῷ. So only the end of the passage provides any plausibility to the assumption of a written source of the scene,[45] and we are entitled to ask which alterations might be due to the evangelists.

It is somewhat plausible that Matthew added ἀμὴν in v. 26.[46] He also seems to have inserted ἂν and dropped the καὶ from the source. Luke might have moved the verb to the end.[47] Quite interesting is the difference in the coins: In Matthew it is a quadrans (κοδράντη), whereas Luke mentions a λεπτόν, the smallest denomination of all, with a value of half a quadrans (see Mark 12:42). Both coins were common in Palestine at the time of Jesus, and it is difficult to decide which of them might have been mentioned in the earliest version of the text. There are however some arguments for the view that the quadrans is the original and that Luke tried to

---

Tradition, SNTSMS 61 (Cambridge: Cambridge University Press, 1989), 105: "Considerable differences in the formulation, context and function of this logion in Matthew and Luke hinder attempts to gain a clear understanding of its use in the underlying tradition." Other exegetes have suggested a reconstruction of the text of the Sayings Source. See S. SCHULZ, *Q* (above, n. 20), 258-60; D. ZELLER, *Die weisheitlichen Mahnsprüche bei den Synoptikern*, FzB 17 (Würzburg: Echter, 1983), 64-65; or, finally, the reconstruction proposed by the International Q-Project in *Edition* (above, n. 35), 394-99.

[45] Thus DAVIES and ALLISON, *Gospel* (above, n. 9), 521 (on the agreement οὐ μὴ ἐξέλθῃς ἐκεῖθεν).

[46] See LUZ, *Evangelium* 1 (above, n. 9), 252. Cf., however, DAVIES and ALLISON, *Gospel* (above, n. 9), 520: "Matthew sometimes added 'amen' (Mt: 30-1; Mk: 13: Lk: 6) to his sources, Luke has sometimes dropped it from Mark so that we cannot be certain whether or not it was here in Q." Whether Matthew also inserted the ταχὺ in v. 25, as LUZ (*Evangelium 1* [above, n. 9]) suggests, cannot be ascertained.

omit the Latin loan word (as he does in Luke 21:2, par. Mark 12:42) and inserted instead the name of the coin with the very smallest value.[48]

Most interesting are the differences concerning the persons involved in the trial. The ἄρχων, mentioned only by Luke, seems to be a Lucan insertion, since Luke felt the need to tell where the two opponents "on their way together" are heading.[49] And if the ἄρχων and the κρίτης are different persons,[50] the Lucan version entails that the trial concerns two different levels of legal authority.

Both versions agree on the terms ἀντίδικος and κριτής. But Luke mentions a πράκτωρ, whereas Matthew uses the word ὑπηρέτης. It was often supposed here that Luke wanted to mention a Roman official instead of a synagogue official, as he was thinking in terms of a Roman court trial.[51] This view may be correct, but it has to be inferred that the term ὑπηρέτης was used not only for an official in Jewish synagogues but also in Hellenistic practice "to describe the court official who executed the sentence imposed by the

---

[47] See DAVIES and ALLISON, *Gospel* (above, n. 9), 521.

[48] See JEREMIAS, *Sprache* (above, n. 31), 225; and DAVIES and ALLISON, *Gospel* (above, n. 9), 521. Unconvincingly, H. MARSHALL, *The Gospel of Luke: A Commentary on the Greek Text*, NIGNT (Exeter: Paternoster, 1978), 552, argues that Luke is more likely to be original because the λεπτόν was said to be equivalent to the Jewish *p^{e}rutah* (cf. *m. Qid.* 1:1).

[49] See BOVON, *Evangelium* (above, n. 33), 362; SCHULZ, *Q* (above, n. 20), 421-22. And see already A. V. HARNACK, *Sprüche und Reden Jesu, Beiträge zur Einleitung in das Neue Testament 2* (Leipzig: Hinrichs, 1907), 43.

[50] Many exegetes thought that the "magistrate" and the "judge" should be interpreted as being the same person. See B. WEISS, *Die Evangelien des Markus und Lukas*, KEK (Göttingen: Vandenhoeck & Ruprecht, 1901), 501; BOVON, *Evangelium* (above, n. 33), 363. Cf., however, J. D. M. DERRETT, *Law in the New Testament* (London: Darton, Longman & Todd, 1970.), 183. But if Derrett thinks that the κρίτης must be God, he comes to a quite problematic understanding of the passage: see ibid., 182-82 and 186, where he refers to G. B. CAIRD, "The Defendant (Matthew 5,25f.; Luke 12,58f.)," *ExpT* 77 (1966), 36-39.

[51] See JEREMIAS, *Gleichnisse* (above, n. 18), 39 n. 3.

court."⁵² So there is no reason to conjecture that the original version must have mentioned a synagogue official. Rather, the difference between the two terms lies in the precise function of the official: A πράκτωρ was the bailiff who dealt with debts and was in charge of the debtors' prison. So Luke's version is not the result of a higher degree of Hellenization; Luke merely chose a more specific term.⁵³

On the beginning of the scene we can only speculate. Some authors think that δὸς ἐργασίαν is a Lucan term.⁵⁴ It is hardly possible to decide whether ἀπηλλάχθαι or εὐνοῦν was the original; but on the whole, it seems more likely that Matthew has preserved the original structure, with an imperative at the beginning, which Luke had to adjust to his context – or at least to his introduction in v. 57.⁵⁵ So we can cautiously assume that the word order and in some parts also the wording of the scene are retained more originally in Matthew.⁵⁶ If this is correct, it is an additional argument for the

---

[52] Thus MARSHALL, *Luke* (above, n. 48), 551. See also K. H. RENGSTORF, "ὑπερέτης κτλ.," in R. KITTEL and G. FRIEDRICH (eds.), *Theologisches Wörterbuch zum Neuen Testament,* 10 vols. (Stuttgart: Kohlhammer, 1933-79), vol. 8, 530-44, esp. 540.

[53] See NOLLAND, *Luke* (above, n. 31), 714; BOCK, *Luke* (above, n. 32), 1199. And see already HARNACK, *Sprüche* (above, n. 49), 43.

[54] See JEREMIAS, *Sprache* (n. 31), 225; MARSHALL, *Luke* (n. 48), 551. ἐργασία is used in Acts 16:16, 19; 19:24-25. δίδωμι ἐργασίαν is a Latinism that had become quite common: see BOVON, *Evangelium* (above, n. 33), 363. The origin of the phrase in the tradition is defended by D. ZELLER, *Mahnsprüche* (above, n. 44), 64.

[55] By inserting γὰρ and changing the word order, Luke seems to have linked the tradition with his redactional transition, v. 57.

[56] See SCHULZ, *Q* (above, n. 20), 421. A possible reconstruction of the traditional wording according to the argument above is: ἴσθι ἐνοῶν (or ἀπαλλάγηθι) τῷ ἀντιδίκῳ σου ταχὺ, ἕως ὅτου εἶ μετ' αὐτοῦ ἐν τῇ ὁδῷ, μήποτέ σε παραδῷ ὁ ἀντίδικος τῷ κριτῇ καὶ ὁ κριτὴς τῷ ὑπηρέτῃ καὶ εἰς φυλακὴν βληθήσῃ· λέγω σοι, οὐ μὴ ἐξέλθῃς ἐκεῖθεν, ἕως καὶ ἀποδῷς τὸν ἔσχατον κοδράντην. However, this is only a "virtual" text, there remain numerous uncertainties. See for example, the different reconstruction of the International Q Project in *Edition* (above, n. 35), 394-99, with the footnotes that mention the doubts about the decisions made.

view that the interpretation was not guided by the Lucan version or its Lucan context.

Consequently, it is more appropriate to read the scene not as a parable but as a prudential or sapiential admonition.[57] This is true for the Lucan version[58] and – even more so – for the passage in the context of the Sermon on the Mount,[59] with the imperative at its beginning (ἴσθι εὐνοῶν). The addressee is admonished, and a negative final clause describes the impending consequences if he does not act according to the advice. All the material, including the threat at the end, is taken from the world of justice and finance.

4. THE SAPIENTIAL BACKGROUND: ADVICE ON LOANS AND SURETY

The sapiential interpretation of the saying is confirmed by comparison with other kinds of sapiential advice on financial matters from Palestinian Judaism.

a) Proverbs

One of the most important passages is Prov 6:1-5, a fundamental warning against standing surety for someone.[60] Shaking hands on a guarantee is an incautious act (see Prov 17:18). It is equated with losing one's liberty (Prov 6:2), and the danger is that the surety may also lose his own living, home or bed (Prov 22:27). So if one

---

[57] Thus LUZ, *Evangelium 1* (above, n. 9), 252. See also ZELLER, *Mahnsprüche* (above, n. 44), 64-67; PIPER, *Wisdom* (above, n. 44), 106; H. V. LIPS, *Weisheitliche Traditionen im Neuen Testament*, WMANT 64 (Neukirchen/Vluyn: Neukirchener Verlag, 1990), 212. It is remarkable that the monograph by M. EBNER, *Jesus – ein Weisheitslehrer?* HBS 15 (Freiburg: Herder, 1998) does not discuss the passage.

[58] See FITZMYER, *Luke* (above, n. 27), 1003: "[it] is best interpreted even here as no more than that."

[59] See BETZ, *Sermon* (above, n. 9), 227 n. 234.

[60] Other passages within Proverbs share this tendency. See Prov. 11:15, 17:18, 20:16, 22:26f., 27:13.

has accepted to stand surety for someone, there is only one urgent course of action: to try to get free by beseeching the debtor to pay his debts. Only thus can the surety also be saved from the claims of the creditor and from the danger of falling into poverty together with his fellow. This kind of advice seems to be given from the perspective of the poor. For them, standing surety means taking a risk that should be avoided at all costs.

b) Ben Sira

A quite different view is taken in the work of Ben Sira. From his perception of contemporary society,[61] it is a good thing to enjoy one's goods (Sir 14:11) and to use these goods to help one's friends (14:13). So lending (Sir 29:1) and standing surety (Sir 29:14) are acts of virtue, even if the risks are seen realistically (Sir 19:18):[62]

> Going surety has ruined many prosperous people
> and tossed them about like the surging sea,
> Has exiled the prominent
> and sent them wandering through foreign lands.

Ben Sira is well informed about how many debtors did not pay their debts on time and kept their creditors waiting (29:5),[63] thus causing hostility between the creditors and themselves (29:6). However, from the perspective of a wealthy man he can give this advice: "Go surety for your neighbor acccording to your means, but take care lest you fall thereby" (29:20).[64] For a wise man it is better to give away his money to help others, before the money gets rusty or is divided by lot among the heirs (14:15).

---

[61] See O. WISCHMEYER, *Die Kultur des Buches Jesus Sirach*, BZNW 77 (Berlin/New York: de Gruyter, 1995), 49-69.

[62] ET according to P. SKEHAN and A. A. DI LELLA, *The Wisdom of Ben Sira*, AncB 39 (New York: Doubleday, 1987), 369.

[63] Sir 29:4ff. enumerates the various tricks by which a debtor tries to win time or escape the duty to repay the loan.

[64] ET according to SKEHAN and DI LELLA, *Ben Sira* (above, n. 62), 369.

A debtor, for his part, is advised to return the loan in due time (29:2). But interestingly, the reason given for this advice is not that the debtor will thereby win back his freedom; it is only an appeal to decency. Repaying one's debts is a social duty and a matter of gratitude to the creditor who earlier offered his help. Only sinners do not act accordingly: "The wicked turns the favor of a pledge into disaster, and the ungrateful schemer abandons his protector" (29:16f.).[65]

But even if Ben Sira usually adopts the viewpoint of the better off, he also knows the moral dangers of financial affairs, which have brought many people into sin (27:1). Occasionally, he will also take the perspective of the powerless. In 8:1-2, he recommends not quarreling with the great or the rich. Similarly, he advises not lending to a person who is more powerful than oneself (8:12); and if this has happened, one should consider the loan as lost. The problem is, obviously, that a weak or poor person has "no way of effectively ensuring repayment".[66]

c) 1Q/4QInstruction

Additional pieces of advice on financial matters are now provided by the sapiential texts from the Qumran library.[67] Most of these documents can be classified as "non-sectarian" or "non-Essene"

---

[65] Ibid.
[66] Thus ibid., 213. See also G. SAUER, *Jesus Sirach/Ben Sira*, ATD (Göttingen: Vandenhoeck & Ruprecht, 2000), 97.
[67] See now the edition of the texts in J. STRUGNELL and D. J. HARRINGTON (eds.), *Qumran Cave 4 XXIV. Sapiential Texts, Part 2: 4Q Instruction (Mūsār lᵊ-Mēḇīn)*: 4Q415ff. DJD 34 (Oxford: Clarendon Press, 1999), esp. the general introduction, 1-41; A. LANGE, *Weisheit und Prädestination: Weisheitliche Urordnung und Prädestination in den Textfunden von Quman*, STDJ 18 (Leiden: Brill, 1995), 45-92; idem, "In Diskussion mit dem Tempel: Zur Auseinandersetzung zwischen Kohelet und weisheitlichen Kreisen am Jerusalemer Tempel," in A. SCHOORS (ed.), *Qohelet in the Context of Wisdom*, BETL 136 (Leuven: Peeters, 1998), 113-59; idem., "Die Weisheitstexte aus Qumran: Eine Einleitung," in C. HEMPEL, A. LANGE and H. LICHTENBERGER (eds.), *The Wisdom Texts from Qumran and the Development of Sapiential Thought*, BETL 159 (Leuven: Peeters, 2002), 3-30.

documents.⁶⁸ This is especially true for the most extensive and important document previously known as 4QSapiential Work A,⁶⁹ or *Mūsār lᵊ-Mēḇīn* ("Instruction for the Knowledgeable") and now edited in the DJD series with the short title 1Q/4QInstruction.⁷⁰

It is not necessary to discuss here the details of the introductory material.⁷¹ The sapiential character of the work is clearly shown by the terminological survey of the editors.⁷² But in spite of the

---

⁶⁸ On this distinction, see D. DIMANT, "The Qumran Manuscripts: Contents and Significance," in D. DIMANT and L. H. SCHIFFMAN (eds.), *Time to Prepare the Way in the Wilderness: Papers on the Qumran Scrolls*, STDJ 16 (Leiden: Brill, 1995), 23-58. On the criteria see, most recently, A. LANGE, "Kriterien essenischer Texte," in J. FREY and H. STEGEMANN (eds.), *Qumran kontrovers*, Einblicke 6 (Paderborn, 2002), 59-70; C. HEMPEL, "Kriterien zur Bestimmung 'essenischer Verfasserschaft' von Qumrantexten," in loc. cit., 71-88. On the origin of the sapiential literature from the Qumran library, see already W. L. LIPSCOMB and J. A. SANDERS, "Wisdom at Qumran," in J. G. GAMMIE (ed.), *Israelite Wisdom: Theological and Literary Essays in Honor of Samuel Terrien* (New York: Scholars Press, 1978), 277-85, esp. 278: "There are no true wisdom texts among the scrolls of undisputed Essene authorship." A possible exception could be the document 4Q420-421 (4QWays of Righteousness). On this document, see T. ELGVIN, "Wisdom in the Yahad. 4QWays of Righteousness," *RevQ* 17 (1996), 205-32, esp. 205f.

⁶⁹ See E. TOV and S. J. PFANN (eds.), *The Dead Sea Scrolls on Microfiche: Companion Volume* (Leiden: Brill, 1993), 43.

⁷⁰ Thus the edition by J. STRUGNELL and D. J. HARRINGTON, in *Sapiential Texts, Part 2* (above, n. 67).

⁷¹ See the general introduction by STRUGNELL and HARRINGTON in *Sapiential Texts, Part 2* (above, n. 67), 1-40; and, most recently, A. LANGE, "Die Weisheitstexte aus Qumran" (above, n. 67). See also the most recent monographs by E. J. C. TIGCHELAAR, *To Increase Learning for the Understanding Ones: Reading and Reconstructing the Fragmentary Early Jewish Sapiential Text 4QInstruction*, StTDJ 44 (Leiden: Brill, 2001); and M. J. GOFF, *The Worldly and Heavenly Wisdom of 4QInstruction*, STDJ 50 (Leiden: Brill, 2003).

⁷² *Sapiential Texts*, Part 2 (above, n 67), 22ff. See also J. STRUGNELL, "The Sapiential Work 4Q415ff. and pre-Qumranic Works from Qumran: Lexicographic Considerations," in D. W. PARRY and E. ULRICH (eds.), *The Provo International Conference on the Dead Sea Scrolls: New Texts, Reformulated Issues, and Technological Innovations*, STDJ 30 (Leiden: Brill, 1999), 595-608.

seven or eight manuscripts preserved,[73] it has, so far, not been possible to clarify the outline and overall structure of the work[74] or the history of its literary development.[75] The suggested dates of composition vary between the late third century and the first half of the second century BCE.[76] The composition is, then, roughly contemporary with the work of Ben Sira,[77] and it demonstrates that the sapiential tradition within Palestinian Judaism of the second century BCE was much more pluriform than we could know before the publication of the fragments from the Qumran library.

The composition combines instruction on practical issues, such as family relations and financial matters, with theoretical reflections, its admonitions being presented within a cosmological and

---

[73] 4Q415, 4Q416, 4Q417, 4Q418, 4Q418a, 4Q423 and 1Q26 are certainly copies of this work, whereas the editors put a question mark after the 4Q418c because it is not totally certain that the single fragment now numbered 4Q418c (formerly 4Q418 fr. 161) represents a separate manuscript. See *Sapiential Texts,* Part 2 (above, n. 67), 501.

[74] "It was loosely structured at best" (J. J. COLLINS, *Jewish Wisdom in the Hellenistic Age,* OTL [Louisville: Westminster John Knox, 1997], 118).

[75] From the material reconstruction of the manuscripts 4Q416, 4Q417 and 4Q418, B. Luassen and A. Steudel suggest that 4Q416 and 4Q417 represent different stages of redaction: 4Q417 seems to be a copy of an earlier version of the work, whereas 4Q416 represents a later stage of redaction, which is also represented by 4Q418. Their article is as yet unpublished; but see the reports by A. LANGE, "In Diskussion mit dem Tempel" (above, n. 67), 127-28; and *Sapiential Texts,* Part 2 (above, n. 67), 19. See also the discussion by E. TIGCHELAAR, "Towards a Reconstruction of the Beginning of 4QInstruction (4Q416 Fragment 1 and Parallels)," in C. HEMPEL, A. LANGE and H. LICHTENBERGER (eds.), *The Wisdom Texts from Qumran and the Development of Sapiential Thought,* BETL 159 (Leuven: Peeters, 2003), 99-126; idem, *To Increase Learning for the Understanding Ones* (above, n. 71).

[76] See LANGE, *Weisheit und Prädestination* (above, n. 67), 47; idem, "In Diskussion mit dem Tempel" (above, n. 67), 129-30.

[77] On the comparison with Ben Sira, see *Sapiential Texts,* Part 2 (above, n. 67), 34-35; and D. J. HARRINGTON, "Two Early Jewish Approaches to Wisdom: Sirach and Qumran Sapiential Work A," *JSP* 16 (1997), 25-38; a slightly revised reprint appears in HEMPEL et al., *The Wisdom Texts* (above, n. 75), 263-76.

eschatological framework.⁷⁸ 1Q/4QInstruction thus provides evidence of an early merging of sapiential with eschatological or even apocalyptic thought. Ususally the person addressed is a (male) junior sage, called מבין. Such a "knowledgeable" person receives advice for different situations in life, one area of advice being financial, including loans, pledges and surety.

First of all, some pieces of advice reflect the situation of a person who finds himself in a position of honor, which may also include some wealth. But 4Q416 2 III 9-12 indicates that the addressee probably comes from a lower social level: his head is lifted up out of poverty, he is raised to splendor and seated with the nobles. So he is advised to consider the origins of the "mystery that is to come"⁷⁹ and to praise God, who glorifies and seek his pleasure continuously.⁸⁰ Prosperity is, then, a gift from God; one should not reject it but "walk in it" and be thankful to God.⁸¹

---

[78] See T. ELGVIN, "Wisdom, Revelation and Eschatology in an Early Essene Writing," *SBL Seminar Papers 34* (1995), 440-63; idem, "Early Essene Eschatology: Judgment and Salvation according to Sapiential Work A," in D. W. PARRY and S. D. RICKS (eds.), *Current Research and Technological Developments on the Dead Sea Scrolls*, STDJ 20 (Leiden: Brill, 1996), 126-65. On the eschatological dualism of the work, see J. FREY, "Different Patterns of Dualistic Thought in the Qumran Library," in *Legal Texts and Legal Issues: Proceedings of the Second Meeting of the International Organization for Qumran Studies, Cambridge 1995. Published in Honour of Joseph M. Baumgarten*, STDJ 23 (Leiden: Brill, 1997), 275-335, esp. 298-99; J. J. COLLINS, "The Mysteries of God: Creation and Eschatology in 4QInstruction and the Wisdom of Solomon," in F. GARCÍA MARTÍNEZ (ed.), *Wisdom and Apocalypticism in the Dead Sea Scrolls and in the Biblical Tradition*, BETL 168 (Leuven: Peeters, 2003), 287-306.

[79] This is a very frequent term in 4QInstruction. See COLLINS, *Jewish Wisdom* (above, n. 74), 121-25; A. LANGE, "In Diskussion mit dem Tempel," (above, n. 67), 134.

[80] רצונו שחר תמיד (4Q416 2 III 12). On שחר רצונו, see Prov 11:27. However, רצונו might mean "pleasure," not "good will" – as it is translated in *Sapiential Texts,* Part 2 (above, n. 67), 113.

[81] 4Q416 2 III 9. See also 4Q416 2 II 3: "And in his poverty thou shalt not make the poor stumble because of it. [Nor] because of [his] shame shalt thou hide thy face ..." (*Sapiential Works, Part 2* [above, n. 67], p. 93).

Most of the instructions, however, reflect a situation of ongoing poverty. Frequently, the addressee is called "poor" (אביון or רָשׁ),⁸² and this term should not be interpreted merely in the sense of the spiritual ideal of poverty and humility. The addressee is even warned: "Do not esteem yourself highly for poverty when you are a pauper, lest you bring into contempt your own life" (4Q416 2 II 20-21). And he is told: "You are needy (אביון אתה): Do not say: 'I am poor, I will not study wisdom'" (4Q416 2 III 12-13); his poverty cannot serve as an excuse for lack of insight. This proves that the poverty mentioned in this document is real, not just a pious ideal. Poverty, obviously, is an element of the social world of this text. (In this respect, there is a marked difference between 1Q/4QInstruction and the work of Ben Sira, which is directed much more toward the well-to-do.) It reflects the severe social discrepancies in the Judean society of later post-exilic times, especially under Hellenistic administration.

The addressee is admonished to be moderate and self-sufficient, not to seek luxury when there is not enough for subsistence:

> Do not sate thyself with food when there is no clothing, and do not drink wine when there is no food. Do not seek after delicacies when thou [*vacat*] lackest (even) bread.⁸³

Here is further proof that there was a real danger of having insufficient food or clothing and being in need of help. In this case, the text encourages borrowing and trusting in God to provide all necessities.⁸⁴ But the dangers of borrowing are also mentioned quite clearly:

---

⁸² See 4Q416 2 III 2, 8, 12, 19 etc. with parallels from 4Q418.

⁸³ 4Q416 2 II 18-20 (*Sapiential Texts,* Part 2 [above, n. 67], 93). See also 4Q416 2 III 8: "Thou art needy; do not desire something beyond thy share/inheritance..." (ibid., 177), and 4Q417 2 I 17: "And thou, if thou lackest food in thy poverty, ..." (ibid., 176).

⁸⁴ If the reconstruction and interpretation of the editors is correct, 4Q417 2 I 19 reads: "And if thou art in poverty, for what thou lackest, borrow without having any money." The reading is ואם תחסר לוא מבלי הון מחסורכה, the editors read לוא as an imperative *qal* of לוה, with a quite unusual spelling, because

> [Do not se]ll thyself for a price. It is good to become a servant in the spirit, And to serve thy oppressors freely. But for [no] price [s]ell thy glory, Or pledge money for thy inheritance. Lest it dispossess also thy body. ...[85]

The passage is difficult to interpret, but the warning clearly points to the danger that a person could lose his inheritance and, consequently, his living and freedom. There is mention of "oppressors" (נוגשים), and the advice is to serve them freely, as a "servant in the spirit" – whatever that might mean. But there is a severe warning not to give away one's inheritance and personal freedom.

In another passages the addressee is warned against taking a loan from a stranger:

> Moreover, from any man whom thou hast not known take no money, Lest he/it increase thy poverty. And if he put the responsibility of it on thy head, Until death take charge of it.[86]

By taking a loan, the pauper could be deprived of his inheritance, his living and his independence. He might also be reproached or even flogged and hit with a rod[87] if he is not able to return the loan on time. So the text urges the addressee to be honest with his creditor and return the due amount as quickly as possible:

---

it fits the theme and language of the subsequent lines (see the commentary on the reading in *Sapiential Texts,* Part 2 [above, n. 67], 187, and the text ibid., 173 [translation, 176]). The subsequent passage is only very fragmentary, but the argument seems to be that God as creator can provide everything that is needed.

[85] 4Q416 1 II 17-18 (ibid., 93). Perhaps something similar is meant some lines earlier (4Q416 2 II 6), where the editors translate: "For no price exchange (?) thy holy spirit, For there is no price equal in value to it" (ibid.). Should this mean that financial problems can lead to sin?

[86] 4Q416 2 III 5-6 (ibid., 112).

[87] See 4Q417 2 I 24ff. The text is very fragmentary here, so the context cannot be further restored.

> If thou borrowest m[e]n's money for thy poverty, Let there be no [sleep for th]ee day or night, and no rest for thy soul, [Until] thou hast restored to [thy] credito[r] his [loan]. Do not lie to him, lest thou shouldst bear guilt (for it)....[88]

Immediate repayment is necessary, not only because lying to the creditor who has helped in a desperate situation is unjust and sinful behavior,[89] but because when the debtor acts dishonestly, the creditor may "close his hand" and refuse to help when help is urgently needed again.[90] And the strong warning "let there be no sleep for thee day or night..." can be understood if we see the danger of severe consequences for the debtor. If he is unable to return what he borrowed earlier, he might suffer under the obligation for a long time, perhaps for the rest of his life, or he might be deprived of his inheritance or freedom. Facing such dangers, the debtor is bound to be restless until he has returned his debt. This formula may be inspired by Prov 6:4 (cf. Ps 132:4), but there is also a close parallel in the Sayings of Ahiqar:

> Do not take a heavy loan from an evil man. And if you take a loan (at all), give yourself no peace until [you have re]pa[id] it.[91]

The same advice is given in the event that the addressee has agreed to stand surety for a friend:

> As much as [a man's creditor has lent him in money, hastily] pay it back, And thou wilt be on an equal footing with him

---

[88] 4Q417 2 I 21-23 (ibid., 177).
[89] Such is the argument in Sir 29:16f.
[90] 4Q417 2 I 24 (ibid., 177).
[91] *Ahiqar* 43, translation according to J. M. LINDENBERGER, in J. H. CHARLESWORTH (ed.) *Old Testament Pseudepigrapha*, vol. 2 (New York: Doubleday, 1985), 479-508, esp. 503. On the parallel with Instruction, see H. NIEHR, "Die Weisheit des Achikar und der *musar lammebin* im Vergleich," in HEMPEL et al., *The Wisdom Texts* (above, n. 75), 173-86, esp. 177.

(i.e. the creditor). If the purse containing thy treasures [thou hast] entrus[ted to thy creditor, On account of thy friends thou hast giv]en away all thy life with it. Hasten and give what is his, And take back [thy] purse....[92]

The reasoning in this analogy is clear: In Hellenistic private law, the surety "rather resembles a joint debtor," because "it was left to the creditor's discretion to seize whom of the two he wished."[93] Standing surety, then, was as dangerous as borrowing, and the surety should see to it that the creditor gets back his money as quickly as possible so the surety himself will be restored to be "on equal footing with him" – that is, free from obligations and independent again.

As we have seen, the text "gives advice about paying back loans or surety bonds quickly, maintaining integrity in business and in serving others."[94] Such advice is "fairly conventional,"[95] as the parallel from the Book of Ahiqar demonstrates. But 1Q/4QInstruction obviously addresses a social situation in which the economic and financial independence of the addressee is greatly endangered. Herein we can see a remarkable difference from the social perception and perspective of Ben Sira. On the other hand, in contrast with other documents from the second century BCE, such as the Epistle of Enoch (1 Enoch 92-106),[96] the text "expresses no anger against the rich."[97] So the perspective of 1Q/4QInstruction on financial affairs differs from the majority of the hitherto known sapiential texts as well as from the apocalyptic traditions. It is clear that our knowledge of the kinds of positions that

---

[92] 4Q416 1 II 4-6 (ibid., 93).
[93] H. J. WOLFF, "Hellenistic Private Law," in S. SAFRAI and M. STERN (eds.), *The Jewish People in the First Century*, CRINT I/1 (Assen: van Gorcum, 1974), 534-60, esp. 552.
[94] D. J. HARRINGTON, *Wisdom Texts from Qumran* (London/New York: Routledge, 1996), 40.
[95] Ibid., 46.
[96] See, for example, 1 Enoch 94:8.
[97] COLLINS, *Jewish Wisdom* (above, n. 74), 119.

could be adopted toward economics in early Jewish literature is considerably broadened by the new sapiential texts from the Qumran library.

5. THE SOCIAL BACKGROUND: DEBT IMPRISONMENT AND DEBT SLAVERY

The above survey of advice on financial matters shows that guidance on borrowing, pledging and surety were an essential part of Palestinian Jewish sapiential tradition. Such advice was necessary for people who shared the experience of their life being often in danger, and that war, famine or "adversaries" could deprive them of their land, shelter or inheritance, even of their personal freedom. This was a real possibility for a large part of the population in Hellenistic and Roman Palestine. Such experiences go back to the Persian era, and especially under Hellenistic administration and Hellenistic law, the problems became quite acute.

The situation under Persian rule is described in Nehemiah 5:1-5.[98] According to this passage, the social gulfs within the society in post-exilic Jehud must have been severe. People had to mortgage their fields to acquire funds to pay the king's tax.[99] Others had to

---

[98] On the passage, see M. HENGEL, *Judentum und Hellenismus*, 3rd ed., WUNT 10 (Tübingen: Mohr Siebeck, 1988), 94-97; H.-G. KIPPENBERG, *Religion und Klassenbildung im antiken Judäa. Eine religionssoziologische Studie zum Verhältnis von Tradition und gesellschaftlicher Entwicklung*, 2nd ed., SUNT 14 (Göttingen: Vandenhoeck & Ruprecht, 1978), 55-62; R. ALBERTZ, *Religionsgeschichte Israels in alttestamentlicher Zeit*, vol. 2, GAT 8, 2 (Göttingen: Vandenhoeck & Ruprecht, 1992), 538-39.

[99] Persian tax policy mandated that taxes had to be paid not in kind but in cash (see Herodotus, *Hist.* 3.89). So the peasants had to produce not only what they needed for subsistence but also a surplus that could be sold for money. It can be assumed that such a change in the economic structure caused severe problems, especially when the harvest was bad or when the labor potential of a family was reduced by illness or by being required elsewhere – for example, in Nehemiah's wall project. See ALBERTZ, *Religionsgeschichte* (above, n. 98), 539.

place their children in bondage or even sell them into slavery to obtain grain during a period of famine. Moreover, the creditors were themselves Judeans who caused their own brethren to be bonded into slavery (Neh 5:7-8). A chasm thus opened up within Judean society.[100] The same incremental stages of poverty are also presupposed in the law of holiness in Lev 25, which shows that an Israelite might sell his land or house (vv. 26, 29, 31) or incur a debt with the obligation to pay interest (vv. 35-37). He could also be claimed as a pledge and possibly be sold to an Israelite (v. 39) or even to a foreigner (v. 47). As interest rates were extremely high,[101] the danger of a debtor becoming unable to return the loan together with the due interest was very real. Quite frequently creditors had to claim the pledge – not only the land and its fruits but also the debtor's labor or that of his family members. Laws such as Deut 15:2 (the canceling of the debts of every Israelite in the seventh year) and Lev 25:26-28 and 25:35-55 (the redemption of the land and the release of personal obligations in the jubilee year)[102] were intended to protect Israelites – but not foreigners[103] – from the social consequences of such practices; and regulations such as Neh 5:6-13 and 10:31-32 represent attempts to root them out. How effective these numerous attempts were, however, remains doubtful. There is no evidence that the Jubilee program described in Lev 25 was ever put into practice.[104] And in the event of an Israelite being unable to obtain a loan from his countrymen, he would have

---

[100] See KIPPENBERG, *Religion* (n. 98), 59-62.

[101] A document from Elephantine (Papyrus Cowley 10) mentions an interest rate of 60 percent. See A. E. COWLEY, *Aramaic Papyri of the Fifth Century BC* (Oxford: Oxford University Press, 1923), 30. See also H. G. KIPPENBERG, *Religion* (above, n. 98), 58.

[102] On the laws of the Jubilee and their social intentions see E. OTTO, *Theologische Ethik des Alten Testaments,* Theologische Wissenschaft 3,2 (Stuttgart/Berlin/Cologne: Kohlhammer, 1994), 249-56.

[103] See Deut 15:3; Lev 25:44-46. See also OTTO, *Ethik* (above, n. 102), 256.

[104] See OTTO, *Ethik* (above, n. 102), 255: "Das AT gibt nicht zu erkennen, ob das Jubeljahrprogramm realisiert wurde. ... Es ist wohl Programm geblieben."

had to resort to foreigners, who were not obliged to adhere to such an ideal. Joel 4:6 attests that in late Persian times Judeans and Jerusalemites were indeed sold into slavery by Phoenician traders.[105]

With the beginning of Hellenistic rule, the economic situation of the majority of Judeans became even worse. Under the rule of the Ptolemees, the administrative system of Ptolemaic Egypt was transferred to the royal province known as Syria and Phoenicia,[106] and the tributes exacted by the new rulers seem to have been much higher than those under Persian rule. In the Hellenistic period, the gap between the small upper class and the rest of the population widened considerably. This was due not only to the intensified trading possibilities but also to the indigenous aristocracy becoming integrated into the system of tax collection.[107] In certain districts tax collection was leased to private individuals who assumed both the risks and the benefits of the enterprise. So their interest was to collect the due amounts rigorously and to obtain their own surplus. The system introduced by the Ptolemees seems to have remained almost unchanged under the Seleucids and also under the Romans.[108] It was developed further under Herod and then remai-

---

[105] On the date of the passage, see H.-W. WOLFF, *Dodekapropheton 2: Joel und Amos,* BK 14,2, 2nd ed. (Neukirchen/Vluyn: Neukirchener Verlag, 1975), 93-94.

[106] See M. HENGEL, *Judentum und Hellenismus* (above, n. 98), 39; and see, generally, ibid., 32-104; idem, *Juden, Griechen und Barbaren,* SBS 76 (Stuttgart: Katholisches Bibelwerk, 1975), 35-63; idem, "The Political and Social History of Palestine from Alexander to Antiochus III (333-187 BCE)," in W. D. DAVIES and L. FINKELSTEIN (eds.), *The Cambridge History of Judaism,* vol. 2 (Cambridge: Cambridge University Press, 1989), 35-78.

[107] On the tax collecting system in Palestine, see F. HERRENBRÜCK, *Jesus und die Zöllner,* WUNT 2,41 (Tübingen: Mohr Siebeck, 1990), 162-227.

[108] The precise character of the tax system under Hasmonean rule remains unclear due to the lack of sources (see ibid., 183f.). However, it is quite possible that they changed only some of the taxes but retained the general system of tax collection: "Wir wissen sehr wenig von dem Besteuerungssystem, das die Hasmonäer schufen, aber es ist sehr wahrscheinlich, daß sie das von den Seleukiden übernommene nicht veränderten und daß Pompeius das gleiche System von ihnen übernahm" (M. I. ROSTOFTZEFF, *Gesellschafts- und*

ned basically untouched until the end of the first century CE.[109] As a consequence, a relatively small number of families were able to increase their wealth and derive profit from their various economic connections, whereas the majority of the population suffered severe economic hardship and indebtedness.

Debts, pledges and surety were thus a severe problem in first century Palestine, and the Jesus tradition "shows an intimate acquaintance and concern with debt in the first half of the first-century CE."[110] This concern is confirmed by various passages from the Sayings Source, not only the passage discussed here but also the story of the unforgiving servant (Matt 18:23-35), the parable of the two debtors (Luke 7:41-42), the episode of the widow's coin (Mark 12:41-44) and especially the two parables of the talents (Luke 19:12-27, par. Matt 25:14-30) and of the unjust steward (Luke 16:1-8). The relevance of the debt problem is confirmed also by Josephus, who recorded that in the Jewish War the *sicarii* burned down the communal archive in order to destroy the debt records and thereby gain support of the poor.[111]

Matt 5:25-26 and Luke 12:58-59 provide an insight into how debts could be recovered if the creditor was unwilling or unable to

---

Wirtschaftsgeschichte der hellenistischen Welt, 3 vols. [Darmstadt: Wissenschaftliche Buchgesellschaft, 1955], vol. 2, 792).

[109] See HERRENBRÜCK, *Jesus und die Zöllner* (above, n. 107), 188-89.

[110] D. E. OAKMAN, "The Lord's Prayer in Social Perspective," in B. CHILTON and C. A. EVANS (eds.), *Authenticating the Words of Jesus*, NTTS 28,1 (Leiden/Boston/Cologne: Brill, 1999), 137-86, esp. 164. See also idem, "Jesus and Agrarian Palestine: The Factor of Debt," in K. H. RICHARDS (ed.), *Society of Biblical Literature 1985 Seminar Papers*, SBLSP 24 (Atlanta: Scholars Press, 1985); idem, *Jesus and the Economic Questions of His Day*, SBEC 8 (Lewiston, NY/Queenston, ONT: Edwin Mellen, 1986), 72-77.

[111] Josephus, *Bell.* 2.425-29. See J. PASTOR, *Land and Economy in Ancient Palestine* (London: Routledge, 1997), 157-58; M. HENGEL, *Die Zeloten*, 2nd ed., AGJU 1 (Leiden/Cologne: Brill, 1976), 368-69. A similar incident from Antioch is also recounted by Josephus. There, some people who were in debt "burned the market-place and the public records, hoping to rid themselves of obligations" (Josephus, *Bell.* 7.60-61). See also PASTOR, *Land and Economy in Ancient Palestine*, 158.

pay his taxes or to return the debts he had incurred. It is often inferred here that imprisonment for debt was not a part of traditional Jewish law.[112] On the other hand, it was an element of the Greek[113] and Roman[114] legal systems, and its use is documented in papyri and inscriptions from Greco-Roman Egypt.[115] From the beginning of the Ptolemean era, Hellenistic private law could also be practiced in Palestine, especially if the person involved was a Greek or a person in the service of the Hellenistic system. Debt imprisonment thus also became a legal practice in Hellenistic and Roman Palestine.[116]

This situation might explain the advice in 4QInstruction not to borrow from a foreigner,[117] because indebtedness to such a person could have much more severe consequences than borrowing from a relative or neighbor. Notwithstanding the Jewish religious traditions, a defaulting debtor (or even his relatives) could be imprisoned until the debt was paid. Such imprisonment was primarily a means to apply pressure on the family of a debtor until they became willing to pay back the loan.[118] Debtors were ususally kept

---

[112] See JEREMIAS, *Gleichnisse* (above, n. 18), 179; LUZ, *Evangelium 1* (above, n. 9), 260; GNILKA, *Matthäusevangelium* (above, n. 9), 157; M. REISER, *Die Gerichtspredigt Jesu,* NTAbh 23 (Münster: Aschendorff, 1990), 264.

[113] See S. ARBANDT, W. MACHEINER and C. COLPE, "Gefangenschaft," *RAC,* vol. 9 (Stuttgart: Hiersemann, 1974), 318-45, esp. 327f., 335f. See also KIPPENBERG, *Religion* (n. 98), 141-42.

[114] On the issue in Roman law, see T. MOMMSEN, *Römisches Strafrecht* (reprint Darmstadt: Wissenschaftliche Buchgesellschaft, 1961), 906 with n. 2 and 960 with n. 2.

[115] See A. DEISSMANN, *Licht vom Osten,* 4th ed. (Tübingen: J. C. B. Mohr [Paul Siebeck], 1923), 229-31; H. LEWALD, *Zur Personalexekution im Recht der Papyri* (Leipzig: Veit, 1910).

[116] On the practice of debt imprisonment, see R. SUGRANYES DE FRANCH, *Études sur le droit palestinien à l'époque évangélique: La contrainte par corps* (Fribourg: Librairie de l'Université, 1946), 114-15.

[117] 4Q416 2 III 5-6 (see above, n. 86).

[118] A similar situation is narrated by Josephus (*Bell.* 2.273) concerning the administration of Albinus.

in a public prison,[119] which means that public courts were in charge of guaranteeing the execution of private contracts.

It is more than plausible, then, that the practice of imprisonment for debt was well known to Palestinian Jews from the time of Jesus and that this practice is also presupposed in Matt 5:25-26, par Luke 12:58-59[120] and, similarly, in Matt 18:30. Douglas E. Oakman plausibly suggests that the episode most likely "refers to the courts within the jurisdiction of Herod Antipas."[121]

6. The meaning of Matt 5:25-26

Against this background, the sapiential advice on financial matters in Matt 5:25-26 and Luke 12:58-59 is quite clear; the passages require no metaphorical interpretation or reading as a parable of the coming eschatological judgment.[122]

The addressee is in a situation of owing a sum of money to another (characterized as his opponent), either as a debtor himself or as a surety for someone else. The opponent, called ἀντίδικος, as the creditor, has the legal right to summon him to court in order to recover the amount owing. It is presupposed that the legal position of the debtor is almost hopeless. He cannot stand "on equal footing" with his creditor. The most likely consequence of a court trial is that the debtor will be imprisoned, and he is likely to remain in prison until the loan has been fully repaid, either by the debtor himself or by someone else. Simple prudence suggests avoiding

---

[119] M. Kaser, *Das römische Zivilprozessrecht*, HAW 10,3,4 (Munich: Beck, 1966), 407 n. 11. Such a public prison might also be presupposed in Josephus' note on Albinus, who set free all those who had been imprisoned because of "robbery" if their relatives were able to pay ransom for them (Josephus, *Bell*. 2.273; see also Kippenberg, *Religion* [above, n. 98], 142).

[120] This was already noted by Deissmann, *Licht vom Osten* (above, n. 115), 229.

[121] Oakman, "The Lord's Prayer" (above, n. 110), 168.

[122] In contrast, Matt 18:23-35 is explicitly presented as a parable of the kingdom of God.

such a trial and resolving the problem quickly, either by paying the amount due or by reaching a settlement out of court.

I cannot see that the text envisages remission as a real possibility. Remission is possible only if the whole matter of obligations is understood as a metaphor for sins. In a real-life setting, the only realistic option seems to be to arrange for deferment of repayment. Every effort should be made to reach an agreement and avoid a court trial with its foreseeable consequences. In Matthew, the adverb ταχύ (sometimes interpreted as alluding to the impending divine judgment) is best understood from the internal logic of the situation. As in Prov 6:4 or in 4QInstruction, there can be no rest for the debtor until he is relieved of the obligation.

The sapiential advice to reach out-of-court settlement is also consistent with the position regarding pagan courts that was held in Diaspora Judaism[123] and in early Christianity.[124] However, in the passage under discussion, whether the judge is a pagan judge is a moot point and is, in any case, irrelevant. The only point is that the debtor will have no chance to avoid imprisonment.

The idea of repaying debts can, of course, be interpreted metaphorically,[125] but in the present context there is no compelling reason for an interpretation whereby the reader should pray to God as the real judge who will finally deliver him from his human opponents;[126] nor is there any reason to see "the way" as a metaphor for the human life that will eventually lead to the throne of God, the judge. All these interpretations go beyond the given text.

In Luke, the advice is embedded in the introduction (v. 57), which urges the addressee to make a just decision and do that, which has to be done. The verse thus takes on a metaphorical

---

[123] On the Jews of Sardes, see Josephus, *Ant.* 14.235; for rabbinic Judaism, the Baraita of R. Tarphon (*b. Gitt.* 88b). See also E. SCHÜRER, G. VERMES and F. MILLAR, *The History of the Jewish People in the Age of Jesus Christ,* rev. ed., 4 vols. (Edinburgh: T. & T. Clark, 1973-87), vol. 2, 208-9; B. COHEN, "Arbitration in Jewish and Roman Law," *RIDC* 5 (1958), 165-222.

[124] See 1 Cor 6:1ff.

[125] This is mentioned by BETZ, *Sermon* (above, n. 9), 229.

[126] Thus DERRETT, *Law* (above, n. 50), 183.

sense, illustrating the urgency of the decision demanded by the Gospel. In Matthew, the saying is used as to demonstrate the urgent need for reconciliation. But basically it is a piece of "prudential advice ... which has lost its specific reference, and is best interpreted ... as no more than that."[127]

Whether such a saying was originally uttered by Jesus[128] or not is hard to decide. Of course, if the passage is understood as simply a piece of "prudential advice," it is difficult to see how it relates to the central themes of Jesus' preaching. But since we cannot assume that Jesus uttered only parables or eschatological sayings, there is no compelling reason to deny that a simple piece of advice of a sapiential nature could also be an authentic saying.

7. CONCLUSION

In closing, I would like to point to the importance of the Dead Sea Scrolls for the interpretation of this short pericope. Matt 5:25-26 does not allude to any specific item of the Qumran texts or even to the Qumran community. The sapiential work discussed here is one of the non-sectarian documents from the Qumran library. But these documents are perhaps even more important than the sectarian texts, because they allow a much more detailed view of the traditions within Judaism in the two or three centuries BCE. In our case, the sapiential instruction entails a considerable change of our view of wisdom traditions in Palestinian Judaism. It provides evidence of a kind of wisdom that is quite different from that in Ben Sira. Moreover, this kind of wisdom seems to relate more closely to the lower strata of Palestinian society and might therefore provide more parallels to the traditions current in the early Jesus movement. In taking the perspective of the poor, this kind of wisdom tradition provides important parallels to the Synoptic texts dealing with the problem of debts and pledges.

---

[127] Thus FITZMYER, *Luke* (above, n. 27), 1002.
[128] As claimed by FITZMYER, loc. cit.

It is obvious that any "companion to the New Testament from Jewish sources" today must include texts from the Qumran library, insofar as they provide real parallels to New Testament texts. For the passage Matt 5:25-26, the texts quoted from Ahiqar, Ben Sira and 4QInstruction provide much closer parallels than most of the rabbinic passages quoted by Billerbeck.[129] They should indeed be included in the series of parallels given in a "new Billerbeck."

---

[129] BILLERBECK, *Kommentar* (above, n. 1) vol. 1, 288-94.

Hermann LICHTENBERGER

MAKARISMS IN MATTHEW 5:3FF. IN THEIR JEWISH CONTEXT

1. INTRODUCTION

4Q525 is generally regarded as a sapiential text that closely follows Proverbs. It has reached us in about fifty fragments that seem to have been copied during the transition from late Herodian to early Hasmonean script – that is, approximately in the first half of the first century BCE. The term "makarism" properly refers only to col 2 of fragments 2 and 3, and since J. Starcky preannounced their publication in 1956, scholarly discussion has focused on these ten lines.[1]

In the following I give the translation according to Florentino García Martínez and Eibert J.C. Tigchelaar (*The Dead Sea Scrolls. Study Edition*, Vol. 2, Leiden 2000, 1053-1055):

> Blessed are those who adhere to her laws, and do not adhere to perverted paths. Bles[sed] are those who rejoice in her,

---

[1] J. STARCKY, "Le travail d'édition des fragments manuscrits de Qumrân," *Revue Biblique* 63 (1956), 67: "Un manuscrit de caractère sapientiel contient une série de macarismes pour ceux qui accomplissent les commandements [...אשרי] et la description des tourments qui attendent les impies." Quoted by E. PUECH, *DJD* XXV, 115A1.

and do not burst out in paths of folly. Blessed are those who search for her with pure hands, and do not pursue her with a treacherous [heart]. Blessed is the man who attains Wisdom, and walks in the law of the Most High, and directs his heart to her ways, and is constrained by her discipline and alwa[ys] takes pleasure in her punishments; and does not forsake her in the hardship of [his] wrong[s], and in the time of anguish does not abandon her, and does not forget her [in the days of] terror, and in the distress of his soul does not loathe [her.] For he always thinks of her, and in his distress he meditates [on her, and in al]l his life [he thinks] of her, [and places her] in front of his eyes in order not to walk on paths [...] [...] together, and on her account eats away his heart [...] [...] ... and with kings it shall make [him s]it [...] [with] his [sc]eptre over ... [...] brothers ... [...] (4Q525 2 II, 1-10).

The makarisms in 4Q525 represent the closest analogy to the makarisms in the Sermon on the Mount and the Sermon on the Plain. This analogy has influenced research on this text with regard to both its form and its context. Yet such research has not, I am afraid, always been carried out with due methodological care. This criticism applies first and foremost to E. Puech's reconstruction of 4Q525 according to Matt 5:3-12 and the reconstructed makarisms in 1QH^a VI, 13-15. Here we have to consider on the one hand that Matthew is about two hundred years later than the composition (not the later copying) of 4Q525 and on the other hand that the Matthean version of makarisms in relation to Luke (in particular Q) is of a secondary nature. It is widely believed that in Luke it is not only the original number (3+1) that has been preserved but, by keeping the address in the second person plural, the more probable text form as well. In contrast, the Matthean arrangement, 8+1, has to be regarded as an enlargement attributable to scribal exegesis; the third person, for instance, was used both in the OT and in rabbinic literature.

The woes in Luke could be of Lucan origin. From a methodological point of view, therefore, it is not appropriate to infer from

the Matthean version the original number of makarisms in 4Q525.²
From a formal point of view, however, there is a remarkable link
between Matthew, Luke and 4Q525 concerning the weight given
to the last makarism: 4Q525 is an extraordinary example of the
hortative enlargement of the last part (1, 3-10), which resembles
Matt 5:11f., Luke 6:23f. and 2 (Slavonic) Enoch 42:14:

> Happy is he who understands all the works of the LORD, performed by the LORD, and glorifies him! For the works of the LORD are right, but the works of mankind – some are good, but others are evil; and by their works those who speak lying blasphemies are recognized.³

For methodological reasons, we have to rule out the eightfold makarism in Sir 14:20-27 (as opposed to Puech, since the makarism formula is not repeated). Otherwise, we are likely to perpetuate the same methodological errors that from the very start impeded our understanding of the relationship between Qumran and the NT.

II. THE EARLY HISTORY OF THE OT GENRE OF MAKARISMS

In my view, the problem of the early history of makarisms has not been convincingly solved. According to Cazelles, "Within the cu-

---

[2] See H.-J. FABRY, "Der Makarismus, mehr als nur eine weisheitliche Lehrform. Gedanken zu dem neuedierten Text 4Q525," in J. HAUSMANN and H.J. ZOBEL (eds.), *Alttestamentlicher Glaube und Biblische Theologie, FS H. D. Preuß* (Stuttgart: Kohlhammer, 1992), 362-71; J. H. CHARLESWORTH, "The Qumran Beatitudes (4Q525) and the New Testament (Mt 5:3-11, Lk 6:20-26)," *Révue d'Histoire et de Philosophie Religieuses* 80 (2000), 13-35. For further bibliography see CHARLESWORTH. I am glad to note several points of agreement with my work. See also H.-J. FABRY, "Die Seligpreisungen in der Bibel und in Qumran," in C. HEMPEL, A. LANGE and H. LICHTENBERGER (eds.), *The Wisdom Texts from Qumran and the Development of Sapiential Thought* (Leuven: Leuven University Press, 2002), 189-200.

[3] From the translation by F. I. ANDERSEN, in J. H. CHARLESWORTH (ed.), *The Old Testament Pseudepigrapha*, 2 vols. (Garden City: Doubleday, 1983) I, 168.

neiform script there are no satisfactory parallels."[4] However, there are such expressions as "May he be happy,"[5] which precede the language of the Psalms, too. References point rather to an Egyptian origin, where in Ptosiris in the 2nd century BCE there are strong resemblances, as in "Happy the man who leads his heart to faithfulness." However, already in Ramses II, a thousand years earlier, we find such formulations as "Happy the man who understands you, Amon!"[6] Taking this hypothesis of Egyptian origin as a starting point, the OT makarisms could stem from sapiential tradition. Klaus Koch pleads for cultic origin because about 60 percent of the OT makarisms are to be found in the book of Psalms;[7] their use in sapiential tradition would therefore be secondary. Yet, especially concerning Psalms, Erich Zenger has contradicted Koch – Zenger finds the "Sitz im Leben" of the makarisms in the realm of the education of the court and in sapiential instruction.[8] The question arises whether there was any cultic use at all outside the Psalter. We can pass over this question here because in 4Q525 the sapiential context is evident.

III. THE FORM OF THE MAKARISMS

Until now makarisms have been mentioned in a general way; they have yet to be defined more precisely. Makarisms are a form of rhetoric characterized by being introduced with אשרי in Hebrew or μακάριος/μακάριοι in Greek. 4Q525 is thus a series of makarisms.

---

[4] H. CAZELLES, *ThWAT* I 483 (translation by H. L.).
[5] *ANET* 387, according to CAZELLES.
[6] According to CAZELLES.
[7] K. KOCH, *Was ist Formgeschichte? Methoden der Bibelexegese* (Neukirchen–Vluyn: Neukirchener Verlag des Erziehungsvereins, 1989), 21 n. 1a.
[8] E. ZENGER, in F. L. HOSSFELD, E. ZENGER, *Die Psalmen I* (Würzburg: Echter, 1993), 45.

1. Individual makarisms

We encounter makarisms in the OT as well as in Greek literature, where the word *makarios* is used for the (immortal) gods in contrast to mortal men such as Homer (Od 5,7 "happy immortal gods"), whereas Hesiod refers to the blissful condition of men in a world to come, on the Islands of the Blessed. Since Aristophanes (5th–4th century BCE), the word *makarios* has been part of the colloquial language describing the carefree life of rich people. Aristotle uses *makariotes* only for the gods, who live in perfect happiness as compared to men, for whom he uses *eudaimonia*.[9] One strict form of makarisms refers to worldly happiness – as in Homer, Od 24,19f.: "Happy are you Odysseus for you are endowed with a virtuous wife" – or refers to children; prosperity, glory, honor and virtue also appear in such a context. The dead too, having escaped the world's vanity, are *makarioi* – hence the expression "blessed" for the dead, as in post-Constantine Christian tradition.

A suffering person or a person in hardship would never be called *makarios*. W. Zimmerli notes: "A makarism of the persecuted is not found in the Old Testament"[10] because אשרי derives from אשר, to praise those who are happy.[11] Frequently, the makarism is either constructed with a suffix or followed by a noun, as in Ps 32:2: "Blessed is the man to whom the Lord imputes no iniquity, and in whose spirit there is no deceit." The OT makarisms have usually to be understood as praising somebody for his happy and salutary condition.[12] In a sapiential context, in particular, makarisms refer to children, beauty and glory as well as to wisdom. He who trusts God, who builds his hopes on him, who fears and loves him, is called *makarios*, a happy man, Ps 2:12: "Blessed

---

[9] F. Hauck, *ThWNT* IV, 365.
[10] W. Zimmerli, "Die Seligpreisungen der Bergpredigt und das AT," in E. Bammel et al. (eds.), *Donum Gentilicium, FS D. Daube* (Oxford: Clarendon Press, 1978), 8-26, esp. 16.
[11] Cf. Cazelles, in *ThWAT* I, 481-485: 481.
[12] M. Sabo, *THAT* I 259.

are those who take refuge in him." God's chosen people is to be called אשרי.

Eventually, in 4 Maccabees 7, the martyr is called *makarios* as well as he who lives in the expectancy of eternal bliss: "O blessed old age, revered gray head, life is loyal to the Law and perfected by the faithful seal of death." Or in 1 En 58:2 "Blessed are you, righteous and elect ones, for glorious is your portion!"[13]

In apocalyptic makarisms, as in sapiential ones, a reason is frequently given, as in 2 En 42:11: "Happy is he who sows right seed, for he shall harvest it sevenfold." Often these makarisms include sapiential or eschatological instructions (for the latter see section 2, "Series of makarisms").

To sum up: In OT-Jewish tradition the makarism is to be found especially in a sapiential or apocalyptic context as a blessing pronounced over a happy person or group and over Israel addressed mainly in the third person but also in the second person. Examples are: "Blessed is the man," "Blessed are you, Israel."

2. Series of makarisms

We encounter series of makarisms in OT-Jewish tradition in both sapiential and apocalyptic texts:
Example of a sapiential text, Sir 25:7-11:

> I can think of nine men I count happy,
> and I can tell you of a tenth:
> a man who can take delight in his children,
> and one who lives to see his enemy's downfall;
> happy the husband of a sensible wife,
> the farmer who does not plough with ox and ass together,
> the man whose tongue never betrays him,

---

[13] There are full makarisms in Jewish epitaphs as a quotation from Ps 83:12 (CIJ II 877), and several occurences of μακάριος (in the basic or the superlative form). See W. AMELING, "Inscriptiones Judaicae Orientis II Kleinasien," *Texts and Studies in Ancient Judaism* 99 (Tübingen: Mohr Siebeck, 2004), 489 n. 26.

and the servant who has never worked for an inferior!
Happy the man who has found a friend,
and the speaker who has an attentive audience!
How great is the man who finds wisdom!
But no greater than he who fears the Lord.
The fear of the Lord excels all other gifts;
to what can we compare the man who has it?

Example of an apocalyptic text, 2 En 42:6ff.:

> Happy is the person who reverences the name of the LORD, and who serves in front of his face always and who organizes his gifts with fear, offerings of life, and who in this life lives and dies correctly!
> Happy is he who carries out righteous judgment, not for the sake of payment, but for justice, not expecting anything whatever as a result; and the result will be that judgment without favoritism will follow for him.
> Happy is he who clothes the naked with his garment, and to the hungry gives his bread!
> Happy is he who judges righteous judgment for orphan and widow, and who helps anyone who has been treated unjustly!
> Happy is he who turns aside from the secular path of this vain world, and walks in the right paths, and who lives that life which is without end!
> Happy is he who sows right seed, for he shall harvest sevenfold!
> Happy is he who has compassion on his lips and gentleness in his heart!
> Happy is he who understands all the works of the Lord, performed by the Lord, and glorifies him! For the works of the Lord are right, but the works of mankind – some are good, but others are evil; and by their works those who speak lying blasphemies are recognized.[14]

---

[14] Quotation according to F. I. ANDERSEN, in *OTP* (see above, n. 3) I, 168.

Woeful and blessed can be placed antithetically. As in Eccl 10:16f.: "Woe the land whose king is a child and whose princes feast in the morning." Blessedness and fatefulness, blessed and woeful can appear side by side or in parallel or can be juxtaposed to damnation. An example is 2 Enoch 52, where the parallelism of blessed and cursed is striking:

> Happy is he who opens his heart for praise, and praises the Lord.
> Cursed is he who opens his heart to insults, and to slander against his neighbor.
> Happy is he who opens his lips, both blessing and praising the Lord.
> Cursed is he who opens his lips for cursing and blasphemy, before the face of the Lord.
> Happy is he who glorifies all the works of the Lord.
> Cursed is he who insults the creatures of the Lord.
> Happy is he who organizes the works of his hand, so as to raise them up.
> Cursed – who looks to obliterate the works of others.
> Happy – who preserves the foundations of his most ancient fathers, made firm from the beginning.
> Cursed – he who breaks down the institutions of his ancestors and fathers.
> Happy – who cultivates the love of peace.
> Cursed – who disturbs those who are peaceful by means of love.
> Happy (is he who) even though he does not speak peace with his tongue, nevertheless in his heart there is peace toward all.
> Cursed – who with his tongue speaks peace, but in his heart there is no peace [but a sword].
> For all these things (will be weighed) in the balances and exposed in the books on the great judgment day.[15]

An example follows from the Qumran texts 1QM XIII 2ff.:

---

[15] Quotation according to F. I. ANDERSON, in *OTP* (see above, n. 3) I, 179f.

> Blessed be the God of Israel for all his holy plan and his truthful works.
> Bl[es]sed be they, all (who) serve him righteously (and) know him faithfully. (vacat)
> Cursed be Belial for the hostile plan and may he be denounced for his guilty authority!
> Cursed be all the spirits of his lot for their wicked plan and may they be denounced for all their service of impure uncleanliness!
> For they are the lot of darkness, but the lot of God is for [everlast]ing light! [16]

A rabbinic example is *b. Berakhot* 61b:

> He replied: Happy are you, R. Aqiva, that you have been seized for busying yourself with the Torah! Alas for Pappus who has been seized for busying himself with idle things!

Early Christian makarisms outside the NT take over the Gospel tradition, for instance, *Gos. Thom.* 54: "Jesus said: Blessed (μακάριος) are the poor, for yours is the kingdom of heaven."
And ibid. 68-69:

> Jesus said: Blessed (μακάριος) are you when (ὅταν) you are hated and persecuted (διώκειν); and no place (τόπος) will be found where you have [not] been persecuted (διώκειν).
> Jesus said: Blessed (μακάριος) are those who have been persecuted (διώκειν) in their hearts; these are they who have known the Father in truth.
> Jesus said: Blessed (μακάριος) are they who are hungry, that the belly of him who desires may be satisfied.[17]

---

[16] Translation according to J. DUHAIME, in J. H. CHARLESWORTH (ed.), *The Dead Sea Scrolls, Vol. 2, The Princeton Theological Seminary Dead Sea Scrolls Project*, vol. 2 (Tübingen/Louisville: Mohr Siebeck, 1995), 123.

[17] Translation according to B. M. METZGER, in K. ALAND (ed.), *Synopsis Quattuor Evangeliorum* (Stuttgart: Württembergische Bibelanstalt, 1990), 524 and 526.

An expanded series of makarisms appears in Acts of Paul 5-6 that take up the content of the makarisms of the Gospels and the Jesus tradition, developing them in accordance with the Acts of Paul's emphasis on the virtue and chastity admonitions.

> Blessed are the pure in heart, for they shall see God.
> Blessed are those who have kept the flesh chaste, for they shall become a temple of God.
> Blessed are the continent, for God shall speak with them.
> Blessed are those who have kept aloof from this world, for they shall be pleasing to God.
> Blessed are those who have wives as not having them, for they shall experience God.
> Blessed are those who have fear of God, for they shall become angels of God.
> Blessed are those who respect the word of God, for they shall be comforted.
> Blessed are those who have received the wisdom of Jesus Christ, for they shall be called the sons of the Most High.
> Blessed are those who have kept their baptism, for they shall be refreshed by the Father and the Son.
> Blessed are those who have come to a knowledge of Jesus Christ, for they shall be in the light.
> Blessed are those who through love of God no longer conform to the world, for they shall judge angels, and shall be blessed at the right hand of the Father.
> Blessed are the merciful, for they shall obtain mercy and shall not see the bitter day of judgement.
> Blessed are the bodies of the virgins, for they shall be well pleasing to God and shall not lose the reward of their chastity.
> For the word of the Father shall become to them a work of salvation in the day of the Son, and they shall have rest for ever and ever.[18]

---

[18] Translation according to J. K. ELLIOTT, *The Apocryphal New Testament* (Oxford: Clarendon Press, 1993), 365 (see in CHARLESWORTH [see above, n. 2], 32f).

To sum up:

1. Both forms, makarisms in the third person singular and in the second person are commonly used in the OT-Jewish and NT traditions, the third person being more frequent.

2. We meet series of makarisms and makarisms paralleled by curses, woes or wise sayings.

3. The sapiential makarism refers to the present condition of an individual person/people/group, whereas the apocalyptic makarism departs from the benediction of, for instance, a person's conduct, actions or qualities and envisages his eschatological destiny – for example, 1 En 58:2: "Blessed are you, righteous and elect ones, for glorious is your portion." The makarisms in the Sermon on the Mount and the Sermon on the Plain, and the woes in the Sermon on the Plain belong to the apocalyptic makarisms.

IV. Makarisms in Rabbinic Judaism

K. Koch's judgment that in rabbinic texts makarisms appear "noticeably seldom"[19] is confirmed (with reference to *b. Hagigah* 14b) by Bertram;[20] Cazelles maintains that אשרי does not occur in Qumranic texts at all.[21] Strecker cites no references, either in *EWNT* II[22] or in his commentary on the Sermon on the Mount.[23] Hengel on the contrary lists an impressive compilation of makarisms.[24]

---

[19] Formgeschichte 9 n. 8; see M. Hengel, "Zur matthäischen Bergpredigt und ihrem jüdischen Hintergrund," *ThR* 52 (1987), 327-400; now in M. Hengel, *Judaica, Hellenistica et Christiana*, Kleine Schriften II (Tübingen: Mohr Siebeck, 1999), 219-92.

[20] G. Bertram, *ThWNT* IV 369.

[21] H. Cazelles, *ThWAT* I 484.

[22] G. Strecker, *EWNT* II 925-932.

[23] G. Strecker, *Die Bergpredigt, Ein exegetischer Kommentar* (Göttingen: Vandenhoeck & Ruprecht, 1985).

[24] Hengel, "Bergpredigt," 332-41.

Three points should be emphasized here:

1. In Mishnah and Tosephta, the address in the second person singular/plural is prevalent; in later texts, however, it is the third person singular/plural.

2. In rabbinic literature, too, there are series of makarisms; they seldom have more than three *stichoi*. The following citation is from *b. Hagigah* 14b, R. Johanan b. Zakkai addressing his pupils:

> Happy are ye, and happy is she that bore you;
> happy are my eyes that have seen thus.

3. Antithetical structures blessed-woeful occur in *b. Yoma* 86a interpreting Deut 6:5:[25]

> And thou shalt love the Lord thy God, i.e., that the Name of Heaven be beloved because of you. If someone studies Scripture and Mishnah, and attends on the disciples of the wise, is honest in business, and speaks pleasantly to persons, what do people then say concerning him? 'Happy the father who taught him Torah, happy the teacher who taught him Torah; woe unto people who have not studied the Torah; for this man has studied the Torah – look how fine his ways are, how righteous his deeds!'

The rabbinic examples show that makarisms have been in use over many centuries. It is not surprising, then, that in the finds of Qumran, too, this biblical form has been preserved.

V. 4Q185: A Sapiential Admonition with Makarisms

Five years after the publication of DJD IV,[26] H. Cazelles erroneously declared that אשרי does not occur in Qumranic literature.[27] In 4Q185, however, only little noticed due to its deplorable state of

---

[25] Ibid., 337.
[26] J. M. ALLEGRO, *Qumrân Cave 4* DJD V (Oxford: Clarendon Press, 1968).
[27] *ThWAT* I 484.

preservation and its poor readability, there are two instances of the use of אשרי in an obviously sapiential context.[28]

Unfortunately, only three columns of the text have come down to us. They comprise an admonition not to contest God's will but to accept it in order to receive salvation and life from it. But how is the will of God manifested? J. Strugnell has demonstrated that the suffixes of the third person feminine singular may refer to wisdom or the Law (Torah).[29] This seems plausible, and we should, according to Deut 4:6, understand it as identical: the promises of the Law are also those of *sapientia*.

The peculiarity of this text is that here not only Israel is being addressed but also the gentiles. Unfortunately the poor state of the text precludes making assessments with certainty, but there is clear evidence for this theory. Perhaps the amazement of which Deut 4:6 speaks has led the author to offer Israel's wisdom to the gentiles. In the language and context of the coming of Yahweh (cf. Nahum 1) or his messengers (cf. Malachi 3), the impossibility of standing before his angels and his judges is stressed, given the vanity and transitoriness of man. Preceded by the address ואתם בני (And you are my sons), the fate of man is mourned in a lamentation (4Q185 1-2, I, 9-13) plainly referring to Isa 40:6-8; Ps 90:5-6 and 103:15-16; and Job 14:1:

> For see, (man) sprouts like grass from the earth and his loveliness blooms like a flower. (But then) his wind blows [over him], his root shrivels, the wind scatters his leaves, until hardly anything remains in [its] pla[ce], and nothing but wind is found. *Blank* They will look for him and not find him, and no hope remains; as for him, his days are like a shadow on the ea[rth].

---

[28] On what follows, see H. LICHTENBERGER, "Eine weisheitliche Mahnrede in den Qumranfunden (4Q185)," in M. DELCOR (ed.), *Qumrân. Sa piété, sa théologie et son milieu* (Paris/Leuven: Duculot, 1978), 151-62; H. LICHTENBERGER, "Der Weisheitstext 4Q185 – eine neue Edition," in C. HEMPEL, A. LANGE and H. LICHTENBERGER (eds.), *The Wisdom Texts from Qumran and the Development of Sapiential Thought* (Leuven: Leuven University Press, 2002), 127-50.

[29] J. STRUGNELL, "Notes en marge du volume V des 'Discoveries in the Judaean Desert of Jordan'," *Revue de Qumran* 7 (1970), 161-276; concerning 4Q185: 269-73.

In face of the vanity, there is a new appeal to follow God's instructions (1-2, II, 1-4) to profit daily from his benefactions.

The makarism "Blessed is the man to whom she had been given" is followed in 4Q185 1-2, II, 9-11 by a sinner's protest. In 4Q185 1-2, I, 8 he who received "her" is blessed, then in 1-2, II, 13 he who "does her (Torah or wisdom)" is אשרי.

The relevant column in 4Q525 presents sapiential makarisms, but it is only part of a large sapiential composition of which only fragments are preserved. Although also only partly preserved, 4Q185 contains such elements as admonition, lamentation, recollection of history, imperative and protest against sinners. The text of 4Q185, despite its Qumranic provenance and a whole string of parallels, cannot be called a typical example of Essene literature; its origins are probably pre-Essene, for the following reasons:

1. The use of defective writing in 4Q185 is striking.

2. Some of its vocabulary appears for the first time in Qumran literature, which might be explained by the text's special subject.

3. The language bears a close resemblance to the late strata of the OT literature, especially its wisdom-centered parts.

4. Its free use of the tetragrammaton (1-2, II, 3) and *Elohim* (1-2, I, 14) outside of biblical quotation is a very important argument for its early origin. The discovery within the Qumran texts proves its usage in the community, and its late Hasmonean script might be a proof that it was copied there.

VI. MAKARISMS IN 1QH VI 13-16 ?

E. Puech,[30] reorganizing the manuscript 1QH^a,[31] believes he discovered a makarism in VI 13-16:

---

[30] "Un hymne essénien en partie retrouvé et les Béatitudes. 1QH V 12-VI 18 [=col XIII-XIV 7] et 4QBéat," *Revue de Qumran* 13, 1988, 59-88.

[31] H. STEGEMANN, "Rekonstruktion der Hodajot. Ursprüngliche Gestalt und kritisch bearbeiteter Text der Hymnenrolle aus Höhle 1 von Qumran" Ph. D. diss. (Heidelberg University, 1963).

13) אשר[י] אנשי אמת ובחירי צדק דורשי
14) שכל ומבקשי בינה בו[נ]י (?) שלום (?) וא[ו]הבי רחמים וענוי רוח מזוקקי
15) עוני וברורי מצרף רחומ[נ]י סליחות (?) ותמימי דרך (?)[(?)] מתאפקים עד קץ משפטיכה
16) וצופים לישועתך

The question arises whether we can be certain that we are dealing here with makarism. The decisive אשרי has been added by Puech, and it would (1) fit perfectly into the sapiential context and (2) prove by its clearly eschatological setting that sapiential and eschatological makarisms are by no means of a contrasting nature.

VII. CONCLUDING REFLECTIONS AND ISSUES

It is evident that makarisms are to be found in Qumran literature – we knew that even before the publication of 4Q525. Our main problem consists on the one hand in the scantiness of evidence and on the other in the impossibility of proving its Essene origin.

I believe 4Q185 to be of pre-Essene origin; if 1QHa VI were a makarism, it would be a piece of evidence for Qumran-Essene provenance. 4Q525 seems to be – because of its relation to the later OT sapiential literature – also of pre-Essene origin even though the tetragrammaton does not occur there. Puech has demonstrated grammatical references to such Qumran texts as S, H, M and CD.[32] The problem calls for further examination.

With regard to the makarisms in the Sermon on the Mount, two observations are striking:

1. The scantiness of makarisms in the DSS.
2. The impressive number of benedictions and curses in the DSS.

Above I quoted 1QM XIII 2ff.; I now refer to the famous passage from 1QS II 1ff., an adaptation of the Aaronite blessing:

> And the Priests shall bless all the men of the lot of God who walk perfectly in all His ways, saying: "May He bless you

---

[32] E. PUECH, DJD XXV 199.

with all good and preserve you from all evil! May He lighten your heart with life-giving wisdom and grant you eternal knowledge! May he raise His merciful face towards you for everlasting bliss!"
And the Levites shall curse all the men of the lot of Satan, saying: "Be cursed because of all your guilty wickedness! May He deliver you up for torture at the hands of the vengeful Avengers! May He visit you with destruction by the hand of all the Wreakers of Revenge! Be cursed without mercy because of the darkness of your deeds! Be damned in the shadowy place of everlasting fire! May God not heed when you call on Him, nor pardon you by blotting out your sin! May He raise His angry face towards you for vengeance! May there be no 'Peace' for you in the mouth of those who hold fast to the Fathers!" And after the blessing and the cursing, all those entering the Covenant shall say, "Amen, Amen!"[33]

Compare also the curses in, for example, 4Q280, 5Q14 and 4Q509. We may refer also to the exorcisms in 11Q11 (PsAp^a), but they may be pre-Essene.

This evidence might not be accidental: whereas Jesus and the Jesus tradition use makarisms and woes to describe a salutary or fateful quality of life or future of man, the DSS make use of blessing and cursing. Let us therefore briefly examine the evidence in the New Testament.

VIII. THE NEW TESTAMENT EVIDENCE

The scantiness of makarisms in the DSS has its counterpart in a prevalent use in the Jesus tradition and a programmatic position at the beginning of the Sermon on the Mount. In Luke the four makarisms are followed by four woes. "Woe" is used also in other

---

[33] Translation according to G. VERMES, *The Dead Sea Scrolls in English*, 3rd ed. (Sheffield: JSOT Press, 1987), 62f.

places in the Jesus tradition, but there is no curse, except Mark 11:21 on the fig tree. This means that Jesus did not use the cultic and priestly manner of cursing but adopted the blessing, as in Luke 6:28: "Bless those who curse you," or in Paul, using Jesus' words in Rom 12:14: "Bless, and do not curse." Also where there are negative pronouncements on people, groups or cities in the Jesus tradition we never find "cursed," but always "woe"; for example, on Chorazin and Bethsaida in Matt 11:21; repeatedly on scribes and Pharisees in Matthew 23; on teachers of the law in Luke; and finally on those through whom temptation (σκάνδαλα) arouse in Matt 18:7, or on those who deliver the Son of Man in Mark 14:21, Matt 26:24 and Luke 22:22. The "woes" are also dominant in Revelation; see especially the three woes in 9:12. Also in Revelation there is the double woe: οὐαί οὐαί (18:10, 16, 19).

Apart from Acts 23:14, Paul is the only New Testament author using ἀνάθεμα, as in Rom 9:3, 1 Cor 12:3, 1 Cor 16:22 and Gal 1:8f.

IX. SUMMARY

The lack of a specific cursing terminology in the Jesus tradition and the scantiness in the rest of the New Testament contrasts with its striking frequency in the DSS. The reason is not to be found in the opinion that the people of Qumran were talking more of judgment and disaster whereas Jesus was a preacher of salvation. An answer to the question must be sought on a sociological level. The blessing and cursing in Qumran is derived from the historical predominance of priestly traditions among the Essenes, a priestly basis that is also to be seen in other instances. On the other hand the use of makarisms and woes by Jesus and the Jesus movement stems from sapiential and laic circles. The difference cannot be explained as resulting from different attitudes to bliss; it derives from different historical and sociological circumstances. To be aware of that leads not to devaluation of either but to a better understanding of both: Qumran and the New Testament.

Hans-Jürgen BECKER

MATTHEW, THE RABBIS AND BILLERBECK ON THE KINGDOM OF HEAVEN

More than eighty years after it first appeared, the famous Strack–Billerbeck Commentary on the New Testament, actually compiled and written by Paul Billerbeck alone, is still widely in use. The reason for its success is the need for a reliable and comprehensive anthology of rabbinic materials on the New Testament among the majority of biblical scholars who are not familiar with the rabbinic sources. In fact, in the secondary literature on the New Testament, the Commentary is often substituted for an examination of the sources. Today, with a growing awareness that investigation into rabbinic literature has led to the questioning of some old certainties, many non-specialists feel uncomfortable with Billerbeck and try to avoid being too obviously dependent upon his dating and evaluation of the texts.

Skepticism and cautious usage is indeed appropriate. As far as dating is concerned, research has shown that in rabbinic literature the attribution of specific sayings or traditions to certain rabbis is not necessarily accurate. Comparison of the medieval manuscripts makes clear that handwritten transmission often corrupted such attributions or changed them deliberately, sometimes under the influence of parallel versions in other rabbinic works, which trace back similar texts to different authorities. In most of these cases it is impossible to reconstruct any "original" version – which, in reality, might never have existed because individual texts were taken from a fluctuating oral tradition and written down in different versions from the very start. Later scribes and redactors of the rabbinic works then strove to standardize and systematize the divergent materials.

But even if all manuscripts and parallel versions unanimously attribute a certain tradition to a certain rabbi, it need not necessarily go back to him. Originally anonymous traditions may have been supplied with the rabbi's name in relatively early stages of their transmission. An especially conspicuous example is the derivation of the famous halakhah according to which the Passover sacrifice overrides the Sabbath law in the event that the 14th Nissan, the eve of Passover, falls on a Sabbath. Examination of the corresponding text in *y. Pes* 6,1 [33a] shows clearly that the attribution of this halakhah to Hillel the Elder belongs to the latest stratum of the text and therefore cannot be regarded as original. Tradition attributed the halakhah to Hillel to provide the reason for his appointment as prince (*nasi*): "When they heard this halakhah from him, they raised and appointed him prince (*nasi*)." Quite obviously, this story as a whole belongs to the realm of historical fiction, because the institution of the *nasi* developed only at a later stage of rabbinic history. This example shows in a striking way that rabbinic literature, as a rule, is not interested in history for its own sake, and certainly not in historiographical correctness. The rabbinic works were molded under the influence of interests quite different from those of historiography. Thus most of the textual references that in earlier stages of research were employed in the writing of rabbinic history are today fundamentally called into question, due to an increased awareness that the respective traditions were neither formulated nor transmitted with the intention of providing historically trustworthy information in the modern sense. For example, the sequence of rabbis in the chain of tradition cited in *m. Avot* 1:1 proves to be a fictionalization of history by later rabbis in the interests of rabbinic self-legitimization. In *Avot de-Rabbi Nathan*, the same chain serves as a framework for the arrangement of additional legendary material and is thus employed in the rabbis' "genealogization" of their narrative tradition. In the Talmud Bavli, eventually, we find a developed system of such interconnections: almost every rabbi mentioned is said to be the son or the student of another rabbi.

These observations alone suffice to indicate that attributions of certain traditions to certain rabbis may not generally be considered as giving reliable information on the life, times and thinking of the respective sages. Rabbinic involvement with genealogy and systematic organization of the learned tradition does not coincide with our interest in historically correct attribution and dating. But even if the rabbi connected to a specific tradition could generally be identified as its author, we would lack an absolute chronology by which to date this tradition and understand it in the framework of a specific historical situation.

In consequence of these reflections, which are the result of research into rabbinic literature after Billerbeck, we can no longer regard the rabbis' names as reliable criteria for dating certain texts or even the kernel traditions taken up in them; nor can we with any certainty derive the biographies of the sages from the sources. Moreover, not only the rabbis' names but also certain events that we might be inclined to accept as historical often serve as a means of accumulating traditions of very different origin. This is the case, for example, with the formula *bo ba-yom* (on that very day), which is repeatedly used with reference to the day on which the rabbis supposedly assembled in the vineyard of Yavneh. Earlier scholars, misjudging the historical reliability of such literary devices in rabbinic literature, made of this the so-called "synod of Yavneh." Similarly, the alleged "occurrences at Bethar" are aggadic legends of diverse origin accumulated around the Bar Kokhba revolt.

Thus neither the rabbis' years of birth or death given in Billerbeck's Commentary nor its link-up of narrative materials and certain historical events taken uncritically from the sources are reliable criteria for the dating of specific texts. In only a very few cases can we derive from the rabbinic sources kernels of traditions that *might* be reminiscent of the temple cult when it was still in existence. But we can never be sure that they are not later projections. In any case, they have been handed down to us in the redactional framework of, at earliest, third-century literature.

For Billerbeck, however, the historical question, especially the possible influence of one or other rabbinic text on New Testament authors, was not the most important concern. This is quite clear from the fact that he cited in great numbers Bavli traditions whose authors, according to Billerbeck himself, lived only in the fourth or fifth century. What was his point in quoting these apparently late texts? This question can be answered by closely examining the (mostly relatively short) comments he himself formulated in order to apply his rabbinic texts to the respective New Testament verses. As a rule, these evaluating comments represent a theological rather than a historical point of view. Billerbeck in many cases tries to show how right or how new Jesus or the New Testament authors were when held against the background of rabbinic literature. In such contexts, the latter serves as the representative of Jewish theology as a whole, which, according to Billerbeck, is a phenomenon very close to New Testament theology but at decisive points in stark contrast to it.

A concrete example of some importance are Billerbeck's comments on the usage of the term "kingdom of heaven" in Matthew and in rabbinic literature, in the framework of his remarks on Matt 4:17, in volume 1 of the Commentary. As regards Jesus' way of speaking of the kingdom of heaven, Billerbeck makes clear from the beginning that his intention is to show how it was distinct from the way the phrase was used in ancient Judaism. He proceeds in two steps typical of his Commentary. First, he emphasizes that Jesus did not create a completely new language or religion from a void but took Jewish thinking as a starting point: "Daß Jesus den Ausdruck 'Gottesherrschaft' nicht selbst gebildet, sondern in der religiösen Sprache seines Volkes vorgefunden hat, bedarf angesichts der unter B gebrachten rabbin. Zitate u. der neutestl. Stellen in Nr. 1 keines weiteren Beweises" (In view of the citations from rabbinic literature I have provided above there is no need of further proof that Jesus did not invent the term "kingdom of God" but took it from the religious language of his people.) Second, the *aber* (but) decisively follows: "Aber ebenso gewiß ist es, daß Jesus den Begriff der Gottesherrschaft vertieft, erweitert u. mit neuem Inhalt erfüllt hat" (But it is just as sure that Jesus heightened and extended the concept "kingdom of God" and gave it a new meaning) (both quotes p. 180). What follows is not a proof of this thesis but an elaboration on it. This elaboration is particularly interesting because it reveals how much the author was indebted to his own Protestant religious tradition. It provided him with the systematic-theological categories for interpreting the relationship of rabbinic texts to the New Testament. In our case, while the rabbis view the kingdom of heaven (*malkhut shamayim*) in terms of acceptance, obedience and submission, Jesus sees it as a gift of God to mankind, "das Heilsgut schlechthin" (p. 181). This is a very German Protestant turn of phrase and therefore hard to translate into English, but it is possibly best rendered as "the ultimate gift of salvation." Therefore, according to Billerbeck's summing up, "Die Malkhut shamayim im jüd. Sprachgebrauch u. die *basileia tôn ouranôn* bezw. *tou theou* in Jesu Mund verhalten sich zueinander wie Gesetz und Evangelium" (The *malkhut shamayim* as a Jewish concept on the one hand and the *basileia tôn ouranôn* or *tou theou* as Jesus taught it on the other relate to each other like Law and Gospel) (p. 181).

This judgment, of course, uses a theological terminology and a pattern of thinking entirely foreign to the Gospel as well as to the rabbis. The hermeneutical *primatus* of Christian systematic-theological reflection is evident here, as is the apologetic intention of the Commentary. Its aim is achieved, on the one hand, by way of a selective perception and tendentious interpretation of the rabbinic material and, on the other, by a dogmatically prejudiced understanding of the Gospel's evidence. As to the latter, it should be taken into account that Billerbeck did not have at his disposal the methodological awareness and the historical critical tools we take for granted in our analyses of the Synoptic Gospels. With regard to the rabbinic texts, though, Billerbeck's interpretation lacks any effort to interpret them in their own right and contexts. There are no grounds to complain that Billerbeck neglected important rabbinic evidence referring to the "kingdom of heaven"; even though he does not cite all relevant texts, he provides the essential ones. But his manner of presenting only the bits and pieces that actually contain the term, disregarding even the immediate literary contexts of those isolated passages, is misleading. It opens the way to their interpretation in categories foreign to the literature they are taken from – "Law" and "Gospel." In consequence, readers lack essential information to form their own opinion on the relationship of the compiled texts to the Matthean conception. Rabbinic literature presents itself as a complex, self-governed system of reference; considering and comparing the different contexts in which certain ideas or terms appear therefore often points to the concepts that stand behind an individual text without their being explicitly mentioned or developed in every single case.

Going through the "kingdom of heaven" texts collected by Billerbeck, attentive readers will find that many of the theologically significant *malkhut shamayim* references show some link to two specific subjects of discussion in rabbinic literature. One is the recitation of the *Shma Yisra'el* (Hear, O Israel), the other the receiving of the Torah at Mount Sinai.

The Mishnah uses the expression *leqabel 'ol malkhut shamayim* (to accept the yoke of the kingdom of heaven) as a circumscription of the recitation of the *Shma*. In *m. Ber.* 2:5 it is told that Rabban Gamli'el recited the *Shma* on the first night of his wedding. His disciples say to him:

> Master, did you not teach us that a bridegroom is exempt from reciting the Shma on the first night? He said to them: I will not hearken to you to cast off from myself the yoke of the kingdom of heaven even for one hour.

Not reciting the *Shma* is equated here with casting off the yoke of the kingdom of heaven; conversely, recitation of the *Shma* is understood as an expression of bearing the yoke of the kingdom of heaven. The most obvious question – one not posed by Billerbeck – is, In what way is the *Shma* related to the kingdom of heaven? To answer this question we need to refer to the context of the quoted Mishnah paragraph; it provides an ample display of traditions concerning the *Shma*. Three paragraphs earlier, in *m. Ber.* 2:2, there is the following reflection:

> Rabbi Yehoshua ben Qorcha said: Why does the section 'Hear, O Israel' precede the section 'And it shall come to pass if ye shall hearken'? – so that a man may first take upon him the yoke of the kingdom of heaven and afterwards take upon him the yoke of the commandments.

This passage presupposes a distinction between the yoke of the kingdom of heaven and the yoke of the commandments, the former relating to the first paragraph of the *Shma* and the latter to the second. If we want to know what is meant here by "the yoke of the kingdom of heaven," we must turn to the central statement of the *Shma* at the beginning of Deut 6:4-9 and clarify its relationship to the acceptance of the commandments, which are essentially dealt with in the second section of the *Shma*, Deut 11:13-21. It is the profession of the unity of God and the unity and integrity of man in his loving relationship to God that dominates the first paragraph of the *Shma*. The unity of God is spoken of not in an abstract way, but in terms of the relationship between God and man. This relationship does not exist in a vacuum; it presupposes and evokes history. God, in the biblical context, had made himself known as the one who created the world, who chose his people and who redeemed it from Egypt.

It is the same historical dimension that is referred to explicitly in an anonymous statement in the *Mekhilta de-Rabbi Yishma'el* on Exod 20:2 (*ba-chodesh* 5), in the framework of a comprehensive discourse on the bestowal of the Torah at Mount Sinai:

> Why were the ten commandments not said at the very beginning of the Torah? The matter may be compared to a king who came into a city. He said to the people: May I rule over you? They said to him: Have you done us any good that you should rule over us? What did he then do? He built a wall for them, brought water for them, fought their battles. Then he said to them: May I rule over you? They said to him: Yes, indeed. So God brought the Israelites out of Egypt, divided the sea for

them, brought manna down for them, brought up the well for them, provided the quails for them, fought for them against Amalek. Then he said to them: May I rule over you? They said to him: Yes, indeed.

First comes the historical act of redemption from Egypt and preservation in the desert, then the acclamation of God's kingship, which brings in its wake the acceptance of his commandments. While past and present are focused in this text, another tradition in its wider Mekhilta context deals with God's kingdom in the light of eschatological future events. The Midrash's commentary on Exod 17:14 relates the following statement in the name of Rabbi Eliezer:

When will the name of Amalek perish? When idolatry will be uprooted, and those who worship it, and when God will be one in the world and his kingdom will be established forever and ever. At that time "the Lord will go forth and fight" (Zech 14:3) "and the Lord shall be king" (Zech 14:9). "You will pursue them in anger and destroy them" (Lam 3:66).

The allusion to the *Shma Yisra'el* in this text ("when God will be one") denotes that profession of the one God relates not only to past and present, to God who is at work in history, but also anticipates the future, when his unity will be evident to everyone and "his kingdom will be established forever." This future aspect is also expressed in the benedictions after the *Shma Yisra'el* in the morning and evening prayer: *emet we-yaziv* and *emet we-emuna*, respectively. Their wording is to be found only in the Siddur, but the opening words of the morning benediction are also referred to in *m. Ber.* 2:2. They deal with redemption history, beginning in the past and ending with a plea for final redemption, citing in this context the biblical verse Exod 15:18: "The Lord is king forever and ever." In Targum Pseudo-Jonathan this verse is paraphrased as follows:

When the people of the house of Israel saw the signs and wonders the Holy, blessed be he, had done for them at the Red Sea, and saw his mighty hand upon the waves, they responded and said one to another: Come, let us put the crown of his majesty on the head of our redeemer, who gives passage, but does not pass away, who changes things, but himself doesn't change; for his is the crown of the kingdom in the world to come, his is the crown, and it will belong to him forever.

The eschatological expectation of God's universal kingdom is expressed in this text with the term "world to come" (*olam ha-ba*). This term, which cannot be further explored here, appears also in a row of relevant texts that deal with rabbinic future expectation, which includes in particular the eschatological expectation of God as universal judge. The rabbinic statements on the kingdom of heaven cannot be separated from this wider context of rabbinic eschatology without reducing its significance.

Another realm of association – one that can only be hinted at here – is evoked by the word *heaven* in the term "kingdom of heaven." In contrast to "kingdom of God" (*malkhut ha-shem*), which is rare in rabbinic literature, "kingdom of heaven" arouses also the image of a spatial reality. Heaven, for the rabbis, is the sphere where God himself dwells on his throne of glory, surrounded by his ministering angels. It is also the place where the righteous will eat from the leviathan in the future.

Last but not least, the idea of martyrdom is inseparably linked to the "kingdom of heaven" concept in the famous story in *b. Ber.* 61b about Rabbi Aqiva, who died as a martyr while he "directed his mind towards accepting upon himself the kingdom of heaven." According to this story, he expired while he was reciting the first paragraph of the *Shma Yisra'el*.

Thus the term *malkhut shamayim* points to a bundle of closely associated and interconnected motifs: God's unity, his presence in his realm, his redeeming acts in past and future, his precepts for Israel by which Israel realizes God's kingdom in the present, his eschatological appearance as universal judge and the idea of martyrdom for heaven's sake.

Surveying Matthew with the contexts and relations of the term *malkhut shamayim* in rabbinic literature in mind, one makes the astonishing observation that he, in his redactional work on Mark and Q, introduced or strengthened exactly those aspects of *malkhut shamayim* stressed by the rabbis. First of all, Matthew is the only one to use the term *basileia tôn ouranôn* at all. It is one of the central and most specific terms in his theology, used no less that 32 times in his Gospel. In 15 of these the Matthean redaction changed *basileia tou theou* into *basileia tôn ouranôn*; in 8 more places it deliberately introduced *basileia tôn ouranôn*; and the term appears 9 times in the framework of material that essentially stems from special Matthean tradition (*Sondergut*). It is most probable that all these occurrences of *basileia tôn ouranôn* in the Gospel stem from Matthean redaction, and its interpretation is obviously crucial to any understanding of Matthew's theological work and intention.

What then are the theological concepts inherent in *basileia tôn ouranôn* in Matthew? Summing up my analysis, I find the most important tendencies in Matthew's redactional work in this regard to be the following:

1. Throughout, Matthew rejects the idea quite prominent in his tradition that the *basileia* is already present. For Matthew it is not yet present but has to be expected in the eschatological future. In only one verse in the whole Gospel did Matthew *not* change his tradition according to this understanding – namely, Matt 12:28, where he retains the formulation found in Q: "If I cast out devils by the spirit of God, then the kingdom of God has come unto you" – but still qualifies it in the immediate context by drawing redactional distinction between this world and the world to come (Matt 12:32: "But whoever speaks against the Holy Ghost, it shall not be forgiven him, neither in this world, nor in the world to come"). In Matthew's own view, the *basileia* may arrive tomorrow or later, there is no speculation on time in the Gospel. The important thing is that everyone should prepare himself, because the *basileia* can come anytime. This leads to the second point:

2. The disciples of the *basileia* are admonished to prepare for its arrival, because only those properly prepared will enter the *basileia*. This is in keeping with the idea strengthened by Matthew's redaction that the coming of the *basileia* will be preceded by a universal judgment of mankind. Only those who pass

this judgment will be heirs to the *basileia*. Repeatedly Matthew emphasizes that the Jesus followers will not automatically pass judgment but will be judged according to their deeds. This eventually leads to the third point:

3. Inheritance of the future *basileia* presupposes a life according to the commandments as interpreted by Jesus, the eschatological teacher. The "righteousness" necessary for the *basileia* can be obtained only by following his Torah. This is not a new Torah, but the old one in his authoritative, messianic interpretation. At its center stands the first sentence of the *Shma Yisra'el* as its governing principle (*klal*, as the rabbis would say), on which, according to Matthew's redaction in Matt 22:40, depends the whole law and the prophets. Jesus' Torah of the *basileia*, which is not yet present, is the standard that must be applied in the present to those who want to be heirs to the *basileia* in the future. In this way, the future *basileia* makes its presence felt. Just as God is and will be king in his *basileia*, he wants to be king in the lives of those whom he chose to keep his ordinances as interpreted by the eschatological teacher. His demand is founded on the redeeming acts of God reported throughout the Gospel – for example, "The blind see, the lame walk, the lepers are cleansed, and the deaf hear" (Matt 11:5), in fulfillment of the prophecies of Isaiah.

Comparing these three matters of concern in Matthew with the rabbinic usage of *malkhut shamayim* reveals a striking conceptual closeness. Realization of God's kingship through observation of the Torah in terms of bearing the yoke of the commandments, future judgment according to one's deeds and expectation of final redemption are all prominent with the rabbis, too. Of course with Matthew, the chosen ones who are called upon to gain the righteousness required for the kingdom of heaven are no longer Israel but the community gathered from Jews and non-Jews who believe in the mission of Jesus as messiah and eschatological teacher of the Torah. Still, Matthew, "the scribe instructed unto the kingdom of heaven" (Matt 13:52), interprets this mission in an entirely "rabbinic" way.

If there is complete agreement between Matthew and the rabbis with regard to the *central* ideas connected with the "kingdom of heaven" concept, may there be a similar closeness regarding the less obvious associations?

As mentioned earlier, heaven, for the rabbis, is the sphere where God himself dwells on his throne of glory. Thus "kingdom of heaven" arouses not only abstract ideas but also the image of a spatial reality. The same is definitely true for Matthew: though the spatial aspect is not foreign to Mark and Q, Matthew emphasizes it. While in 8:11 he merely approves of his Q tradition in telling us that "many shall come from the east and west and sit down at the table with Abraham, Isaac and Jacob in the kingdom of heaven," he introduces the spatial aspect in his own verses 5:20 about the just, who will "enter the kingdom of heaven," and 18:3, according to which those who do not convert and become like little children will not enter the kingdom of heaven. The "locking up" of the kingdom of heaven in Matt 23:13 also points to a spatial conception.

The close association of martyrdom with the idea of taking upon oneself the kingdom of heaven that we find in the rabbinic story of Rabbi Aqiva's death might explain the similar connection in Matt 5:10, which stems entirely from the Matthean redaction: "Blessed are they who are persecuted for righteousness' sake, for theirs is the kingdom of heaven." A combination similar to that found in the Talmud was apparently on Matthew's mind, and he found it important enough to formulate a separate beatitude to stress it – at least I don't see any other satisfactory answer to the question of why Matthew here redoubled the promise of v. 3 and the motif of 11-12.

To sum up: There is no way of proving literary dependencies between rabbinic literature and the New Testament. Nevertheless, I think we can benefit greatly from comparing these sources, on condition that we sharpen our hermeneutical awareness and define our position. Billerbeck's was the standpoint of a Christian theologian who, in many instances, was concerned with revealing in his New Testament texts the essentials of Protestant theology and, sadly enough, thought it would be helpful to outline them against the dark background of what he perceived and depicted as Jewish theology. Obviously, this was a prejudiced position.

In my view, an unprejudiced interpretation of ancient texts belongs to the realm of illusion. Every interpretation will necessarily be biased, depending on the particular questions posed and the educational background of the questioner. Under these circumstances, a most appropriate education and predisposition for interpreting the Gospel of Matthew is a thorough knowledge of rabbinic literature. It can be achieved only by studying the sources on their own terms and for their own sake. Eventually, familiarity with them will make it possible to discern aspects and connections in the Gospel that would otherwise have been missed, thus widening one's exegetical imagination and inspiring a wide-ranging interpretation of Matthew.

Such interpretation, however, is to be carefully weighed, in every case, against Matthew's text and the evidence of his redactional work.

Berndt SCHALLER

THE CHARACTER AND FUNCTION OF THE ANTITHESES IN
MATT 5:21-48 IN THE LIGHT OF RABBINICAL EXEGETIC
DISPUTES *

In Matthew's version of the Sermon on the Mount, following the nine beatitudes (Matt 5:3-12) and some basic exhortations to the disciples on their mission (Matt 5:13-16) and the lasting value of the commandments (Matt 5:17-20), the reader finds another group of utterances outstanding in character and unique in form. Six logia – dealing with such matters as murder, adultery, divorce, swearing of oaths, retaliation and love of one's enemies – follow the same linguistic pattern (Matt 5:21-48). Each is constructed in the classical mode of thesis and antithesis, position and contra-position. The position is always introduced by a variation on the same phrase – twice given in full: ἠκούσατε ὅτι ἐρρέθη τοῖς ἀρχαίοις· (You have heard that it was said to those of ancient times; Matt 5:21-33), three times reduced to ἠκούσατε ὅτι ἐρρέθη (You have heard that it was said; Matt 5:27, 38, 43) and once simply as ἐρρέθη (It was said; Matt 5:31); the contra-position is signaled by ἐγὼ δὲ λέγω ὑμῖν (But I say to you; e.g., Matt 5:22).

---

* In preparing a readable English text I am greatly indebted to Elisabeth Eck, Göttingen, who was helpful not only in brushing up my English but also in clarifying the presentation of the argument.

In New Testament research this bundle of "antitheses," as they are called,[1] has become a focus of scholarly attention. Two aspects are most prominent: (1) the literary character of the antitheses and their traditional and historical background; and (2) their theological impact. This paper attempts to explore the latter: What is the function and aim of the antithetically shaped six logia, and what implications do they have for the issue of Jesus' relation to the Torah, the biblical commandments and the fundamental statutes of contemporary Judaism – at least with regard to the picture presented by Matthew?

At first sight the answer seems simple. Given that in every case the dictum of Jesus opposes a sentence referring to biblical law, it appears logical to conclude that those "antitheses" reflect an explicit contradiction between Jesus and that law, the Torah of Moses. Thus it is not surprising to find Matt 5:21-48 grouped under headings like "The Lord stands above the Torah"[2] or "Jesus is against the Law"[3] and therefore not astonishing to find Matt 5:21-48 used

---

[1] Exactly when the word came into use as a technical term for Matt 5:21ff. is still an unresolved issue. The first occurence I found in the commentaries on Matthew was in J. WELLHAUSEN, *Das Evangelium Matthaei* (Berlin: Georg Reimer, 1904), 19, and in E. KLOSTERMANN and H. GRESSMANN, *Die Evangelien: Matthäus*, HNT 2 (Tübingen: Mohr Siebeck, 1909), 188-94. On the question of a Marcionitic background, see below n. 8.
As I have recently discovered, Martin VAHRENHORST provided an excursus on this subject in his seminal dissertation on Matt 5:33-37; 23:16-22: *'Ihr sollt überhaupt nicht schwören'* – *Matthäus im halachischen Diskurs*, WMANT 95 (Neukirchen/Vlyn: Neukirchener Verlag, 2002), 217ff., in which he refers to the treatment of the term "antithesis" in the philosophical language of the 18th and 19th centuries.

[2] G. STRECKER, *Die Bergpredigt*, (Göttingen: Vandenhoeck & Ruprecht, 1984), 65 [= *The Sermon on the Mount* (Nashville: Abingdon, 1988), 63].

[3] J. JEREMIAS, *Neutestamentliche Theologie, Erster Teil: Die Verkündigung Jesu* (Gütersloh: Gütersloher Verlagshaus Gerd Mohn, 1971[= 1973]) 242 [= *New Testament Theology. Part One: The Teaching of Jesus* (London: SCM Press, 1971) (= 1996), 253]; L. GOPPELT, *Theologie des Neuen Testaments* 1 (Göttingen: Vandenhoeck & Ruprecht, 1975), 150 [= *Theology of the New*

to prove Jesus' opposition to Judaism, to portray Jesus as a critic of the Torah.

On closer inspection of the texts however, this Torah-critical interpretation becomes highly questionable. It is loaded with incongruities and paradoxes especially on three counts.

First, the Torah-critical interpretation does not work with all of the antithetical sayings. In at least two of the six antitheses – the first, about murder, and the second, about adultery – Jesus does not criticize the Torah, much less does he advocate the abolition of the biblical commandments.

Second, the assertion that the sayings of Jesus in Matt 5:21-48 are opposed verbatim to texts of the Torah does not fit in all cases; it is true only in regard to the second and fifth sayings. All the others have to do either with biblical citations supplemented by additional sentences (the 1st and 6th sayings) or simply with free allusions to biblical texts (the 3rd and 4th sayings).

Third, in Matthew 5 the group of six antithetically shaped sayings is preceded by statements in which the lasting value of the Torah and the Prophets (Matt 5:17-20) is proclaimed as a hermeneutical principle. This combination would not make sense if the antitheses were basically antinomistic by nature.[4]

But that is not all. When we assign a Torah-critical function to the antitheses, we are confronted with a further problem of considerable theological import. In characterizing the sayings of Jesus in Matthew 5 one routinely speaks of Jesus as being opposed to the Torah or as placing himself above the Torah. But these expressions cloud rather then clarify the decisive point. Who is the logical subject in the formula ὅτι ἐρρέθη (that it was said)? The question is not only what was said but also who is standing in the back-

---

Testament I (Grand Rapids: Eerdmanns, 1981), 104].

[4] On attempts to untie this knot in terms of literary criticsm and history of tradition, see. H. T. WREGE, *Die Überliefungsgeschichte der Berpredigt*, WUNT 9 (Tübingen: Mohr Siebeck, 1968), 44-57. See also, G. RÖHSER, "Jesus – der wahre 'Schriftgelehrte'. Ein Beitrag zum Problem der Toraverschärfung in den Antithesen der Bergpredigt," *ZNW* 86 (1995), 20-33, esp. 22f.

ground? Some scholars maintain that the reference is to Moses.⁵ But that is certainly not the case; since ὅτι ἐρρέθη is specifically defined with regard to the contemporary linguistic code – in the same way as the Hebrew equivalent שנאמר is in rabbinic literature, – the subject behind it must be God himself. As an introductory formula for a biblical commandment, "it was said" is a *passivum divinum*, a divine passive, which is used in Jewish literature and also in Christian sources to paraphrase God's actions.⁶ This is by no means a new observation, but its significance with respect to the antitheses in Matthew 5 has rarely been perceived or has been played down.⁷ Hans Windisch was one of the few scholars who realized what was at stake in this special context. Windisch, in his excellent and still important book *Der Sinn der Bergpredigt* (The

---

⁵ See J. SCHNIEWIND, *Das Evangelium nach Matthäus*, NTD 2 (Göttingen: Vandenhoeck & Ruprecht, 1937/196812), 57; K. BERGER, *Die Gesetzesauslegung Jesu*, WMANT 40 (Neukirchen/Vlyn: Neukirchener Verlag, 1972), 589; STRECKER (above, n. 2), 67 [65].

⁶ On the use of שנאמר, see W. BACHER, *Die exegetische Terminologie der jüdischen Traditionsliteratur. Erster Teil: Die bibelexegetische Terminologie der Tannaiten* (Leipzig: Hinrichs, 1899) [= Darmstadt: Wissenschaftliche Buchgesellschafts, 1965], 6. In the New Testament it is especially Matthew who makes use of this parlance, in addition to Matt 5 see 1:22; 2:17, 23; 8:17; 12:17; 13:35; 21:4; 22:31; 24:15; 27:9. See further Acts 2:16 and 13:40; Gal 3:16; Rom 9:12.

⁷ See, for example, G. DALMAN, *Jesus-Jeschua* (Leipzig: Hinrichs, 1922) [= Darmstadt: Wissenschaftliche Buchgesellschaft, 1967], 68: "Bei Jesus stehen nicht menschliche Autoritäten einander gegenüber, sondern der Gesetzgeber vom Sinai, also der dort redende Gott, steht auf der einen Seite, auf der anderen Jesus als einer, der überzeugt ist, Gott auch hinter sich zu haben, nämlich als den, der seine Königsherrschaft endgültig aufrichtet." [= *Jesus-Jeshua* (London: Society for Promoting Christian Knowledge, 1929), 70: "Our Lord does not place His authority in opposition to that of others; it is the Law-Giver of Sinai (i.e. God) who is on the one side, and on the other Jesus; He being at the same time convinced that the same God is, in fact, in agreement with His, Jesus', purpose, which is to establish God's kingdom for ever."]

meaning of the Sermon on the Mount), published in 1929 and again with some revisions in 1934,[8] pointed out that in the opposing sequence "It was said (to those of ancient times) ... but I say to you," Marcion is anticipated, because in this sequence Jesus is opposed to God, if one takes it literally. Are the antitheses in the Gospel of Matthew a forerunner of Marcion's *antitheseis*?[9] Understandably, this conjecture was not well received. Windisch himself admitted: "Der Radikalismus der Antithesen ... (sei) doch nicht so ernst, so marcionitisch ... gemeint, wie es der Wortlaut fordert" (The radicalism of the antitheses ... is not so grave, so Marcionitic as the wording indicates).[10] Windisch maintained this view merely with regard to Matthew, observing that in Matthew 5 the antithetical sayings of Jesus are closely connected with Jesus'

---

[8] H. WINDISCH, *Der Sinn der Bergpredigt*, UNT 16 (Leipzig: Hinrichs, 1929), 96f.

[9] It is obvious that in the modern exegesis of Matt 5:21ff., the Marcionitic context played, consciously or unconsciously, an important role (see H. FRANKEMÖLLE, "Die sogenannten Antithesen des Matthäus (Mt. 5,21ff.)," in *Die Bibel. Das bekannte Buch – das fremde Buch* (Paderborn: Ferdinand Schöningh, 1994), 62-92, esp. 69-75 [= *Jüdische Wurzeln christlicher Theologie. Studien zum biblischen Kontext neutestamentlicher Texte*, BBB 116 (Bodenheim: Philo, 1998), 295-328, esp. 303-10]. But whether the designation of Matt 5:21-48 as "antitheses" was from the beginning chosen in accordance with the title of Marcion's work is still an open question (above, n.1). – In any case it is highly doubtful that Marcion himself was inspired by Matt 5:21ff. (see A. VON HARNACK, *Das Evangelium vom fremden Gott*, TU 44 (Leipzig: Hinrichs, 1924) [= Darmstadt: Wissenschaftliche Buchgesellschaft, 1985], 89 n. 2. Regarding the few and second-hand relics of Marcion's *Antitheseis* that have been preserved (containing at best faint echoes of Matt 5:21ff.), I don't see how Marcion's supposed dependence on Matthew 5 could be proven (contrary to H. D. BETZ, *The Sermon on the Mount*, [Minneapolis: Fortress Press, 1995], 200). And this holds even more for the suggestion that Marcion introduced the term *antithesis* with the exclusive meaning of "abolition," especially in view of Matt 5:21ff. See H. FRANCKEMÖLLE, *Matthäus Kommentar 1*, (Düsseldorf: Patmos, 1994), 226.

[10] WINDISCH (above, n. 8), 97

statements about the lasting value of the Torah and the Prophets (Matt 5:17-20). Consequently, he concluded that the opposition between Jesus and the law stated in Matthew 5 has nothing to do with a real antagonism but describes a phantom. As far as I can see, only Wellhausen has risked giving his comment on Matt 5:21 48 a similar direction by creating one of his typical aphorisms: "Die Folie wird verdunkelt, um das Licht heller strahlen zu lassen." (The foil is darkened in order to brighten the light).[11] In general, New Testament scholars have simply overlooked this consequence of the Torah-critical interpretation of the antithetical sayings in Matthew 5, or they have underestimated its relevance.[12] But that provides no solution to the problem.

In short, it is quite evident that the Torah-critical interpretation of the antithetical pattern in Matthew 5 leads, in terms both of theology and of hermeneutics, into a dead end. In this situation, one either has to admit that the antitheses in Matthew 5 are fictitious, because they don't correspond in fact to what they promise in form, or to look about for a different interpretation. Is that possible?

Initial hints of another mode of interpretation were given already by John Lightfoot and Christian Schoettgen, the early collectors of rabbinic parallels to the New Testament, the Billerbecks of the seventeenth and eighteenth centuries. Lightfoot in his *Horae Hebraicae et Talmudicae in Quattuor Evangelistas* commented as follows on Matt 5:21: "Particulae Legis, quae hic citantur a Salvatore, non adducuntur ut nuda verba Mosis, sed ut vestita glossematibus Scribarum" (The particular words of the Law that are here quoted by the Savior are not used as the naked words of Moses but as [words] clothed by explanations of the Scribes),[13] but

---

[11] WELLHAUSEN (above, n. 1), 19.

[12] John P. MEIER presents a remarkable example in his study *Law and History in Matthew's Gospel: A Redactional Study of Mt. 5:17-48*, Analecta Biblica 71 (Rome: Biblical Institute Press, 1976), 131ff.

[13] J. LIGHTFOOT, *Horae Hebraicae et Talmudicae in Quattuor Evangelistas*, J. B. CARPZOV (ed.) (Leipzig: Fridricus Lankisius, 1684), 262f.; for English translation, see *A Commentary on the New Testament from Talmud and Hebraica II* (Oxford: Oxford University Press, 1859), 107.

without listing proofs from rabbinical sources. These, however, were provided by Schoettgen in his *Horae Hebraicae et Talmudicae in universum Novum Testamentum*. He equated the Greek passive ἐρρέθη in Matthew 5 with the Aramaic אתאמר, which in the talmudic sources "non de verbo divino, sed tantum de traditionibus Rabbanistarum adhibetur" (is not related to the divine word, but only to the traditions of the rabbis)[14] Although this identification does not hold with respect to the antitheses of Matthew 5 – אתאמר is an introductory formula that obviously was first used in the Amoraic period[15] – Schoettgen deserves mention because it was he who initiated the search for parallels to the antithetical scheme, especially to the introductory formulas of Matt 5:21-48.

To anticipate the results of the present study: No precise parallel was found. The antithetically formulated sayings in Matthew 5 are, in terms of their linguistic character, unique. There are no counterparts, either in Matthew or in other parts of the New Testament or further early Christian writings, nor in the whole bulk of Jewish literature. What can be found are parallels to certain elements of the antithetical matrix.

It was the famous Salomon Schechter who commented, in an aside, that the way in which the verbs ἀκούειν (to hear) and λέγειν (to say, to speak) are used in Matt 5:21-48 seemed to him very close to the manner in which their Hebrew equivalents שמע and אמר are used in the rabbinical sources to express understanding by hearing, and interpreting by saying.[16] Schechter referred at this point to the phrase שומע אני תלמוד לומר (I have heard [and under-

---

[14] C. SCHOETTGEN, *Horae Hebraicae et Talmudicae in universum Novum Testamentum*, (Dresden/Leipzig: Christoph. Henkelii Filius, 1733), 32f.

[15] Cf. BACHER (above, n. 6), 189.

[16] S. SCHECHTER, "The Rabbinic Conception of Holiness," *JQR* 10 (1897/98), 11 n. 2; idem, "On the Study of Talmud (1899)," in *Studies in Judaism II* (New York: Jewish Publications Society of America, 1908), 117 [= *Studies in Judaism: Essays on Persons, Concepts, and Movements of Thought in Jewish Tradition* (New York: The Jewish Publications Society of America, 1958), 65].

stood], but the teaching says), which in tannaitic midrashim serves to describe, and solve, an exegetic or halachic dispute.

Somewhat later, Gustav Dalman pointed out another substantial linguistic parallel.[17] He indicated that the phrase ἐγὼ δὲ λέγω ὑμῖν (But I say to you), with the emphatic "I" at the beginning of Jesus' statement, is by no means exceptional. Indeed, in early as well in later rabbinical writings nearly the same phrase is used.[18] In the Tosefta and the midrash *Sifre*, in the Palestinian and the Babylonian Talmud, and in other rabbinical sources, we repeatedly find the phrase ואני אומר, in all cases in the adversative sense of "But I say."[19] This ואני אומר is like the phrase שומע אני תלמוד לומר, a for-

---

[17] DALMAN (above, n. 7), 68f.

[18] The same observation was already made by LIGHTFOOT (above, n. 13), 263, but again without providing any proof: "ואני אומר: Confutantis est, vel quaestionem determinantis, frequentissime apud scriptores Hebraeos." This was noticed also by F. NORK, *Rabbinische Quellen und Parallelen zu neutestamentlichen Schriftstellen* (Leipzig: Ludwig-Schumann, 1839), 31, and by E. BISCHOFF, "Jesus und die Rabbinen. Jesu Bergpredigt und 'Himmelreich'," in idem, *Unabhängigkeit vom Rabbinismus*, Schriften des Institutum Judaicum in Berlin 33. But DALMAN [(above, n. 7), 68 n. 4.5] was the first to present a collection of relevant passages mainly from the Tosefta (see also below, n. 19).

[19] The number of references to this formula is not as small as sometimes stated (see, for example, M. HENGEL, "Zur matthäischen Bergpredigt und ihrem jüdischen Hintergrund," *ThR* 52 1987, 376). It can be found in the following variety of rabbincal sources: *t. Bik.* 1:2 (ed. ZUCKERMANDEL 100,6); *t. Pes.* 1:6 (155,17); *t. Sota* 4:6 (304,15), 7 (305,2), 9 (305,20), 11 (306,3.9); *t. Bekh.* 2:12 (536,26); *t. Miq.* 3:4 (655,20); *Sifre Bemidbar* 95 on Num 11:21 (ed. HOROVITZ, 95,3); *Sifre Devarim* 31 on Deut 6:4 (ed. FINKELSTEIN 50,4.7.13); *Sifre Zuta* 19, 3 (ed. HOROVITZ, 302,8); *Mek. R. Sh.* 19, 17 (ed. EPSTEIN-MELAMED, 143,1); *y. Er.* 1, 1 [18d 8]; 2,1 [20a 29]; *y. Pes.* 5,2 [32a 50]; *y. Yoma* 1,1 [38d 41]; *y. R. Ha-Shan.* 3,1 [58d 11]; *y. Ta'an.* 4,8 [68c 67]; *y. Hag.* 3,4 [79c 48]; *y. Yev.* 15,1 [14d 13]; *y. Git.* 1,2 [43c 2]; *y. B. Qam.* 1,1 [2b 46]; *y. Sanh.* 11,7 [30b 45]; *y. Mak.* 2,7 [31d 41.46]; *y. Hor.* 3,3-5 [47d 46]; *b. Ber.* 38b (2x); *b. Shab.* 25b; *b. Pes.* 66b-67a (3x); *b. Yoma* 43b; *b. Hag.* 19b; *b. Yev.* 52b; 70a; *b. Ket.* 106a; *b. Qid.* 4a; *b. B. Qama* 11a(2x); *b. B. Mez.* 41b (2x); 59a; *b. Av. Zar.* 16b; *b. Zev.* 44b (5x); 82b; *Ber. Rab.* 53 on Gen 21:9.

mula of discussion. It is used in the context of disputes among sages over the meaning and interpretation of biblical texts, concerning both halachic and haggadic matters. ואני אומר comes into play in distinguishing an interpretation held by a single scribe in order to contrast his position against the view taken by other scribes, in most cases the majority position.

In his huge collection of rabbinical parallels to the New Testament, Paul Billerbeck oddly enough ignored both Schechter's idea and Dalman's proposal.[20] Two generations passed before Morton Smith,[21] David Daube[22] and Eduard Lohse[23] came back to these suggestions. However they did not pay enough attention to the importance of these parallels for the character of the antitheses in Matthew 5.

Of course one cannot ignore the fact that the introductory phrases in Matt 5:21-48 concur only partially with the rabbinical parlance used in scribal discussions. But the question is whether this can be used as an argument to deny a substantial connection between the rabbinical and the New Testament phrases.

Here we are confronted with a basic problem of methodology. Using rabbinical texts to understand New Testament texts has again and again been a matter of dispute. Naming the early Bous-

---

[20] In his comments on the introductory formula of Matt 5:21ff., Billerbeck merely repeated Schoettgen's remarks on ἐρρέθη (above, n. 14), adding some new references from the talmudic literature (see H. STRACK and P. BILLERBECK [eds.], *Kommentar zum Neuen Testament aus Talmud und Midrasch, I Das Evangelium nach Matthäus* [Munich: C. H. Beck, 1926], 253; also NORK [above, n. 18], 30f.)

[21] M. SMITH, *Tannaitic Parallels to the Gospels*, JBL Monograph Series 6 (Philadelphia: Society of Biblical Literature, 1951), 27-30.

[22] D. DAUBE, "Ye Have Heard – But I Say Unto You," in idem, *The New Testament and Rabbinic Judaism* (London: Athlone Press, 1956), 55-66.

[23] E. LOHSE, "Ich aber sage euch," in E. LOHSE, C. BURCHARD and B. SCHALLER (eds.), *Der Ruf Jesu und die Antwort der Gemeinde*, FS J Jeremias (Göttingen: Vandenhoeck & Ruprecht, 1970), 189-203 [= idem, *Die Einheit des Neuen Testaments. Exegetische Studien zur Theologie des Neuen Testaments I* (Göttingen: Vandenhoek & Ruprecht, 1973/1976), 73-87].

set[24] and the more recent Neusner[25] may suffice for illustration. There are good reasons both pro and con. Certainly one has to be very careful on this point. "Parallelomania" is, without doubt, a danger. But a general and complete ban on using rabbinical material cannot be validated. In the case under consideration I think it is well justified to take the above-mentioned rabbinic linguistic parallels into account in interpreting the introductory formulas in Matthew 5. The decisive question in such cases is not whether the phrases are precisely identical but whether the corresponding phrases reflect the same cultural or intellectual perspective of language and thought.[26] In my judgment this is the case for Matthew 5. The phrases used in the context of rabbinical disputes and the phrases used in the introduction to the sayings of Jesus in Matthew 5 are tangential in terms of both language and circumstances. In both instances they are related to and included in the interpretation of biblical dicta, of words of the Torah. In both cases, apparently, they reflect one and the same intellectual milieu: the language, thought and practice of the scribes.

This conclusion strikingly supports the above suggestion that the antithetically constructed sayings in Matthew 5 do not imply an opposition of Jesus to the Torah. Quite the contrary. What those sayings present is Jesus' struggle with and refutation of other interpretations and interpreters of the biblical law. No more and no less.

---

[24] W. BOUSSET, *Die Religion des Judentums im neutestamentlichen Zeitalter* (Berlin: Reuther and Reichard, 1903, 41ff.); idem, *Volksfrömmigkeit und Schriftgelehrtentum. Antwort auf Herrn Perles' Kritik an meiner "Religion des Judentums im N.T. Zeitalter"* (Berlin: Reuther and Reichard, 1903), 3ff.

[25] J. NEUSNER, "Are There Really Tannaitic Parallels to the Gospels?" in *South Florida Studies in the History of Judaism* 80 (1993).

[26] The objection of HENGEL ([above, n. 19], 376), that the rabbinical introductory formula cannot be compared with the formula in Matt 5 because the latter has additionally the personal pronoun is in my view not very well founded. Hengel ignores not only the fact that the personal pronoun in Matt 5:21-48 is conditioned by the introductory ἠκούσατε (You have heard) but also that in Matt 5, as in the rabbinical texts in question, the formula is related to the meaning of biblical commandments.

Under this presupposition one has to rephrase the introductory formulas of the antithetical scheme in Matthew 5 in the following way: "You have heard and interpreted what God said to the men of old ... But I say to you in regard to that which you understood...." This rephrasing means, first, the phrase ἠκούσατε (You have heard) implies hearing and understanding, hearing as understanding; second, the phrase ἐρρέθη (It was said) is related to God and introduces the matter concerned, the biblical text referred to; and third, the antithetical phrase ἐγὼ δὲ λέγω ὑμῖν (But I say to you) bears not upon ἐρρέθη (It was said), but – addressing the same persons – upon ἠκούσατε (You have heard); consequently it is opposed not to the sentence of the Torah itself being cited or alluded to, but to some aspect of its interpretation.

Of course, objections to this proposal may be raised. One can ask, and it has been asked, whether the distinction between opposing the Torah and opposing interpretations of the Torah, between criticism of the Torah and criticism of its interpreters, holds what it seems to promise.[27] Where does this distinction stand with respect to the concept of the two תורות מסיני (Torahs from Sinai), as it is found in rabbinical discourses that place the Torah and the Halakhah in an extraordinarily close relationship? At first glance this question seems reasonable, as long as one proceeds on the assumption that rabbinical utterances can be handled like a system of theological dogmata. But that is notoriously problematic, given the range of controversies within and between the rabbinical schools about the proper understanding of the divine commandments.[28]

---

[27] W. KÜMMEL, "Jesus und der jüdische Traditionsgedanke," *ZNW* 33 (1934), 105-30, esp. 125ff. [= idem, E. GRÄSSER, O. MERK and A. FRITZ (eds.), *Heilsgeschehen und Geschichte. Gesammelte Aufsätze 1933–1964*, Marburger Theologische Studien 3 (Marburg: Elwert, 1965), 15-35: 31f.].

[28] An early example of explicit controversial regulations introduced by the formula אנחנו אומרים (We say) is found in the "Halakhic Letter" from Qumran: 4QMMT^b 55.64f.73 (DJD X, 52.54). On this formula see the remarks by E. QIMRON and J. STRUGNELL, *Qumran Cave 4. V: Miqṣat Ma'aśe Ha-Torah*, DJD X (Oxford: Clarendon Press, 1994), 97.

As far as I can see the only real challenge to the suggested meaning of the antitheses in Matthew 5 lies in the question: To what extent is it possible that the antitheses themselves provide evidence in favor of this understanding? To what extent are the six antithetical statements related to the biblical commandments preceding each of them? And in particular, to what extent can those statements be understood as interpretations of those commandments?

What follows is an attempt to address these questions.

That interpretation is inherent can be plainly detected in the first antithesis, relating to the issue of murder (Matt 5:21ff). Both thesis and antithesis reflect the reasoning typical of scribes. It is evident in the former in the way the biblical instruction quoted by Jesus is amplified, giving notice of the punishment ordained against murder: "and whoever murders shall be liable to judgment."[29] And it is evident in the latter in the character of Jesus' own injunction "to regard the feeling of anger as no less terrible a crime than murder." As C. G. Montefiore in his commentary on the Synoptic Gospels has pointed out: "Such paradoxical equivalencies were quite usual among the Rabbis."[30]

The same holds for the second and the third antitheses, concerning adultery (Matt 5:27ff.) and divorce (Matt 5:31f.). Here too an interpretative character is evident.[31]

The fourth antithesis, concerning the issue of oaths (Matt 5:33-37), poses problems at several points. First, it is the only saying not based on a specific biblical quotation.[32] Second, as is widely

---

[29] See M. McNamara, *The New Testament and the Palestinian Targum to the Pentateuch*, Analecta Biblica 27(A) (Rome: Biblical Institute Press, 1965/1978), 126-30. And see further esp. S. Ruzer, "The Technique of Composite Citation in the Sermon on the Mount (Mt. 5:21-22, 33-37)," *RB* 103 (1996), 65-75, esp. 66ff.

[30] C. G. Montefiore, *The Synoptic Gospels*, vol. 2, 2nd ed. (London: Macmillan, 1927), 60.

[31] See Ruzer (above, n. 29), 71f.

[32] οὐκ ἐπιορκήσεις has no biblical counterpart, but it squares with the summary of Exod 20:7 and Lev 19:12 in *PsPhoc* 16. See P. W. van der Horst, *The Sentences of Pseudo-Phocylides*, SVTPs 4 (Leiden: Brill, 1978), 123f.

thought, in its essence it seems to go far beyond what a contemporary Jew could have said. How should we deal with this text? Was Serge Ruzer on the right track arguing against this view by demonstrating a close connection with rabbinic discussions about vows and oaths?[33] I leave that question open for the time being.

I will restrict my inquiry to the last two sayings, the fifth antithesis, concerning non-retaliation (Matt 5:38-42), and the sixth antithesis (Matt 5:43-48), concerning love of one's enemies. In both cases we have to do with statements of a most impressive and outstanding character: μὴ ἀντιστῆναι τῷ πονηρῷ· (Do not resist an evildoer) – ἀγαπᾶτε τοὺς ἐχθροὺς ὑμῶν (Love your enemies). They seem to be absolutely exceptional. But that is true only with regard to their wording, not with regard to their substance. Similar or at least comparable utterances, as we all know, are to be found here and there in ancient Jewish sources.[34] The crucial problem of these statements lies not in their uniqueness but in their relation to the quoted biblical precepts. Would it be possible to define this relationship in terms of interpretation?

At first sight to do so looks far-fetched, especially in view of Jesus' saying formulated in opposition to the biblical rule "An eye for an eye, a tooth for a tooth." Among the antitheses in Matthew 5 no other saying can so clearly be classified as contradicting or abrogating the Torah. Taking all this into consideration, how can one assume an interpretative attitude behind this saying?

Two observations, I think, support the assumption of an interpretative attitude. First, in contemporary Jewish literature we find

---

[33] RUZER (above, n. 29), 72ff. See also esp. VAHRENHORST (above, n. 1).
[34] On the concept of non-retaliation, see BILLERBECK, vol. 1 (above, n. 20), 341f.; U. LUTZ, *Das Evangelium nach Matthäus*, EKK I.1 (Zürich/Neukirchen/Vlyn: Benzinger-Neukirchener Verlag, 1985), 293ff. [= *Matthew 1-7* (Minneapolis: Augsburg, 1989), 326-29]; M. GORDON, *Non-Retaliation in Early Jewish and New Testament Texts: Ethical Themes in Social Context*, PSP Suppl. 13 (Sheffield: Sheffield Academic Press, 1993), 39-44. On the virtue of loving enemies, see BILLERBECK, vol. 1 (above, n. 20), 368ff.; A. NISSEN, *Gott und der Nächste im antiken Judentum*, WUNT 15 (Tübingen: Mohr Siebeck, 1974), 304-29.

some pronouncements that, in their substance, are very close to the saying of Jesus. In the love story of Joseph and Aseneth, probably written by an Egyptian Jew, the concept of non-retaliation is verbalized several times, both in taking up and in reversing the biblical *ius talionis*.[35] The admonition addressed by Levi to his brother Benjamin while the latter is drawing his sword to strike Pharaoh's son provides the best example: μηδαμῶς ἀδελφὲ ποιήσεις τὸ πρᾶγμα τοῦτο διότι ἡμεῖς ἄνδρες θεοσεβεῖς ἐσμεν καὶ οὐ προσήκει ἀνδρί θεοσεβεῖ ἀποδοῦναι κακὸν ἀντὶ κακοῦ οὐδὲ πεπτωκότα καταπατῆσαι οὐδὲ ἐκθλίψαι τὸν ἐχθρὸν αὐτοῦ ἕως θανάτου (By no means, brother, will you do this deed, because we are men who worship God, and it does not befit a man who worships God to repay evil for evil nor to trample underfoot a fallen [man] nor to oppress his enemy till death) (*JosAs* 29:3).[36] This admonition, which explicitly invokes the biblical *ius talionis* and simultaneously expresses just the opposite, shows quite clearly that in ancient Judaism it was not unusual to attack or abrogate the principle of *ius talionis* while invoking the biblical phrasing itself.[37]

Second, comparing the antithetical saying with the corresponding biblical thesis one senses a subtle linguistic allusion to the former in the latter. The phrase μὴ ἀντιστῆναι τῷ πονηρῷ (Do not resist an evildoer) is reminiscent of the wording ὀφθαλμὸν ἀντὶ ὀφθαλμοῦ ὀδόντα ἀντὶ ὀδόντος (An eye for an eye and a tooth for a tooth). However this is true only on the basis of the Greek text. A more evident connection occurs elsewhere. The special rule of the *ius talionis* occurs in the Bible in Exod 21:23-25, Lev 24:19,20

---

[35] See *JosAs* 28:5,10,14; 29:3.

[36] The Greek text follows the new critical edition of C. BURCHARD, *Joseph und Aseneth*, PsVTG 5, (Leiden: Brill, 2003); the English translation is also indebted to C. Burchard: see OTP, vol. 2, 246.

[37] A similar case is to be found in a dictum ascribed to Rabbi Meir in *Exod. Rab.* 26,2, where God himself gives the advice: הוי דומה לי מה אני משלם טובה תחת רעה אף אתה הוי משלם טובה תחת רעה (Resemble Me; just as I repay good for evil, so do thou also repay good for evil) (translation: S. M. LEHRMAN, *Midrash Rabba. Exodus* [London: Soncino Press, 1951], 318.)

and Deut 19:21. Closer inspection of these specific texts and their settings strikingly reveals, in the proximate context of Deut 19:21, the very words used in Jesus' saying: in Deut 19:16 and 18 the verb ענה occurs in the Hebrew text in the sense of opposing someone in court, which is translated in the Septuagint either by καταλέγειν (v.16) or by καθιστάναι (v.18); and in Deut 19:19 and 20 the noun רע plays an essential role; in the Septuagint it is treated first as the masculine gender (τὸν πονηρόν) and then as neuter (τὸ πονηρόν).

This concurrence of motives is too peculiar to be brushed off as purely accidental. In ancient times, as opposed to our era, pious and learned people were so well acquainted, so intimate, with the biblical texts that they recognized and appreciated this type of allusion. And if that is true with regard to the wording of the fifth antithesis, then we can go a step further and ask whether Jesus' saying about non-retaliation may be understood as an interpretation of the biblical *ius talionis*. At first sight this proposition looks abstruse and absurd, but I think it is defendable.

In what follows I am especially indebted to David Flusser.[38] The basis of Flusser's reasoning with regard to the fifth antithesis is the text of the *talio* in Exodus 21. There the *talio* starts with ונתתה נפש תחת נפש (Then you shall give life for life ...). To whom is it said? Originally, of course, it was directed to the evildoer. However, if the saying is isolated as a maxim – and this apparently happened – then it could also be understood, paradoxically, to be directed to the victim. According to Flusser, Jesus took this position in opposing "the cruel understanding" of the *ius talionis*, as was promulgated mainly by the Sadducees. And in this way he not only intended to refute his Saducean adversaries but also risked changing the meaning of the biblical rule to the very opposite.

This is certainly an unusual way of reasoning, but it is nevertheless worth considering, at least if we take into account that the

---

[38] D. FLUSSER, "Die Tora in der Bergpredigt," in H. KREMERS (ed.), *Juden und Christen lesen dieselbe Bibel*, Duisburger Hochschulbeiträge 2 (1977), 103 [= idem, *Entdeckungen im Neuen Testament 1: Jesusworte und ihre Überlieferung* (Neukirchen/Vlyn: Neukirchener Verlag, 1987), 21f.].

logic of interpretation reflected in early Jewish and also in early Christian sources often goes along highly artificial paths. Further, given that the ancient interpreters read their Bible as an integrated complex, one could even go a step further. But once again, of course, some imagination is needed and also a biblical concordance.

In Isa 50:6 the servant (עבד) of the Lord speaks thus about himself: גוי נתתי למכים ולחיי למרטים; LXX: τὸν νῶτόν μου δέδωκα εἰς μάστιγας, τὰς δὲ σιαγόνας μου εἰς ῥαπίσματα (My back I gave to those who struck me and my cheeks to those who pulled out my beard). Whether this saying itself alludes to the text of the *talio* is an open question. But it is quite obvious that in reading this text one is reminded of the *talio*. In Isa 50:6 the parlance used is the same as in the *talio*: here MT נתתי, LXX δέδωκα (I gave); there MT נתתה, LXX δώσεις (You shall give). But the tenor is the opposite. Apparently Isa 50:6 is highly proximate to the reversal of the classical *talio* as stated in Matthew 5 (and *JosAs* 28 and 29). One may thus ask whether this prophetic saying is the source of this kind of reversal. The fact that in Matt 5:39b (ὅστις σε ῥαπίζει εἰς τὴν ... σιαγόνα) (If any one strikes you on the ... cheek) we find the same motives used as in Isa 50:6b makes it very likely.[39] But I leave that point open. For the present purpose it is sufficient to have shown that the fifth antithesis, by opposing the *ius talionis* and thus seemingly abrogating the Torah – incidentally, the only one among the antitheses in Matthew 5 to do so – can be understood in the setting of Torah-related interpretation.

Finally, in this connection, what about the sixth antithesis: ἀγαπᾶτε τοὺς ἐχθροὺς ὑμῶν (Love your enemies)? Can this saying

---

[39] After finishing the first draft of this paper, I found that this contextual relation had already attracted the notice of M. D. GOULDER. In his *Midrash and Lection in Matthew* (London: SPCK, 1974), 293, Goulder classified Matt 5:39 as "a development of Isa 50:6" on the basis of the LXX. I doubt that the reference to the LXX version is necessary, but the entire question of the textual underpinning of the antithetical sayings is indeed worthy of investigation.

also be understood as resulting from interpretation? In Matthew 5 the principle of love also including love of one's enemy is related to Lev 19:18: ἀγαπήσεις τὸν πλησίον σου (You shall love your neighbor), but of course it does not stand in opposition to this biblical commandment. It is opposed to a second part of the "thesis," which is appended in Matt 5:43 to the precept of Leviticus 19: καὶ μισήσεις τὸν ἐχθρόν σου (And you may hate your enemy). This sentence is not to be found in Leviticus 19 or anywhere else in the Bible. Much effort has been exerted to find its source. An Essene background has been discussed and is to some degree likely.[40] But whatever the case, there is yet another point, which is relevant to the context of our inquiry. The riddle of Matt 5:38, 39 could possibly be solved by taking a closer look at Leviticus 19. Both the mix of loving one's neighbor and hating one's enemy, as well as the idea of loving one's enemy, can be understood in terms of interpretation related to Leviticus 19.

Concerning the peculiar addition to Lev 19:18 cited in Matt 5:43, it has been scarcely noted[41] that the motive of hate plays a role in Leviticus 19 too. In v. 17, immediately before v. 18, it is written: "You shall not hate your brother in your heart" (MT לא תשנא את אחיך בלבבך; LXX οὐ μισήσεις τὸν ἀδελφόν σου τῇ διανοίᾳ σου). Reading these two verses together it is not so far-fetched to conclude that the precept of love in v. 18 is restricted exclusively to one's kinsmen or to one's folk, and that hatred is allowed toward other people, foreigners and potential or actual enemies. In fact, with regard to the Jewish sources known to us this interpretation sounds very strange. But that does not mean it could not have occurred. If Matt 5:38 is not totally out of order, it is quite likely that in some Jewish circles this way of interpreting Lev 19:18 was current. Unlike Billerbeck (and also Betz)[42] I doubt whether one can speak of "a popular maxim, according to which the average Israelite of Jesus' day understood their conduct towards friend and

---

[40] See Lutz (above, n. 34), 311; Betz (above, n. 9), 304.
[41] A rare exception is found in Betz (above, n. 9), 306f.
[42] Ibid., 302 n. 809.

foe."[43] In my view it is more likely that the extended saying of Matt 5:43 reflects an interpretation of scribal origin, perhaps "in the spirit of some contemporary Shammaites"[44] or with Sadducean background.[45] In the bulk of the early rabbinic traditions there is, as Paul Fiebig has noted,[46] at least one text (*Sifra* to Lev 19:17b) showing that some rabbis in dealing with Leviticus 19 restricted the commandment of love to one's own kinsmen, "the children of thy people," and in the same passage permitted hatred against "the others": לא תקום ולא תטור את בני עמך נקום ונטור לאחרים ואהבת לרעך כמוך (You shall not take revenge on nor be hateful to the sons of thy people. You may take revenge on and be hateful to other men. And you shall love your neighbor as yourself).[47]

---

[43] BILLERBECK, vol. 1 (above, n. 20), 353.

[44] See MONTEFIORE (above, n. 30), 79.

[45] See FLUSSER (above, n. 38), 22.

[46] P. FIEBIG, *Jesu Bergpredigt. Rabbinische Texte zum Verständnis der Bergpredigt* (Göttingen: Vandenhoeck & Ruprecht, 1924), 9.

[47] *Sifra*, Qedoshim IV,12, WEISS (ed.), 98b, 12ff. On this saying and a parallel tradition in *Qoh. Rab.* 8, 8, note the comment of Heinz-Wolfgang KUHN in "Das Liebesgebot Jesu als Tora und Evangelium. Zur Feindesliebe und zu christlichen und jüdischen Auslegung der Bergpredigt," in H. FRANKEMÖLLE and K. KERTELGE (eds.), *Vom Urchristentum zu Jesus, FS Joachim Gnilka*, (Freiburg: Herder, 1989), 206ff. Possibly *ARN* A 16 offers an example of a similar restriction of Lev 19:18 with the following dictum (text according to the *editio princeps* Venice 1550/SCHECHTER 1887, 64): ושנאת את הבריות כיצד מלמד שלא יכוין אדם לומר אהוב את החכמה/ החכמים ושנא את התלמידים אהוב את התלמידים ושנא את עמי הארץ [אלא אהוב את כולם] ושנוא את המינים ואת המשומדים וכן המסורות ... הלא הוא אומר ואהבתה לרעך כמוך אני ה' בראתיו [מה מעס אני] בראתיו ואם עושה מעשה עמך אתה אהובו אם לאו אי אתה אהובו (And hatred of mankind. [What is that?] That teaches that no man should think of saying: "Love the wisdom/wise men, but hate the disciples" or "Love the disciples and hate the *am ha-arez*." [Schechter adds: "On the contrary, love all of these"]. But hate the sectarians, apostates, and informers.' ... But has He not said: "And you shall love your neighbour as thyself. [Because] I have created him"? Indeed, if he acts as your people do, you shall love him; but if not, you shall not love him.) (Translation after J. GOLDIN, *The Fathers according to Rabbi Nathan*, Yale Judaic Series 10 [New Haven: Yale University Press, 1955], 86).

By proclaiming, "Love your enemies," Jesus' logion is attacking this interpretation. And in this case too it is very likely that the pronouncement has its basis in Leviticus 19. In Lev 19:34 the commandment of love is repeated, but it is now related to the גר – the foreigner or the alien. Of course it is not aimed at every foreigner, it speaks about the foreigner who resides with you. There is no question, however, that this commandment, which requires one to love not only one's kinsman and one's folk but also the foreigner, offers a good argument against any restricted understanding of the love commandment. And seen from this aspect it was quite possible to include also the enemy in the commandment to love.

The purpose of the above inquiry was to test whether the antithetical sayings in Jesus' Sermon on the Mount can be understood in the light of scribal disputes about the meaning and appropriate understanding of the Torah, and whether Jesus' own pronouncements are themselves related to a special interpretation of the biblical text under discussion. I have tried to show that this can indeed be the case, if one takes into account the various ways in which the ancient scribes handled biblical texts.

Whether the arguments I have presented hold water will be a matter a dispute. I know that many questions remain open, especially with regard to the traditional and historical character of the six antithetical sayings and also with regard to the author or authors standing behind them.

I am likewise aware that there are many open questions also from the methodological point of view, especially with regard to what I call constructive imagination, which sometimes played an important role in my arguments. But I consider it worth the attempt, in order to stimulate discussion about the problems of the "Jewish setting of New Testament traditions."

Serge RUZER

ANTITHESES IN MATTHEW 5:
MIDRASHIC ASPECTS OF EXEGETICAL TECHNIQUES

This study addresses the exegetical techniques applied in a number of antithetic sayings from the Sermon on the Mount as well as in a passage from Matthew 19. The discussion relates mainly to the structure of the text as it stands now, its redactional history being beyond the scope of this investigation. A number of parallels in Jewish sources are reviewed and the question is raised of their relevance to the study of the Sermon. It is suggested that even when the conclusions drawn and the regulations derived from Torah exegesis in different traditions vary radically, the exegetical techniques applied seem to constitute a shared element of religious discourse, its basic syntax inherited from earlier generations. Finally, a typology of the antitheses' polemical stance is suggested.

I

While instances of Jesus' *separate* treatment of some of the issues involved in Matthew 5 are attested elsewhere in the Gospels,[1] their

---

[1] See, for example, Matt 19:3-9 (cf. Mark 10:2-12) for the divorce issue or Matt 22:34-40 (cf. Mark 12:28-34; Luke 10:25-37) for the discussion on the love-your-neighbor precept.

thematic combination within a unifying exegetical framework stands out as the trademark of the compiler (editor) of the Sermon on the Mount. The thematic combination includes a discussion of three prohibitions from the Decalogue (Exodus 20/Deuteronomy 5) and their parallels, the "eye for an eye" issue (also from Exodus 20) and the "love your neighbor" precept from the Holiness Code (Leviticus 19).[2] In Matthew, the discussion is presented as an uninterrupted sermon initiated by Jesus himself, as opposed to instances where a discussion of various religious topics is reported in the same Gospel and Jesus is portrayed as *responding* to a question addressed to him as a rabbi.[3] Whereas this latter mode of discourse in that period seems mainly to have characterized actual oral interaction between the general populace and those considered the embodiment of the (legal) tradition – Jewish sages or, in the wider context, Roman jurists[4] – the thematic arrangement of material may reflect the later editorial process.[5]

---

[2] Cf. *Mekhilta de-Rabbi Ishmael* Ithro 8 (ed. by H. S. HOROVITZ [Jerusalem: Sifre Wahermann, 1970], 233-34): כתיב לא תשא את שם ה' אלהיך לשוא וכנגדו כתיב אל תגנוב, מגיד הכתוב שכל מי שהוא גונב לסוף בא לידי שבועת שוא, שנאמר הגנוב רצוח ונאוף והשבע לשקר) [On the one tablet] was written: "You shall not take the name of the Lord your God in vain. And opposite it [on the other tablet] was written: "You shall not steal." This tells that he who steals will in the end also swear falsely. For it is said: "Will you steal, murder and commit adultery and swear falsely" [Jer 7:9]). English translation is indebted to LAUTERBACH: see J. Z. LAUTERBACH, *Mekilta de-Rabbi Ishmael*, vol. 2 (Philadelphia: The Jewish Publication Society of America, 1961), 267.

[3] See, for example, Matt 22:16-22 and parallels, Matt 22:23-33 and parallels, and Matt 22:34-40 and parallels. Cf. Matt 22:41-46 and parallels, where Jesus poses a question to other rabbis, who fail to give a satisfying response.

[4] See C. HEZSER, "The Codification of Legal Knowledge in Late Antiquity: The Talmud Yerushalmi and Roman Law Codes," in P. SCHÄFER (ed.), *The Talmud Yerushalmi and Graeco-Roman Culture* (Tübingen: Mohr Siebeck, 1998), 583-84.

[5] In her illuminating study Hezser deals mainly with a later period, but some of her suggestions may turn out to be at least partly relevant for the first century CE. See, for example, ibid., 619-24.

The first antithesis is introduced in Matt 5:21 by the formula: "You have heard that it was said to the men of old (τοῖς ἀρχαίοις)." Whereas the first part of the saying that follows ("You shall not kill") is obviously taken from Exod 20:13 (=Deut 5:18), the rest cannot be found in any Old Testament text.[6] M. McNamara was the first to point to the targumic paraphrase of Gen 9:6 as a clear parallel to the Matt 5:21 ending.[7] *Tg. Onqelos* interprets the biblical "Whosoever sheds man's blood, by man shall his blood be shed..." as relating to a juridical procedure in which "by man" means "following the testimony of witnesses according to the decision (sentence) of judges."[8] The targumic paraphrase of the Torah seems to have been one of the pillars of public teaching in the synagogue already in the late Second Temple period. Biblical passages, therefore, could often be remembered in their Aramaic form, and it is highly probable that the popular exegetical tradition concerning Gen 9:6 (attested in *Tg. Onqelos* and also in *Tg.*

---

[6] R. J. BANKS (*Jesus and the Law in the Synoptic Tradition* [Cambridge: Cambridge Univeristy Press 1975], 186) calls it "a legal pronouncement... whose source is uncertain"; J. P. MEIER (*Law and History in Matthew's Gospel* [Rome: Biblical Institute Press, 1976], 131-32) claims, in line with his general thesis but without providing any substantiation, that "what is cited each time [in Matt 5 antitheses] – with the exception of the last part of vs. 43 – is a passage (or paraphrase) from the written Torah."

[7] See M. MCNAMARA, *The New Testament and the Palestinian Targum to the Pentateuch* (Rome: Pontifical Biblical Institute, 1966), 127-29. It is worth noting that Gen 9:6 was perceived already by Philo as posing an exegetical problem: in *Questiones et Solutiones in Genesim* 61, Philo explains that the murderer will be punished by the "dissolution of his soul" (i.e. he himself will be "shed"). The LXX version of Gen 9:6 reads: ὁ ἐχέων αἷμα ἀνθρώπου ἀντὶ τοῦ αἵματος αὐτοῦ ἐκχυθήσεται ("Whoever sheds the blood of man, will be [himself] shed like [or instead of, against] his blood").

[8] The Aramaic reads: דיישוד דמא דאנשא בסהדין (נ.א. + על) מימומר דייניא דמיה יתאשד ארי בצלם אלהים עבד ית אנשא, see A. SPERBER (ed.), *The Bible in Aramaic*, vol. 1: *The Pentateuch* (Leiden: Brill, 1959), 13. The Old Syriac Gospel of Matthew, which has ܒܝܬ ܕܝܢܐ in Matt 5:21, seems to understand the received tradition in exactly this way. *Tg. Neofiti* here closely follows the Hebrew.

Pseudo-Jonathan – see below) was in great part responsible (together with Exod 20:13) for the quotation form in Matt 5:21.[9]

There is evidence that already in the early rabbinical tradition, discussing Gen 9:6 vis-à-vis Exod 20:13 constituted an accepted exegetical procedure. More than that, *Mekhilta de-Rabbi Ishmael*, quoted by McNamara,[10] perceives these verses to be essentially two parts of the same commandment:

> "You shall not murder." Why is this said? Because it says [before]: "Whoever sheds man's blood," etc. [Gen 9:6]. We have thus [i.e. in Gen 9:6] heard the penalty for it but we have not heard the warning against it. Therefore it says here: "You shall not murder."[11]

In the *Mekhilta* the same technique is applied to the seventh, eighth and ninth commandments of the Decalogue. However, in the *Mekhilta de-Rabbi Shimeon ben Yohai*, it is Num 35:16 and not Gen 9:6 that is juxtaposed to Exod 20:13.[12] It is clear from the *Mekhilta*

---

[9] See S. RUZER, "The Technique of Composite Citation in the Sermon on the Mount (Matt 5:21-22, 33-37)," *Revue biblique* 103.1 (1996), 67 and n. 5 there.

[10] See above, n. 7.

[11] *Mek. R. Ishmael* (HOROVITZ, 232): לא תרצח למה נאמר, לפי שנאמר שופך דם האדם, עונש שמענו אזהרה לא שמענו, תלמוד לומר לא תרצח. English translation is indebted to LAUTERBACH (above, n. 2), 260.

[12] See *Mek. R. Shimeon b. Yohai*, ed. J. N. EPSTEIN and E. Z. MELAMED (Jerusalem: Meqize Nirdamim, 1955), 152: לא תרצח מכלל שנאמר מות יומת הרוצח למדנו עונש אזהרה מנין תלמוד לומר לא תרצח. מנין אמר הריני רוצח על מנת ליהרג הרי זה מותרה תלמוד לומר לא תרצח. מנין ליוצא ליהרג ואמר מנין הרי זה מותרה תלמוד לומר לא תרצח. ("You shall not kill" (Exod 20:13). From what is said: "the murderer shall be put to death" (Num 35:16), we have learned [only] about the punishment but what about the warning? Hence, [the Scripture] says: "You shall not kill." And if someone says: I am going to commit murder being ready to be killed for that, in this case it is permitted? [To prohibit that the Scripture] says: "You shall not kill." And if someone is going to be killed anyway, in this case it is permitted (for him to kill)? [To prohibit that the Scripture] says: "You shall not kill.")

evidence that the existence of seemingly parallel or close Torah ordinances concerning murder was seen as a problem by rabbinic exegetes. One of the solutions offered for Gen 9:6 vs. Exod 20:13 was to declare these two verses components of the same commandment. According to this approach the Decalogue prohibition does not widen the scope of the definition of murder established by the traditional understanding of Gen 9:6.

However, other conclusions also seem to have been drawn from the juxtaposition of Gen 9:6 and Exod 20:13. Thus, for instance, *Pesiqta Hadta*, a midrashic composition of uncertain provenance, contains a midrash that suggests (relating to the four letters composing the word תרצח [לא]) that Exod 20:13, in fact (unlike Gen 9:6?), speaks of murder as something committed not only "by hand and by foot" but also by word of mouth and lack of psychological involvement in the fate of the other.[13] Indeed, the midrash sees these moral deficiencies as actually leading to the death of the "other," and they may therefore be considered murder in the legal sense. And of course there is that famous talmudic saying (*b. B. Mez.* 58b): "If one offends his fellow man in public, it is as if he sheds a man's blood."[14] The choice of words ("sheds a man's blood") is rather telling: it attempts to deal with the "moral offense" usually discussed – as in *Pesiqta Hadta* – in connection with Exod 20:13 as belonging to the legal realm of Gen 9:6.

It is worth noting that Philo was already of the opinion that – or was familiar with a tradition according to which – the prohibition in the Decalogue "forbids murder, and under it come the laws, all of them indispensable and of great public utility, about violence, insult, outrage..."[15] However, unlike Matthew and the rabbinical

---

[13] See *Pesiqta Hadta*, Shevuot, *Beth ha-Midrash*, ed. A. JELLINEK (Jerusalem: Bamberger & Wahermann 1938), v. 6, p. 45.

[14] The Hebrew reads: כאילו שופך דמים.

[15] Philo, *De Decalogo* 170. Philo calls the Exodus 20 prohibition of murder "the second head" – he seems to have had the μοιχέω–φονέω–κλεψέω (adultery–murder–stealing) order in his Greek text.

sources quoted above, Philo does not establish here any exegetical connection to Gen 9:6.[16]

Returning to Matt 5:21, I suggest that what we have here is a juxtaposition of Exod 20:13 and Gen 9:6 – the latter being represented by its more or less standard interpretation, attested, inter alia, in the Targum. Thus the polemic here should be seen as directed against the exegetical tendency that presented Exod 20:13 and Gen 9:6 as having the same scope of application, a tendency similar to the one attested in the *Mekhilta*. Denying the validity of this tendency, Matthew's Jesus suggests instead widening the scope of the Exod 20:13 application (vis-à-vis that of Gen 9:6) to "murder committed also by word of mouth." He does so while adopting an approach similar to the one attested in the passages from *Pesiqta Hadta* and the Babylonian Talmud discussed above.

Another characteristic structural feature of Matt 5:21-22 is the gradual transition from the jurisdiction of an ordinary court to the Sanhedrin to the Court on High, where Gehenna is the punishment. This transition corresponds to the changes in the nature of the transgressions mentioned: from hard-core crimes, tried in a court of law with the testimony of witnesses, to offenses against fellow men that may not be witnessed by a third party. It is worth noting that a similar transition occurs in the *Tg. Pseudo-Jonathan* interpretation of Gen 9:6:

> Whoever sheds the blood of man with witnesses, the judges will find him guilty of murder. And he who sheds blood without witnesses, the Lord of Eternity will call him to account on the day of Great Judgment.[17]

---

[16] Cf. ibid., 132: "But man, the best of living creatures, through that higher part of his being, namely, the soul, is most nearly akin to heaven also to the Father of the world, possessing in his mind a closer likeness and copy than anything else on earth of the eternal and blessed Archetype."

[17] The Aramaic reads: דיישוד דמא דאינשא בסהדין דייניא מחייבין ליה קטול ודיישוד דמא בלא סהדין מרי עלמא עתיד לאתפרע מניה ליום דינא רבא.

The tradition from the Babylonian Talmud equating public offense with murder, on the one hand, and the fact that "Gehenna" was quite interchangeable in this context with the "Day of Great Judgment,"[18] on the other, allow us to posit that a similar basic logic governs the transition from earthly to heavenly jurisdiction both in Matt 5:21-21 and in the *Tg. Pseudo-Jonathan* interpretation of Gen 9:6.

Having discerned these structural parallels, we should now inquire about their meaning. All rabbinical parallels discussed above are attested in compositions belonging to a later period than the Gospel account. Although in some cases we may reasonably assume that they represent an earlier tradition – as, for example, when a similar motif is attested in Philo's writings[19] – if we attempt to prove a specific literary link between them and the Gospel pericope, we will find ourselves on shaky ground. To my mind this is less so if we focus neither on the form of a particular saying nor on a specific literary link, but on issues of religious discourse and on the exegetical techniques applied. It is unlikely that Jesus – or the compiler of Matthew for that matter – was the first to recognize the problem of parallel Torah precepts or the problem of jurisdiction in cases of "transgressions of the heart" that could not be tried in a court of law. It is also unlikely that the author of the Gospel text invented the method of playing a Decalogue precept against its extra-Decalogue parallel in order to widen the scope of the commandment, while later proponents of the same technique followed his lead or invented the method independently. The opposite seems

---

[18] Whereas in the *Mek. R. Ishmael* (above, n. 2, 169) it is claimed that those who observe the Sabbath will be saved from "the birth pangs of the Messiah, the day of Gog and Magog, and the Day of Great Judgment," according to *b. Shab.* 118a they will be saved from "the birth pangs of the Messiah, the judgment of Gehenna (= the punishment in Gehenna), and the war of Gog and Magog." So Matthew's "Gehenna" and *Mekhilta*'s "Day of Great Judgment" seem to have been interchangeable in this context.

[19] See above, n. 15 and 16 and discussion there.

much more probable:[20] Matt 5:21-22 presents its argument in accordance with an existing exegetical format; it fights a current exegetical tendency – the one perceiving Gen 9:6 and Exod 20:13 as the same prohibition – and follows an alternative one that tries to widen the scope of Exod 20:13. Thus Matt 5:21-22 may or even should be seen as an early witness to the exegetical techniques in question, attested in later rabbinic sources.[21]

The meaning of τοῖς ἀρχαίοις (to/by the men of old) may thus be assessed as relating to an existing exegetical opinion – in our case, the claim that Gen 9:6 and Exod 20:13 constitute one prohibition with the same subject matter – established by previous generations of exegetes and seen by our preacher as mistaken. And indeed that has been the opinion of a number of scholars.[22] As D. Flusser pointed out, in some rabbinical sources the polemical juxtaposition of לקיים את התורה (to fulfil the Torah) and לבטל את התורה (to abolish the Torah) stands for opposition between the true and the mistaken interpretation of the Torah;[23] this,

---

[20] Inter alia, in view of the evidence from Philo's writings. Cf. P. SIGAL (*The Halakah of Jesus of Nazareth* [Lanham: University Press of America, 1986], 21), who agrees with the notion that in this antithesis (as well as in others in Matt 5) we have what is to be understood as a juxtaposition of different interpretations of the Torah and not an attack on the Torah itself. At the same time he perceives in the Sermon a *radical departure* from the body of existing oral tradition as a whole: "Since he (Jesus) was soon to urge norms of conduct (halakha) that were significantly more difficult than those of both the written Torah and the oral interpretative Torah, he anticipated both inevitable protest and neutral inquiry as to why." Sigal does not discuss the particularities of the exegetical procedure in Matt 5:21-22, and it is unclear whether he considers innovative only the results of the halakhic procedure applied there or also the method itself.

[21] See RUZER, "Technique of Composite Citation," (above, n. 9) p. 71 and n. 20 there.

[22] See, for instance, J. P. MEIER, *Law and History in Matthew's Gospel* (Rome: Biblical Institute Press, 1976), 132 and n. 2 there.

[23] See D. FLUSSER, "Torah in the Sermon on the Mount," in *Jewish Sources in Early Christianity* (Tel Aviv: Sifriyat Poalim, 1979) (in Hebrew), 230 and n. 11 there.

then, may be the meaning of Matt 5:17 ("Think not that I have come to abolish the law ... I have come not to abolish ... but to fulfil").

Flusser, however, quotes also the *Sifra* for Lev 15:33, where to my mind the opposition is more between different stages of gradual revealing of the Torah's true meaning within the same school of interpretation than between true and false exegesis:[24]

> The elders of old used to say: during her monthly period a woman should not make her eyes... until she immerses herself into the water. [That was the rule] until R. Aqiva had come and taught...[25]

Another telling example of the distinction between an opinion of the "first generation(s) of a school of exegetes" and the "ultimate exegesis" is found, this time with clear messianic overtones, in a famous passage from the *Rule of Congregation*: "... shall be ruled by the first directives which the men of the Community began to be taught until the prophet comes, and the Messiahs of Aaron and Israel."[26] Here, as in Matthew 5, the "first directives" seem to stand for the interpretations propagated by earlier exegetes belonging to the community (school of interpretation) of Qumran and not to the "Sinai generation."

---

[24] See D. FLUSSER, "Es wurde zu den Alten gesagt," *Entdeckungen im Neuen Testament*, vol. 2 (Neukirchen-Vluyn: Neukirchener Verlag, 1992), 83-88. See also idem, "'Den Alten ist gesagt' Interpretation der sogenannten Antithesen der Bergpredigt," *Judaica* 47 (1985), 35-39.

[25] *Sifra* Metsora 5, 12, ed. J. H. WEISS (Vienna: Ya'akov ha-Cohen Schlosberg, 1862), 79c, זקנים ראשונים היו אומרים ... עד שבא ר"ע ולימד. In contradistinction to this case the *Sifra* for Lev 15:29 ordains that those are not the "innovators," but הראשונים (the first ones) one is supposed to follow: בן עזאי אומר הולכים אחר הראשונים: אחד לעולה ואחד לחטאת.

[26] 1QS IX 10-11. The Hebrew reads: ונשפטו במשפטים הרשונים אשר החלו אנשי היחד לתיסר בם עד בוא נביא ומשיחי אהרון וישראל. English translation is derived from F. GARCÍA MARTÍNEZ and E. J. C. TIGCHELAAR (eds.), *The Dead Sea Scrolls: Study Edition*, 2 vols. (Leiden: Brill, 1997-1998), 1:93.

II

I will now briefly discuss one more example of applying the midrashic technique described above, one that I have elsewhere called a "technique of composite citation"[27] – namely, Matt 5:33-37 (the fourth antithesis), where the issue of swearing is addressed. Examples of early Jewish biblical exegesis dealing with the issue again bear witness to the juxtaposition of two Torah ordinances: Exod 20:7 ("You shall not take the name of the Lord your God in vain for the Lord will not hold him guiltless that shall take the name of the Lord in vain") and Lev 19:12 ("You shall not swear falsely by my name").

Here is the targumic evidence:

> You shall not swear by the name of the Lord your God in vain (למגנא) for the Lord will not hold him guiltless that shall swear by his name falsely (לשקרא). (*Tg. Onq.* Exod 20:7)
>
> My people, House of Israel, no one of you shall swear by the name of the Memra of the Lord your God in vain (על מגן) for the Lord... will not hold guiltless at the Day of Great Judgment any one who swears by his name in vain (על מגן). (*Tg. Pseudo-Jonathan* Exod 20:7)

We may observe (a) that in the Targum, Exod 20:7 was routinely interpreted as relating to "swearing"; and (b) that the parallel between Exod 20:7 (לשוא = in vain) and Lev 19:12 (לשקר = falsely) was recognized. *Tg. Onqelos* indicates that these two prohibitions should be seen as synonymous – although a certain ambivalence may be discerned here: the Targum speaks of punishment only in connection with false (and not "vain") swearing.[28]

There were also attempts, however, to use the obvious differences between the Exod 20:7 and Lev 19:12 wording to widen the

---

[27] See S. RUZER, "Technique of Composite Citation" (above, n. 9), 65-75.
[28] Cf. *Peshitta*, which, not unlike *Tg. Pseudo-Jonathan*, uses the slightly ambiguous ܒܫܘܩܪܐ in both cases.

scope of the Decalogue precept. Thus, among other sources, *Pesiqta Rabbati*, a Palestinian midrash of the sixth century, stresses that in contrast to "falsely" of Leviticus, "in vain" of the Decalogue covers also certain cases where no lie is involved but nevertheless the swearing is considered a transgression.[29] Cases of sinful "empty" or "obvious" swearing are related to, inter alia, in the Jerusalem Talmud:

> (... in the name of R. Yohanan): anything which is known to the two of them constitutes "vain swearing"... Hizkiya used to say: if somebody swears that "two is two," he is guilty against this [Decalogue] commandment. (*y. Sheb.* 3, 8 [34d])

The Talmud not only widens the scope of the Decalogue commandment but also, unlike the Targum, leaves no doubt about the punishment that is due for "empty" swearing:

> In the name of R. Shmuel b. Nahman: twenty-four cities (city councils) existed in the South and all of them were destroyed because of vain swearing that was true to the facts. (ibid.)

The demand, reported in *Sifra* (91a), for "'no' which is truly so and 'yes' which is truly so" may be seen as a logical step in this direction. This *Sifra* saying constitutes a clear tannaitic parallel to the "yes, yes; no, no" of Matt 5:37.[30] Philo's writings, however, may testify that this demand reflects a long-standing religious concern:

---

[29] See *Pesiqta Rabbati*, ed. M. FRIEDMAN (Tel Aviv: Esther Press, 1963 [reprint of the original Vienna 1880 edition]), 113a: "Hizkiah said: even if someone states with oath concerning an olive tree that it is an olive tree... it constitutes a 'vain swearing' [prohibited in the Decalogue]."

[30] Cf. Jas 5:12 and 2 Cor 1:17. M.-É BOISMARD ("Une tradition para-synoptique attestée par les pères anciens," in J.-M. SEVRIN [ed.], *The New Testament in Early Christianity*, Bibliotheca Ephemeridum Theologicarum Lovaniensium 86 [Leuven: Leuven University Press, 1989], 191-94) showed that the Matthean formula represents an early tradition and not the final redaction of the text, in spite of its not being supported by patristic writings, where the form of the logion corresponds to its para-synoptic variant attested in Jas 5:12.

There are some who without even any gain in prospect have an evil habit of swearing incessantly and thoughtlessly about ordinary matters where there is nothing at all in dispute, forgetting that it were better to submit to have their words cut short.[31]

But the difference between "in vain" and "falsely" is not the only difference between Exod 20:7 and Lev 19:12 discussed in rabbinical sources. While "the name of the Lord your God" from the Decalogue is understood as a reference to the Tetragrammaton proper (see *Tg. Pseudo-Jonathan*, quoted above), "my name" from Lev 19:12 covers – according to *Sifra*, where the two ordinances are explicitly juxtaposed – swearing by "every name which belongs to God and not only the Holy Name"; and this is in addition to what is already covered by the prohibition in Exod 20:7![32] In contradistinction to the exegesis attested in Philo, *Sifra* presents its argument as based on the midrashic juxtaposition of what are perceived as parallel Torah ordinances;[33] in this case, however, the extra-Decalogue verse is being used to widen the scope of a Decalogue precept and not vice versa. We may thus observe two basic

---

[31] Philo, *De Decalogo*, ad loc. Cf. *De Specialibus Legibus* 2, 2 and the discussion that follows.

[32] *Sifra*, Qedoshim 2: לא תשבעו בשמי לשקר מה ת"ל לפי שנאמר לא תשא את שם ה' אלהיך לשוא שיכול אין לי חייבים אלא על השם המיוחד בלבד מנין לרבות את כל הכינויים ת"ל בשמי כל שם שיש לי ("And you shall not swear by my name falsely" [Lev 19:12]. What is the point of Scripture? Since it is said: "You shall not take the name of the Lord your God in vain" [Exod 20:7], I might have supposed that one incurs liability only if he takes in vain the ineffable name of God. How do I know that all of the euphemisms for God's name also are involved in a false oath? Scripture says: "[And you shall not swear] by my name [falsely]"). English translation is according to J. NEUSNER, *Sifra: An Analytical Translation*, vol. 3 (Atlanta, Georgia: Scholars Press, 1988]), 103-4.

[33] Widening of the scope of the commandment is argued for by Philo without explicit appeal to the juxtaposition of Exod 20:7 and Lev 19:12. See also above, n. 16 and discussion there.

directions in which rabbinical exegesis tries to widen the understanding of Exod 20:7: from "false" to "empty" swearing and from swearing by the Holy Name itself to swearing by any name that "belongs to God."[34]

With regard to the exegetical position represented in Matt 5:33-37, then, we may conjecture that here, as in the first antithesis, not the biblical prohibition as such but one of its current interpretations is being addressed – namely, the "minimalistic" interpretation, which does not distinguish between לשוא of the Decalogue and לשקר of Lev 19:12. In fact, the interpretation in question seems to represent an even more "restrictive" position, as it brings into the picture a third parallel from Deut 23:22 ("If you make a vow to the LORD your God, do not postpone fulfilling it"). The problem of "using the Lord's name" then becomes restricted to the realm of vows. Against this interpretation, Matthew's Jesus suggests widening the scope of the prohibition by moving in two directions:

1. In Matt 5:33 and 5:37 he moves from "false" through "empty" swearing to the ultimate conclusion that any swearing is suspected of "emptiness."

2. In Matt 5:34-35 he states that not only swearing by the Holy Name itself but also swearing by God's Temple, etc. – wherever it may be said that שמי נקרא עליו (my name is called upon it) – is covered by the prohibition (with a peculiar development in Matt 5:36, where an additional motif is introduced).

The Gospel does not refer explicitly to Lev 19:12 (as noted, it refers instead to Deut 23:22), but Lev 19:12 is clearly present in Matt 5:33 and 5:37 thinking. The interpretation of the Decalogue commandment here has the same agenda and is construed along the very lines of thinking that characterize rabbinical exegesis, which is forever trying to determine what kind of swearing (swearing about what and by what "name") is prohibited in Exod 20:7.

---

[34] On the transition "from old to new halakha" on swearing, see Y. N. EPSTEIN, *Introduction to Tannaitic Literature* (in Hebrew) (Tel Aviv: Magnes Press, 1957), 377-78.

Here again I tend to believe that while it would be preposterous to try to prove any specific link between the pericope in question and exegetical traditions attested in later rabbinical sources, Matt 5:33-37 – despite the undeniable originality of the discourse – presents its argument in accordance with an existing exegetical format.[35] To my mind, it is with regard to the basic characteristics of this format, attested also later in rabbinic sources, that Matt 5:33-37 may be seen as an early witness. And vice versa: the logic and the structure of Jesus' reasoning in Matt 5:33-37 as well as in Matt 5:21-22 may be better understood if the tendencies of rabbinic thinking discussed above are given proper consideration.

III

Let us turn now to Matt 5:27-32 – a passage that contains the second and third antitheses of the Sermon on the Mount. I have dealt elsewhere[36] with the traditions presenting idolatry and lust as two basic expressions of the evil impulse. Moreover, since in a number of sources from the late Second Temple period and later, idolatry was presented as having become obsolete, lust came to be portrayed in these sources as the main outlet of the evil impulse – or at least as the first of the capital sins.[37] The prohibition "You shall not commit adultery" might in certain contexts – in Qumran, for example – have come to represent the Torah prohibitions in general;[38] hence the centrality of the adultery issue, discussed also in other parts of the New Testament.[39]

---

[35] I would stress again that Philo may definitely be seen as an early witness to the trend of widening the scope of the commandment – not, however, for the technique of "composite citation."

[36] See S. RUZER, "The Seat of Sin in Early Jewish and Christian Sources," in J. ASSMAN and G. G. STROUMSA (eds.), *Transforming the Inner Self in Ancient Religions* (Leiden: Brill, 1999), 367-91.

[37] See, for example, CD-A IV 15-18 and Luke 16:14-18. In both these texts lust is coupled with greed as a major temptation ensnaring the man.

[38] See CD-A VII 6-9, XVI 10-12.

[39] See, for instance, Matt 19, Rom 7, 1 Cor 6, 1 Thess 4.

In Matt 5:27-32 one comes across the same basic exegetic technique already discerned in the passages relating to murder and "vain swearing": to prove his point Matthew's Jesus juxtaposes various Torah ordinances perceived as related to the same issue. In addition to obvious references to Exod 20:14/Deut 5:18 (Matt 5:27) and to Deut 24:1 (Matt 5:31), there is Matt 5:28 πᾶς ὁ βλέπων γυναῖκα πρὸς τὸ ἐπιθυμῆσαι αὐτήν (every one who looks at a woman lustfully), which points to Exod 20:17/Deut 5:21 לא תחמד אשת רעך=οὐκ ἐπιθυμήσεις τὴν γυναῖκα τοῦ πλησίον σου (You shall not covet your neighbor's wife). In the tannaitic sources, which discuss the commandments from the second part of the Decalogue (e.g., *Mekhilta*), we find the argument served by the same basic technique of juxtaposing parallel Torah ordinances. More exactly, the *Mek. R. Ishmael* connects "You shall not covet" from Exod 20:17 (as a first step toward "hard-core" adultery) with "You shall not commit adultery" from Exod 20:14.⁴⁰ Further on the *Mekhilta* connects "You shall not commit adultery" to Lev 20:10, which stipulates that in a case of adultery with a married woman both the adulterer and the adulteress should be put to death. The *Mekhilta* quotes the opinion that Exod 20:14 speaks about the same issue: "We have heard about the punishment but did not hear the warning – now we hear it."⁴¹ This last opinion is also cited in the *Mek. R. Shimon b. Yohai*:⁴² Exod 20:14 and Lev 20:10 have the

---

⁴⁰ See *Mek. R. Ishmael* (above, n. 2), p. 232.

⁴¹ Ibid.: לא תנאף למה נאמר, לפי שהוא אומר מות יומת הנואף והנואפת, עונש שמענו אזהרה לא שמענו, תלמוד לומר לא תנאף ("You shall not commit adultery." Why is this said? Because it says: "Both the adulterer and the adulteress shall surely be put to death" [Lev 20:10]. We have thus heard the penalty for it but we have not heard the warning against it; therefore it says here: "You shall not commit adultery"). English translation is indebted to LAUTERBACH (above, n. 2), 260.

⁴² *Mek. R. Shimeon b. Yohai* Ithro 20 (above, n. 12), 152-153: לא תנאף מכלל שנאמר מות יומת הנאף והנאפת למדנו ענש אזהרה מנין תלמוד לומר לא תנאף. מנין אמר הריני נואף על מנת ליהרג הרי זה מותרה תלמוד לומר לא תנאף. מנין האוכל בקערו ורואה את עצמו כאלו אוכל בקערה שלחבירו והיה שותה בכוסו ורואה את עצמו כאלו הוא שותה בכוסו שלחבירו הרי זה מותרה תלמוד לומר לא תנאף. ("You shall not commit adul-

same subject matter, but one is an absolute imperative while the other describes the punishment. According to this interpretation the true importance of Exod 20:14 is that with it adultery becomes absolutely forbidden – even if one is ready to accept the punishment and be executed for the transgression. Philo testifies to a different trend, but he also seems to have been of the opinion that Exod 20:14 and its parallels outside the Decalogue have the same subject matter: he interprets the Decalogue prohibition in light of the list of illicit types of intercourse found in Lev 18:10-16.[43]

However, an alternative interpretation is also reported in *Mek. R. Shimon b. Yohai*: the prohibition in the Decalogue is addressed to someone who eats/drinks from his own plate/glass (a standard metaphor for sexual intercourse) but *imagines* that he eats/drinks from the plate/glass of another.[44]

Thus the tannaitic sources take the discussion, presented as the exegesis of Exod 20:14, in two different directions. First, adultery equals adultery proper – illicit intercourse with another man's wife – and the transgressors should be punished by death. The ordinances of Lev 20:10 and Exod 20:14 have, according to this line of thinking, the same substance – except that the one relates to the penalty whereas the other provides the warning. Second, compared to Lev 20:10 there is more to the Exod 20:14 ordinance, and

---

tery" (Exod 20:14). From what is said: "[If a man commits adultery with the wife of his neighbor,] both the adulterer and the adulteress shall be put to death" (Lev 20:10), we have learned [only] about the punishment but what about the warning? Hence, [the Scripture] says: "You shall not commit adultery." And if someone says: I am going to commit adultery being ready to be killed for that, in this case it is permitted? [To prohibit that the Scripture] says: "You shall not commit adultery." And if someone eats from his own plate but imagines himself eating from his friend's plate, drinks from his own cup but imagines himself drinking from his friend's cup, is that permitted? [To prohibit that the Scripture] says: "You shall not commit adultery.")

[43] See Philo, *De Decalogo*, 164; *De Specialibus Legibus*, 7. In his deliberations Philo relates to a variety of adulterous acts but not to *adulterous thoughts/intentions*.

[44] *Mek. R. Shimon b. Yohai* (above, n. 42).

this additional substance can be seen as connecting the adultery issue with the mental/sensual sphere of coveting/lust related to in Exod 20:17.[45]

As in the two cases discussed above, the *Mekhilta* evidence here makes possible a better appreciation of the exegetical structure of Matt 5:27-32. Some exegetes seem to have claimed (as later documented in *Mekhilta*) that the substance of the precept is "adultery proper" – meaning illegal intercourse with a married woman – a transgression for which the death penalty would be the punishment ordained by the Torah, as specified in Lev 20:10. Jesus is portrayed in Matt 5:27-30 as one who is not satisfied with this solution – which is presented as something other exegetes have been saying – but chooses instead the second solution, also attested in the *Mekhilta*, that the subject matter of Exod 20:14 should be widened to accord with the prohibition in Exod 20:17.[46]

---

[45] The absence of the second of these two trends in Philo's deliberations on Exod 20:14 has already been observed (see above, n. 43). This second trend, however, is also attested in a later talmudic source (*b. Ber.* 61a): "Adultery means to look on a woman. Every one who walks behind a woman [to look at her] loses his share in the world-to-come... One, who gives her money from hand to hand while counting the coins in order to (have an opportunity) to look at her, even if he has done good deeds and studied Torah like Moses our Teacher – he will not escape the judgment of Gehenna." English translation is according to Soncino ed.

[46] Transgressions of the heart, which cannot be proved in court, such as anger (as opposed to real murder), bring to the fore – both in early rabbinical sources and in the Sermon – the question of the judgment of Gehennah (instead of regular juridical procedure). Switching from "hard-core adultery" to "coveting" produces the same results both in the Sermon and in a number of rabbinical passages, such as the talmudic passage just quoted. The issue of the hand and the eye as agents of lust has been thoroughly investigated. Inter alia, the connection with the tradition attested in *m. Nid.* 2:1 and *b. Nid.* 13b has been pointed out ("It was taught in the School of R. Ishmael, 'You shall not commit adultery' means that there should be in you *no adultery*, neither with the hand, nor with the foot.") It is worth noting that in Matthew the prohibition emphasizes lustful glances! I dealt with this issue in "The Seat of Sin in Early Jewish and Christian Sources" (above, n. 36).

Further on, however, the Sermon returns to the connection, rejected earlier, between Exod 20:14 and Lev 20:10, bringing up the issue of a married woman who commits adultery. It may be suggested that with the practice of putting to death both lovers losing its grip, other measures came to the fore – in particular, divorce. Hence the reference to Deut 24:1 in Matt 5:31-32 – whether originally part of the pericope or not – justly belongs to the discussion bearing witness to the compiler's versatility in the current Exod 20:14 exegesis.[47]

Matt 5:27-32 and the discussion in the *Mekhilta* differ not only in certain important details[48] but in general tone: polemics in the Sermon, as opposed to reporting different opinions without attempting to establish which interpretation is the true one in the *Mekhilta*. The latter attitude, sometimes defined as "classicist," characterizes legal discourse in both rabbinical and Roman law compendia of late antiquity,[49] and it is clearly at variance with the attitude attested in the Gospel tradition, which seems to represent an earlier period. All these differences notwithstanding, the Sermon and the tannaitic sources have been shown to share both agenda and basic exegetical technique. I suggest that here too they all bear witness to the same traditional exegetical structure that was routinely used as early as the first century CE.

IV

It has been observed in the research[50] that Jesus in Matt 5:31-32 adopts the interpretation of ערות דבר (something indecent[?]) from

---

[47] J. A. FITZMYER, *To Advance the Gospel*, 2nd ed. (Cambridge: Eerdmans, 1998), 83: "Matthew... has modified it to make it better suit his Jewish-Christian concerns, casting it in terms of [the] Hillel-Shammai dispute."

[48] Cf. SIGAL, *Halakah of Jesus* (above, n. 20), 92.

[49] See HEZSER, "Codification" (above, n. 4), 612, 628-29, 633-36.

[50] See, for example, the Davies–Allison commentary (W. D. DAVIES and D. C. ALLISON, *The Gospel according to Saint Matthew*, ICC, 3 vols. [Edinburgh: T.&T. Clark, 1997], I: 522-32, esp. 530). See also SIGAL, *Halakah of Jesus* (above, n. 20), 21.

Deut 24:1 as well as the position with regard to divorce ascribed by *m. Gittin* 9:10 to the school of Shammai, as against the interpretation ascribed by the same mishnah to the school of Hillel:

> The school of Shammai say: A man may not divorce his wife unless he has found unchastity in her, for it is written, *Because he has found in her **indecency** in anything* (Deut 24:1). And the school of Hillel say: [He may divorce her] even if she spoiled a dish for him, for it is written, *Because he has found in her indecency **in anything*** (ibid.).
>
> R. Akiva says: Even if he found another fairer than she, for it is written, *And it shall be if she find no favor in his eyes...* (ibid.)[51]

Thus according to the school of Shammai, only adultery constitutes a sufficient reason for divorcing a wife, whereas Hillel is presented in the Mishnah as initiating a chain of authorities (including R. Akiva) who believed that almost any reason would suffice – a position presented in Matt 19:3 as that of the Pharisees. It stands to reason that from the outset this position, far from being characteristic only of Hillel, was widely held; it is only later, and in view of the importance ascribed to Hillel in the rabbinic perception of the history of halakhic controversies, that it became strongly connected with this particular sage.[52] It is also worth noting that Philo does not discuss at all the reasons for the divorce but,

---

[51] English translation is indebted to H. DANBY, *The Mishnah* (Oxford: Oxford University Press, 1974), 321. The Hebrew text of the Mishnah reads: בית שמאי אומרים לא יגרש אדם את אישתו אלא אם כן מצא בה דבר ערוה, שנאמר כי מצא בה ערות דבר. ובית הלל אומרים אפילו הקדיחה תבשילו, שנאמר כי מצא בה ערות דבר. רבי עקיבא אומר אפילו מצא אחרת נאה הימנה, שנאמר והיה אם לא תמצא חן בעיניו.

[52] See A. GOSHEN-GOTTSTEIN, "Hillel and Jesus: Are Comparisons Possible?" in J. H. CHARLESWORTH and L. L. JOHNS (eds.), *Hillel and Jesus: Comparative Studies of Two Major Religious Leaders* (Minneapolis: Fortress, 1997), 31-55, esp. 39, 41-47. For a discussion of Hillel's hermeneutical stance, see D. R. SCHWARTZ, "Hillel and Scripture: From Authority to Exegesis," *Hillel and Jesus*, 335-62.

not unlike the passage from Deuteronomy 24 itself, concentrates instead on what happens after divorce.[53]

Mishnah *Gittin* reports a number of additional instances of polemics between the school of Shammai and the school of Hillel relating to the marriage-divorce issue:

1. m. Git. 4:5 – The world was not created except for the sake of procreation (so Shammai, referring to Genesis 1), so one is supposed to allow half-slave half-bondman to marry (and procreate).

2. m. Git. 8:4-5 – A difference of opinion is attested with regard to which kind of divorce is legally sound and which is not. The "wrong" divorce creates a situation where a divorced woman who remarries may be considered an adulteress, and her children – bastards (cf. Matt 5:31).

3. m. Git. 8:8 – A husband gives his wife a divorce and then changes his mind.

Unlike the Mishnah, the earlier Gospel tradition does not mention by name the two sages, who might have been older contemporaries of Jesus or belonged to the previous generation;[54] but it does seem to relate to a yet unsolved exegetical controversy, siding with one of the existing opinions.

In contradistinction to the pericopes discussed above, in Matt 5:31-32 it is the existence of conflicting interpretations of a difficult biblical expression (ערות דבר) that constitutes the exegetical crux of the polemic; neither composite citation nor the widening of the scope of the precept is employed here. This demonstrates the variegated nature of both the polemical patterns and the exegetical methods used in the Gospel. To better appreciate this variety, let us

---

[53] Philo, *De Specialibus Legibus* 30: "... for any cause whatever, after parting from her husband and marrying another..."

[54] In these instances also, the attribution to the *schools* of Shammai and Hillel may indicate a later attempt to overcome the anonymity of the longstanding tradition; see above, n. 52 and the discussion there. Cf. HEZSER ("Codification" [above, n. 4], 610-611, 628), who discusses the return to anonymity in later stages of construction of the meta-discourse in the Jerusalem Talmud.

consider a pericope from outside the Sermon that addresses the same adultery-divorce issue.

V

In Matt 19:3, Pharisees ask Jesus' opinion on the interpretation of Deut 24:1 (ערות דבר), which *m. Gittin* 9:9 ascribes to the school of Hillel.[55] But as opposed to the Sermon on the Mount,[56] Deut 24:1 is presented in Matt 19:7-8 as an ad hoc regulation with only a limited period of application. The notion of ad hoc Torah regulation (הוראת שעה) is attested in later rabbinical sources, and even Philo created a tripartite division of the Torah material: God's words, Moses' own deliberation and a mix of the two.[57] To my mind, it is vis-à-vis these tendencies that one must examine the "liberal" position with regard to the Holy Writ attested in our pericope.[58] Could it be that in this instance also the reasoning of Matthew's Jesus reflected an inherited exegetic pattern?[59] This is

---

[55] Matt 19:3: "And Pharisees came up to him and tested him by asking, 'Is it lawful to divorce one's wife for any cause?'" B. REPSCHINSKI ("Taking On the Elite: The Matthean Controversy Stories," in *Society of Biblical Literature Seminar Papers* [Atlanta: Scholars Press, 1999], 1-23), suggests that the prominence given to the Pharisees in the "controversy stories" by the compiler of Matthew reflects the closeness of the former to the Matthean community and hence the acuteness of the polemics (p. 14). To my mind, Repschinski overamplifies the controversy aspect in some of the pericopes he discusses (incl. Matt 19:3-9); but in general his suggestion is convincing. Moreover, this polemical closeness may account for the reliance on shared exegetical patterns.

[56] Matt 5:18: "For truly, I say to you, till the heaven and earth pass away, not an iota, not a dot, will pass from the Torah (law) until all is accomplished."

[57] See Philo, *De Vita Mosis* II, 188-91.

[58] Cf., DAVIES–ALLISON, *Matthew* (above, n. 50), 1:527; 3:11-12, where a reference to Mal 2:16 is discerned here.

[59] The Gospel, which elsewhere is more than ready to report on Jesus' controversies with the Pharisees, does not here give the slightest indication that Jesus' statement provoked a resentment or any other negative reaction.

a question that cannot be addressed here; it necessitates further investigation.[60]

Beyond that "liberal" quality of the statement in Matt 19:7-8, verses 4-6 establish that for the true eternal principles of marital union one has to look to the story of the creation. This is one of the characteristic midrashic features to be discerned in traditions ascribed to the school of Shammai in *m. Gittin* referred to above. The saying from Gen 1:28 is used in *m. Gittin* 4:5 to create a halakhic midrash: man finds his fulfillment in procreating, hence one should adopt a lenient attitude toward an additional marriage union. Although the specific halakhic decision at which the Mishnah arrives here may characterize only Shammai (or certain followers of his), using the creation story to define basic principles of Jewish marriage seems to represent a wider midrashic trend.

Let us have a closer look at Matt 19:4-6. The argument here is presented as a midrashic combination of Gen 1:27 and 2:24:

> He answered, "Have you not read that he who made them from the beginning made them male and female, and said, 'For this reason a man shall leave his father and mother and be joined to his wife, and the two shall become one flesh'? So they are no longer two but one flesh. What therefore God has joined together, let not man put asunder."

The Strack–Billerbeck's *Kommentar* provides a number of references to rabbinical sources where Gen 2:24 is put to halakhic use

---

[60] A development in the opposite direction – namely, instead of Moses' initiative to add to the "initial Torah," a move aiming at concealment of the "existing Torah" (with the similar purpose of "adjusting God's demands" to Israel's real abilities) – is described in CD-A V 1-8. This latter perception seems to reflect the CD programmatic stance, according to which the written Torah, the one the members of the group share with the rest of Israel, forever retains its status, while in actuality it is reinterpreted according to the revelation of the new covenant. See P. R. DAVIES, "The Judaism(s) of the Damascus Document," in J. M. BAUMGARTEN, E. G. CHAZON and A. PINNICK, *The Damascus Document: A Centennial of Discovery* (Leiden/Boston/Cologne: Brill, 2000), 33-34.

with regard to problems pertaining to marriage,[61] whereas Gen 1:27 is referred to mostly in connection with the androgyne-centered notion of the first man's nature; the *Kommentar* supplies a number of references to the Midrash where Gen 1:27 is used in this way. As far as I can see, the only midrashic use of Gen 1:27 pointed out by the *Kommentar* in connection with the issue of *marriage* is in *b. Yeb.* 63a, where R. Elazar refers to Gen 5:2 (=Gen 1:27): "One who does not have a wife is not a man (Adam) because it is said, 'Male and female He created them'." It is worth noting that the talmudic discussion here centers on encouragement to marry – seemingly detached from the call to procreate – not on the prevention of divorce and/or second marriage.

Hence the importance of the evidence from the *Damascus Document*, where Gen 1:27 is used, as in Matthew 19, to establish the marital halakha (CD-A IV 15-18):[62] הם ניתפשים בשתים בזנות לקחת שתי נשים בחייהם ויסוד הבריאה זכר ונקבה ברא אותם (They... are caught twice in fornication: by taking two wives in their lives, even though the principle of creation is [Gen 1:27] 'male and female he created them').

The exact meaning of the above admonition has been much discussed. Does it refer to remarriage and thus directly correspond to

---

[61] For example, the following is an interpretation in *b. Sanh.* 58a attributed to R. Elazar (an early tannaitic authority from the second half of the first century?): "He should leave his father and mother and cling to his wife and the two should become one flesh". "His father" – i.e. the one who belongs to his father, his father's sister (r. Aqiva: his father's wife); "his mother" – his mother's sister (or his mother herself); "and cling" not to male but to female; "to his wife" – and not to his fellow's wife; "one flesh" – not to a beast or an animal, they never become "one flesh." See H. STRACK and P. BILLERBECK, *Kommentar zum Neuen Testament aus Talmud und Midrash* (Munich: C. H. Beck, 1922), ad locum.

[62] M. KISTER ("Some Observations on Vocabulary and Style in the Dead Sea Scrolls," in T. MURAOKA and J. F. ELWOLDE (eds.), *Diggers at the Well* [Leiden: Brill, 2000] 157-158) even suggests that the corresponding descriptions of the initial ideal state of affairs in Matt 19 (ἀπ' ἀρχῆς) and CD-A IV (יסוד הבריאה) might have been derived from the same formula.

the Gospel pericope? If so, the prohibition derived from Gen 1:27 pertains to "their lives," meaning that it is not absolute. If read in light of 11QTemple 57:15-19, the text may be understood as suggesting that second marriage after the death of the first wife is not forbidden.[63] Should we then suppose that the same position is taken by Matt 19:9 (absent in the Marcan parallel, where it sounds like a total rejection of remarriage?)[64] Other scholars, however, put forward strong arguments for the anti-bigamy (anti-polygamy?) leaning of the *Damascus Document* passage.[65] Whatever the true intention of the CD admonition, it can be stated that while halakhic and non-halakhic decisions derived from discussions of the marriage-divorce issue might have differed from tradition to tradition, the appeal to Genesis 1 and 2 and, even more specifically, to Gen 1:27 is attested in at least some of those discussions, including Qumranic, New Testament and later tannaitic evidence.[66] So it may

---

[63] So FITZMYER, *To Advance the Gospel*, 83. 11QTemple 57:15-19: לכול עצה חוץ מהמה vacat ואשה לוא ישא מכול בנות הגויים כי אם מבית אביהו יקח לו אשה ממשפחת אביהו ולוא יקח עליה אשה אחרת כי היאה לבדה תהיה עמו כול ימי חייה ואם מתה ונשא לו אחרת מבית אביהו ממשפחתו ולוא יטה משפט (15 ... in all his councils outside of them. *Blank* And he shall not take a wife from among all 16 the daughters of the nations, but instead take for himself a wife from his father's house 17 from his father's family. He shall take no other wife in addition to her 18 for she alone will be with him all the days of her life. And if she dies, he shall take 19 for himself another from his father's house, from his family. And he shall not pervert justice.) English translation is according to GARCÍA MARTÍNEZ and E. J. C. TIGCHELAAR [above, n. 26], 2:1279.

[64] Mark 10:2-12.

[65] See, for example, A. SCHREMER, "Qumran Polemic on Marital Law: CD 4:20–5:11 and Its Social Background," in E. CHAZON and J. BAUMGARTEN (eds.) *The Damascus Document: A Centennial of Discovery* (Leiden: Brill, 2000), 147-60.

[66] W. D. DAVIES (*The Setting of the Sermon on the Mount* [London: Cambridge University Press, 1964], 252) presented certain isolated sayings of the Sermon as expressions of polemics with the Essenes. J. KAMPEN ("A Reexamination of the Relationship between Matthew 5:21-48 and the Dead Sea Scrolls," in D. J. LULL [ed.], *Society of Biblical Literature Seminar Papers* [1990], 34-59) reaches the conclusion that "there are larger bodies of mate-

be suggested – with even greater probability than with regard to the pericopes discussed earlier – that in this case also the exegetical move in Matt 19:4-6 represents an inherited midrashic feature.

Conclusion

Five pericopes from the Gospel of Matthew were examined, four of them from the Sermon on the Mount and one from Matthew 19. In every one of them the argument is presented in the form of an interpretation of the Torah, suggesting a Jewish-Christian milieu sensitive to the characteristic late Second Temple features of the art of exegesis. The investigation centered less on the text form and more on the general agenda and structural features of New Testament exegetical passages, as well as on the techniques applied. Juxtaposing two or more parallel Torah precepts as a means of widening the scope of the commandment was shown to be one of the most important exegetical tools used in Matthew 5. Other exegetical moves, such as moving from a juridical procedure dealing with hard-core transgressions to judgment in Gehenna as punishment for transgressions that cannot be tried in the court of justice, choosing one of two possible interpretations of a difficult biblical expression (Deut 24:1: ערות דבר), or appealing to the story of the creation – always used for backing the tougher religious standards – were also outlined.

A number of relevant Jewish exegetical traditions from outside the New Testament were also reviewed. These traditions might differ from the Gospel sayings in tone (non-polemical in *Mekhilta* but polemical in CD) and in the details of their halakhic and other conclusions, but it turned out that they deal with the same exegetical problems and follow the same basic structure of argument. In the

---

rial in the Gospel of Matthew which reflect some debate with a viewpoint we find represented in the preserved writings of Qumran" (58). Both Davies and Kampen, however, analyze primarily the ideas expressed and positions taken (hence "debate"), while the present study emphasizes the issue of shared exegetical structures and presuppositions underlying the debate.

case of appealing to Genesis 1 and 2 for the sake of establishing the marriage law (Matthew 19) it appears that the same exegetical technique was applied in the rabbinical sources and in Qumran, which enables us more or less safely to define the technique applied in Matt 19:4-6 as an inherited one.

In the other cases, those were mostly rabbinic parallels, attested in tannaitic and amoraic (i.e. later) sources that were available. Philo supplied only half-parallels: similar ideas but not necessarily the same exegetic techniques applied. Nevertheless, it would be preposterous to see the shared *technical features* of the exegetical discourse as first invented either by Jesus or by the transmitters of the Gospel tradition and later reinvented or picked up by certain tannaitic authorities. It is much more plausible that both New Testament and rabbinic sources bear witness to an existing midrashic device – a midrashic pattern that should be described as Palestinian rather than Hellenistic. Thus one may apply Fitzmyer's suggestion – that Matthew has modified the discussion of the divorce issue to make it better suit his Jewish-Christian concerns, casting it in terms of a known exegetical polemic – also to the first, second and fourth antitheses.

It should be emphasized again that what is observed here is not necessarily an inherited *opinion* on the issues under discussion (the period was one of a great fluidity and variety of opinions!) but inherited technical or structural characteristics of exegetic discourse. The Sermon material may, therefore, be seen as early witness to – or as witness to an early stage in the development of – certain exegetical techniques otherwise attested only in later rabbinical sources, thus providing us with an important link in the history of Jewish exegesis that was hitherto missing. The midrashic device of composite citation observed in the Sermon on the Mount – namely, the polemically flavored juxtaposing of parallel Torah precepts – is one of these techniques. The importance of the First Gospel evidence is here further enhanced, given the absence of this exegetical technique in Luke's version of the Sermon as well as in Philo's exegesis – in spite of the latter's obvious inclination to see the Decalogue in light of the extra-Decalogue "special laws," and vice versa.

The foregoing analysis lends support to the opinion that the intention of the compiler of Matthew 5 was to present the polemics as directed not against the Torah but against certain contemporaneous exegetical tendencies. Such tendencies include opinions that do not recognize in the Decalogue commandments additional meanings vis-à-vis the parallels outside the Decalogue, or refer to hard-core transgressions only or, just the opposite, ascribe too broad a meaning to the difficult ערות דבר from Deut 24:1. My analysis therefore supports an interpretation of τοῖς ἀρχαίοις (to/by the men of old) (Matt 5:21, 33) as relating to a long chain of exegetical tradition, and of καταλῦσαι τὸν νόμον – πληρῶσαι τὸν νόμον (to abolish the law – to fulfil the law) (Matt 5:17) as relating to a wrong (lacking, incomplete) *interpretation of the Torah* as against the true (profound, exhaustive) one.[67]

Berndt Schaller has suggested a different explanation for the opening formula, one based on his reading of ἠκούσατε ὅτι ἐρρέθη τοῖς ἀρχαίοις ... ἐγὼ δὲ λέγω ὑμῖν (You have heard that it was said to the men of old ... But I say to you) as analogous to the rabbinic expression שומע אני ... תלמוד לומר (I have heard and understood ... but the teaching/text instructs otherwise).[68] If accepted, this suggestion would modify my conclusions regarding the polemical aspect of the antitheses. However, in this case also, the conclusions regarding basic exegetical patterns employed in Matt 5:21-37 (juxtaposition of parallel Torah precepts, using differences in wording to widen the scope of the precept) would remain valid.

The passage from Matthew 19 differs in this respect from the first four Matthew 5 antitheses. This passage was chosen for discussion (a) because its subject matter (the divorce issue) and its immediate context (Jesus' conversation with a young man in Matt

---

[67] DAVIES–ALLISON (above, n. 50, 480) mention this interpretation of the Sermon's intention as only sixth among nine possibilities and then dismiss it altogether in a footnote, claiming: "However, in the following paragraphs Jesus' words are much more than exegesis." I believe that this interpretation deserves to be upgraded.

[68] See B. SCHALLER, "The Function and Character of the Antitheses in Matt 5:21-48 in the Light of Rabbinical Exegetic Dispute," in this volume.

19:16-20) point to a link with the Sermon on the Mount tradition; and (b) because of its antithetical structure. However – unlike Matt 5:31-32 – the polemically flavored argument is presented here not as disclosing the true meaning of Deut 24:1 but as dismissing Deut 24:1 as an ad hoc palliative of Moses' invention for the sake of a more profound and truly godly ordinance from elsewhere in the Torah. The question as to the extent to which this position might have had a standing in a broader Jewish milieu in the first century CE needs further deliberation. In any case, the variegated nature of the antithetical constructions attested in Matthew warrants emphasis. It is, of course, instructive that the "liberal" attitude toward certain "secondary" parts of the Torah is documented only in Matthew 19 – that is, it is relegated to a position far outside the Sermon on the Mount with its programmatic/apologetic statement: "For truly, I say to you, till the heaven and earth pass away, not an iota, not a dot, will pass from the Torah until all is accomplished."

Menahem KISTER

WORDS AND FORMULAE IN THE GOSPELS
IN THE LIGHT OF HEBREW AND ARAMAIC SOURCES*

To William Horbury

Jesus knew both Hebrew and Aramaic well, probably both of them as a native speaker.[1] There can be little doubt that Jesus' sayings were originally uttered in a Semitic language, either Aramaic or Hebrew (or rather, the most ancient traditions of Jesus' sayings were originally in a Semitic language). Naturally, there are many doubts concerning the details; for instance: whether a certain saying was translated from Aramaic or from Hebrew; the extent to which the Semitic background can be reconstructed; and how the reconstructed text is related to Jesus' *ipsissima verba*.

The Aramaic background of the wording of the Gospels is axiomatically presumed by the vast majority of scholars; the minority view is that some of Jesus' sayings may well have had a Hebrew original. It should be emphasized at the outset that the

---

* This article is a slightly elaborated version of a lecture delivered in the Faculté Universitaire de Theologie Protestante de Bruxelles in May 2004.
[1] For a lucid summary of the research into the Hebrew and Aramaic behind the Greek Gospels, see the forthcoming article of Jan Joosten, originally a lecture delivered in the Faculté Universitaire de Theologie Protestante de Bruxelles.

vocabularies of Hebrew and Aramaic are rather close. Hebrew borrowed many Aramaic words in the Second Temple period. In the Aramaic texts of Qumran we find some words (and forms) borrowed from Hebrew.[2]

Thus, for instance, in the phrase ולא איתי [כ]ל מחיר נגדה (4Q213 frg 1 ii, 4)[3] the word נגדה means "equal to it (i.e., to wisdom),"[4] כנגד in Mishnaic Hebrew.[5] This is especially interesting because it does not fit the meaning of the root נגד in Aramaic, "to draw."[6] This state of affairs in Hebrew and Aramaic makes it often very difficult, if not totally impossible, to determine whether a specific saying was translated from the former language or from the latter. Another example is the usage of על (from the root עלל). This is the normal word for "enter" in Aramaic, but now it also occurs in a Hebrew calendrical text in the same sense (while others use the Hebrew word בא and its infinitive ביאה).[7]

Moreover, our knowledge of the Hebrew of that period is not satisfactory. For instance, the Hebrew word *'amen* is used in the Gos-

---

[2] S. FASSBERG, "Hebrew in the Aramaic Documents from Qumran," in T. MURAOKA (ed.) *Studies in Qumran Aramaic*, Abr Naharain Supplement 5 (Louvain: Peeters, 1992), 48-69.

[3] M. E. STONE and J. C. GREENFIELD, "Aramaic Levi Document," in *Qumran Cave 4.XVII: Parabiblical Texts, Part 3*, DJD 22 (Oxford: Oxford University Press 1996), 18.

[4] Cf. וכ]ול מח[יר לוא ישוה בה] (1Q27 ii, 6; see J. T. MILIK, *Qumran Cave 1*, DJD 1 (Oxford: Oxford University Press, 1955), 105.

[5] For example, *m. Ma'aser Sheni* 2:9 and the idiom שקול כנגד current in Mishnaic Hebrew.

[6] The editors translate: "and it is priceless. He who acquires it" (p. 19), deriving the word נגדה from the Aramaic root נגד (although the meaning they attribute to it is rather unusual; see pp. 16, 20). This suggestion is stylistically awkward. Other translations are closer to the one suggested above: "compared to it" (F. GARCIA MARTINEZ and E. J. C. TIGCHELAAR, *The Dead Sea Scrolls Study Edition* [Leiden: Brill, 1998], 1:447).

[7] 4Q325 frg. 1 (eds. S. TALMON and J. BEN-DOV, DJD 21 [Oxford: Oxford University Press, 2001], 127, lines 9-10). JOOSTEN considers the rendering of עלו as εἰσελεύσεται (Josh 6:5) as an "Aramaic word that is not attested in

pels in a manner unknown from Jewish writings: in the Gospels the word means "truly" (ἀληθῶς), usually in the expression "truly I say to you,"[8] whereas in biblical and mishnaic Hebrew it is known only as a liturgical response to blessings or to oaths (Greek γένοιτο). It may well be that the usage attested in Hebrew is but a remnant of a wider Hebrew usage reflected in the Gospels, as a normal adverb: "true, truly." Interestingly, a hitherto unnoticed parallel to the formula "truly I say to you" is the formula אבל אומר אני לך, put in the mouth of Rabban Yohanan ben Zakkai when he is described as addressing his disciple in a tradition recorded in *Avot de-Rabbi Nathan*,[9] the word אבל being elsewhere a synonym of בקושטא.[10]

A fundamental methodological problem is the chronological gap between Jesus' time and rabbinic literature. Even the earliest strata of rabbinic literature are considerably later than Jesus. Some exceedingly interesting parallels to the New Testament occur in later midrashim, many of them redacted in the Byzantine period. Yet it can be demonstrated by abundant examples that rabbinic literature often reproduces and reworks material that originated in the Second Temple period, and that later works often include ancient material (albeit in reshaped form). Unintelligible passages in the Gospels often become intelligible when read in the light of these parallels. This is the best proof that the method employed is adequate, and it would be a grave mistake to disregard rabbinic literature, without which no Jewish text of the Second Temple period (including Jesus' saying traditions) can be correctly interpreted.

Hebrew at all," although he aptly notes: "Admittedly, the absence of attestation does not mean that the word was never used in any Hebrew text (J. JOOSTEN, "On Aramaizing Renderings of the Septuagint," in M. F. J. BAASTEN and W. T. VAN PEURSEN [eds.], *Hamlet on a Hill: Semitic and Greek Studies Presented to Professor T. Muraoka on the Occasion of His Sixty-Fifth Birthday* [Leuven: Peeters, 2003], 596-97). The occurrence of the Aramaic word על in a *Hebrew* context in a newly found text from Qumran thus illustrates the difficulty of deciding whether a word is Aramaic or Hebrew.

[8] Cf. ἀμὴν λέγω ὑμῖν (Mark 9:1 par. Matt 16:28) // λέγω δὲ ὑμῖν ἀληθῶς (Luke 9:27).

[9] *Avot de-Rabbi Nathan*, Version B, ch. 13 (ed. SCHECHTER, p. 31).

[10] *Targum Onkelos* to Gen 42:21; cf. *Gen. Rab.* 91:8 (ed. ALBECK, p. 1130).

In this article I will deal with words or expressions in the Gospels that can be better understood in their original Semitic context (either Aramaic or Hebrew). Much of my discussion, however, will not be confined to words but will deal with Hebrew and Aramaic formulae and figures of speech (or of thinking), in an effort to demonstrate their contribution to the interpretation of some New Testament passages. Although I have not confined myself to the Sermon on the Mount, many of the passages discussed below are related to this central text.

* * *

1. A good starting point for discussing the Semitic background of the New Testament is the few Aramaic and Hebrew words transliterated into Greek. It would be instructive to discuss one of these, namely, the word *hosanna*.[11]

In Matthew we read:

Most of the crowd spread their garments on the road, and others cut branches from the trees and spread them on the road. And the crowds that went before him and that followed him shouted: "Hosanna to the son of David! Blessed is he who comes! Hosanna in the highest." (Matt 21:8-9 and, similarly, Mark 11:8-10)

It is clear that the word *hosanna* is the Hebrew word *hosha'-na*, meaning "save!" but the relation between the literary meaning of this word (namely, an imperative form of the Hebrew verb) and its usage in the Gospel narrative as an exclamation (rather than a request) has puzzled interpreters and scholars, both ancient and modern. One possible way of solving this riddle has been to assume a mistranslation or a mistake in the tradition of the Gospels. Another has been to suppose, ostensibly without any documenta-

---

[11] For additional details see M. KISTER, "Lexicographical Problems – Early and Late," in M. BAR-ASHER (ed.), *Studies in Mishnaic Hebrew*, Scripta Hierosolymitana 37 (Jerusalem: Magnes, 1998), 252-63.

tion, that the Hebrew word was used as an exclamation. Such a shift in meaning cannot be easily explained. Naturally, the scholars who have favored a Semitic approach to the Gospels (i.e., who have sought the Aramaic or Hebrew originals of Jesus' sayings) have tended to opt for the former solution, while for those less acquainted with Hebrew the latter solution has sounded more plausible.

Paradoxically, however, a Hebraist may demonstrate that the latter solution is indeed the right one: the Hebrew word was used as an exclamation. Manuscripts of *Avot de-Rabbi Nathan* Version A (chap. 4 [ed. SCHECHTER, 10a]) read ואחז בידו שרביט של הדס והיה משענן בו, "He was holding a stick of myrtle in his hand and was waving it" in a marriage procession. Similarly we read in the Targum to Isa 55:12: "the mountains and the hills shall exult before you and the trees of the fields shall wave their branches (ישענון בענפיהון)." A parallel passage, referring to the same verse, in the late midrash *Otiyyoth de-Rabbi Aqiva*, reads ואומרים לפניהם הושענא, "and they exclaim to them, Hosanna."[12] It can be demonstrated with certainty that the verb שענן is derived from *hosha'na* (the verb שענן is used for waving the Hosha'na in the Hebrew and Arabic of Yemenite Jews, and the verb שענן in the Targum is paralleled by הושענא in the late midrash).

It remains now to explain this shift of meaning. In the Hellenistic and Roman period the custom was to wave branches during joyous events (Judith 15:12-13; 1 Macc 13:51). This custom was associated with the Jewish practice of waving palm branches on Sukkoth while uttering the word *hosha'na*.[13] The verb *shi'nen*, derived from the *ritual* utterance *hosha'na*, was also used for the "secular" waving of branches. The word *hosha'na* as a sec-

---

[12] *Otiyyoth de-Rabbi Aqiva, Version A* (ed. WERTHEIMER, p. 374). Similarly in a late aggadic addition to the targum of Isa 61:10 that alludes to Isa 55:12: דטורי ורמתא יחדון ביום פורקניך ... יאי ושפיר יומא ההוא כד אנת אתי ברישנא ואנחנא כולנא בתרך ואמרין הושענה הושיעה נא (R. KASHER, *Targumic Toseftot to the Prophets* [Jerusalem: World Union of Jewish Studies, 1996], 175).

[13] The exclamation in the liturgy is derived, of course, from the root יש"ע, meaning "save (us)." This meaning was obviously lost in the secular usage of this word.

ular exclamation is documented in a very late source, *Midrash Otiyyot de-Rabbi Aqiva*, based on Isa 55:12, which is interpreted in a way similar to the Targum.[14] But even if this source is ignored, the verb derived from *hosha'-na* in Mishnaic Hebrew and in Aramaic and the occurrence of *hosha'-na* in the Gospels are complementary evidence for the employment of this word as an exclamation. As is quite often the case, the Gospels supply considerably earlier evidence than rabbinic literature, but the latter is of crucial significance for understanding the former.

2. Jesus' saying to Peter, ἐπὶ ταύτῃ τῇ πέτρᾳ οἰκοδομήσω μου τὴν ἐκκλησίαν, καὶ πύλαι ᾅδου οὐ κατισχύσουσιν αὐτῆς, "On this rock I will build my church, and the gates of death shall not prevail against it" (Mt 16:18), can be illuminated by the Dead Sea Scrolls:[15] ונ[פשי תגיע] עד שערי מות ... כי אתה תשים סוד על סלע ... לבנו[ת חומת] עוז ללוא תתזעזע וכול באיה בל ימוטו (1QH^a XIV 25-26 [= Sukenik ed., 6:25-26]) or כי אתה תשים[סודי]על סלע] (4Q429 4 2:7).[16] The word סוד at Qumran has the meaning of both "foundation" and "community." The words ἐπὶ ταύτῃ τῇ πέτρᾳ οἰκοδομήσω μου τὴν ἐκκλησίαν may be reconstructed, then: אבנה סודי על סלע, assuming that the word סוד was used here, unlike in the *Hodayot*, in the sense of "community." This is, however, a secondary interpretation of the word סוד in this sentence (which is ultimately based on Isa 28:16). In the *Hodayot* (whose wording is derived from the verse in Isaiah) the meaning of the word is "foundation," but it can be demonstrated that the double meaning of the word was significant for the authors of Qumran writings related to the *Hodayot* passage (1QS

---

[14] My argument is based not on *Otiyyot de-Rabbi Aqiva* but on the cumulative evidence of *Avot de-Rabbi Nathan*, the targum to Isa 55:12 and the usage of the verb שענן by Yemenite Jews. It is intriguing to note, however, that the late sources, namely *Otiyyot de-Rabbi Aqiva* and the addition to targum Isa 61:10 (above, n. 12), use the word הושענא as an exclamation, and the Gospels teach us that this usage is very ancient.

[15] As has been observed by O. Betz, "Felsenmann und Felsengemeinde: Eine Parallele zu Mt. 16:17-19 in den Qumranpsalmen," *ZAW* 48 (1957), 49-77.

[16] E. Schuller, *Qumran Cave 4.XX: Poetical and Liturgical Texts, Part 2*, DJD 29 (Oxford: Oxford University Press, 1999), 192.

XI 4). Moreover, the fact that the expression "gates of death," which is problematic in the context of Jesus' saying, occurs in the Qumranic text in juxtaposition to the expression cited above (1QH^a XIV 24 [=Sukenik, 6:24]) demonstrates that Matt 16:18 is derived from a *literary unit* similar to the *Hodayot* passage.[17] For the present discussion, it is important to note that the double meaning of the word סוד is attested only in Hebrew. This, as well as the affinity of this text to the *Hodayot*, indicates that this saying may well have a Hebrew, rather than an Aramaic, source.

3. As is well known to any student of rabbinic literature, the word *rav* in Mishnaic Hebrew (and Jewish Aramaic) has two meanings: (1) master, (2) teacher.[18] This polysemy is the clue to the translations of the word רבי in the Gospels. The words רבי and רבוני are transliterated in Mark as ῥαββι and ῥαββουνί, respectively. The same words are translated in John as διδάσκαλος.[19] Similarly, Matt

---

[17] For a more detailed argumentation, see M. Kister, "Some Observations on Vocabulary and Style in the Dead Sea Scrolls," in T. Muraoka and J. F. Elwolde (eds.), *Diggers at the Well: Proceedings of a Third International Symposium on the Hebrew of the Dead Sea Scrolls and Ben Sira* (Leiden: Brill, 2000; STDJ 36), 163-65. This saying probably represents material current in the early Christian community in relation to Peter.

[18] To give only one well-known example: in the phrase כעבדים המשמשים את הרב (*m. Avot* 1:3) the meaning of *rav* is "master," whereas in the phrase עשה לך רב (*m. Avot* 1:6) the word means "teacher." Compare Dalman: "רבי is a deeply-deferential form of address, the full force of which is in nowise expressed by the Greek διδάσκαλε. ... He who was addressed as רבי is thereby acknowledged to be the superior of the speaker. To some extent the Latin 'magister' corresponds, as it denotes superiors of various kinds, among others the teachers especially" (G. Dalman, *The Words of Jesus Considered in the Light of Post-Biblical Jewish Writings and the Aramaic Language* [Edinburgh: T & T Clark, 1902], 334). The word רב in the sense of "master (of a slave)" is current in Hebrew, but it occurs also in Jewish Aramaic (*contra* Dalman; see M. Sokoloff, *A Dictionary of Jewish Palestinian Aramaic of the Byzantine Period* (Ramat-Gan: Bar-Ilan University Press, 1990), 512.

[19] ῥαββί, ὃ λέγεται μεθερμηνευόμενον Διδάσκαλε, John 1:38; ῥαββουνί, ὃ λέγεται Διδάσκαλε, John 20:16. In rabbinic literature, רבוני is attested only in the sense of "master, sir" (in addressing one's superior), but not as a title for a

23:8: "You are not to be called *rabbi*, for you have one teacher (διδάσκαλος)"[20]; the word διδάσκαλος, "teacher," translates the word *rav* in the original Semitic saying. The words κύριε in another passage of Mark and διδάσκαλος in its Matthean parallel (Mark 9:17 par. Matt 17:15) are probably two renderings of *rabbi*, as may be the case with many occurrences of the vocative διδάσκαλε and with some of the occurrences of κύριε[21] in the Synoptic Gospels.[22]

The polysemy of the word רב ("teacher" and "master") is evident in the saying: כל מלאכות שהעבד עושה לרבו, תלמיד עושה לרבו (*b. Ketubbot* 96a) "All the services that a slave renders his master, a disciple should render to his teacher."[23] The polysemy can also be seen in some other passages in rabbinic literature, where the same phrases are used for master-slave and disciple-teacher relations. This derives, at least partly, from the polysemy of the word *rav*.[24]

rav = master (versus slave)	*rav* = teacher (versus disciple)
משל למי שאמר לו רבו: תביא לי אלא חיטים, והלך והביא לו חיטים ושעורים[25]	לתלמיד שאמר לו רבו אל תביא לי אלא חיטין והביא חיטין ושעורין[26]
שיהא העבד נוטל הפנס ומאיר לקונו[27]	תלמיד טוען פנס לפני רבו[28]
אנת ... שליט באמתה הדא דזבנת לך ... ולמעבד בה כל דתצבא[29]	והרב שליט לעשות בתלמיד מה שהוא רוצה[30]

---

teacher or sage (but cf. חד רבן, DALMAN, *The Words of Jesus*, 335; SOKOLOFF, *Dictionary*, 514). Apparently, at the time of the Gospels there was no clear differentiation between the two synonyms. It seems to me likely that the word *rabbi* in the sense of "teacher" reflects the era of the Second Temple rather than that of Jamnia, even if it became a rabbinic official title only in Jamnia (cf. P. TOMSON, "The Wars against Rome: The Rise of Rabbinic Judaism and of Apostolic Gentile Christianity, and the Judaeo-Christians: Elements for a Synthesis," in P. J. TOMSON and D. LAMBERS-PETRY [eds.] *The Image of the Judaeo-Christians in Ancient Jewish and Christian Literature* [Tübingen: Mohr Siebeck, 2003], 13).

[20] The identification of the "teacher" with Jesus that occurs in several MSS is textually secondary.

[21] Needless to say, the Greek words have different denotations and connota-

In Matt 10:24 we read: Οὐκ ἔστιν μαθητὴς ὑπὲρ τὸν διδάσκαλον οὐδὲ δοῦλος ὑπὲρ τὸν κύριον αὐτοῦ. ἄρκετον τῷ μαθητῇ ἵνα γένεται ὡς ὁ διδάσκαλος αὐτοῦ καὶ ὁ δοῦλος ὡς ὁ κύριος αὐτοῦ, "A disciple is not above his teacher, nor a slave above his master; it is enough for a disciple to be like his teacher and a slave like his master."[31] In rabbinic literature we find an identical proverb: דיו

---

tions, and could be influenced by the style and message of each Gospel; but basically the rendering of the word *rabbi* in the Gospels as either "teacher" or "master" simply reflects Semitic usage. Contrast W. FOERSTER, *Herr ist Jesus: Herkunft und Bedeutung des Urchristlichen Kyrios-Bekenntnisses* (Gütersloh: Bertelsmann, 1924), 11-56; 227-36; E. LOHSE, *TDNT*, vol. 6, s.v. ῥαββι, 964-65; W. FOERSTER, *TDNT* vol. 3, s.v. κύριος, 1093.

[22] To be sure, the word κύριος may translate also the Aramaic מר and the Hebrew אדון. It should be noted, however, that the Aramaic word מרי (my lord, sir) does not occur in the Gospels. This is especially remarkable given that the word μαράν (our Lord) was an epithet of Jesus in the early Christian period even in a Greek-speaking milieu (1 Cor 16:22). One wonders: would not a Christian translator have left this word untranslated had it occurred in his Semitic text?

[23] Similarly, a sage is asked during persecution: "Why are you called *rabbi*," and answers: "I am the weavers' master" (רבן של תרסיים אני; *b. Avoda Zara* 17b).

[24] These changes may be, at least in some cases, the product of medieval scribes; but even if this be so, they illuminate the phenomenon being dealt with here.

[25] *Sifra* ad Lev 1:2, *Dibbura di-Nedava*, *Parasha* 2:6 (ed. FINKELSTEIN, p. 22). According to the context, the original meaning was "slave/master."

[26] *b. Zevahim* 34a.

[27] *Num. Rab.* 16:27; cf. also *Tanna de-Be Eliyahu* 13 (ed. Friedmann, p. 60).

[28] *Ex. Rab.* 25:6 (but later עבד ... רבו as in the parallel source!); *Midrash Ps.* 18:29 (ed. BUBER, p. 156).

[29] A Syriac bill of sale from the year 243 CE; see J. A. GOLDSTEIN, "The Syriac Bill of Sale from Dura Europos," *JNES* 25 (1966), 2, lines 11-12.

[30] *Midrash ha-Gadol* ad Deut 3:21 (ed. FISCH, p. 66). See M. KISTER, "'Let Us Make a Man': Observations on the Dynamics of Monotheism", *Issues in Talmudic Research: Conference Commemorating the Fifth Anniversary of the Passing of E. E. Urbach, 2 December 1996* (Jerusalem: The Israel Academy of Sciences and Humanities, 2001), 31-37 (in Hebrew).

[31] The parallel in Luke 6:40 has different wording but includes only one pair – namely, "disciple/teacher."

לעבד שיהיה כרבו, "It is enough for a slave to be like his master." This mundane proverb, current in rabbinic literature,[32] is applied in some passages to religious matters.[33] A parallel to the proverb "It is enough for a disciple to be like his teacher" occurs in tannaitic sources. According to *Mekhilta de-R. Shimʿon ben Yohai*, a disciple might think (פלוני) דיי שאהיה כרבי, "It is enough that I will be like *my teacher*."[34] According to the *Tosefta* (*t. Sanhedrin* 3:8), the reading is דַּיִּי שֶׁאֲרָאֶה כְרַבִּי, "It is enough that I consider (the verdict) like my teacher"; but MS Vienna of the *Tosefta* reads דיו לעבד להיות כרבו, "It is enough for a *slave* to be like his *master*,"[35] a proverb inappropriate in the context of the *Tosefta*, probably the result of replacing the phrase דיי שאהיה כרבי by the common proverb relating to the slave. Evidently, the proverb in Matthew can be reconstructed: דיו לתלמיד שיהיה כרבו ודיו לעבד שיהיה כרבו.[36] The

---

[32] *Sifra* ad Lev 25:23 (*Behar* 4:8; ed. WEISS, p. 108b); *b. Berakhot* 58b; *Ex. Rab.* 42:5; *Tanhuma, Hayye Sara* 4; *Ki Tissa*, 21; *Tanhuma* ed. BUBER, *Lekh Lekha*, 23; *Midrash Ps.* 27:5 (ed. BUBER, 226). See also M. GRUENEWALD, "'It Is Enough for the Servant to Be Like His Master'," in S. LIEBERMAN (ed.), *Sallo Wittmayer Baron Jubilee Volume* (New York and London: Columbia University Press, 1974), 573-76.

[33] In *b. Berakhot* 58b the context is: Jews are supposed to suffer no less than God himself (whose temple is ruined and whose land is desolate; this may be implied already in the *Sifra* ad Lev 25:23). This is very similar to John 15:20, where the context is that Christians are supposed to suffer no less than Christ himself.

[34] The asterisks indicate the original reading (without the word פלוני) that can be reconstructed in *Midrash ha-Gadol*, on the basis of the parallel in the *Tosefta*. The text in *Mekhilta de-Rabbi Shimʿon ben Yohai* (ed. EPSTEIN-MELAMED, p. 214) is problematic (see textual notes to line 22). The text of *Midrash ha-Gadol* is corrected according to a citation in Moses NAJARA, *Leqah Tov* (Jerusalem: Yeshivat Suvi Nafshi, 1999), 100 [ad Exod 23:2]), noted in Epstein-Melamed's edition, ad loc. In *t. Sanhedrin* 3:8 the word רבי means "my teacher"; in the *Mekhilta* as we have it, it means "a certain rabbi," but the word פלוני (certain) is probably secondary.

[35] The word רב acquires here the sense of "master" by the change of *student* to *slave*.

[36] Contrast Dalman's reconsruction: לית תלמידא לעיל מן רביה ולית עבדא לעיל מן מריה (G. DALMAN, *Jesus-Jeshua: Studies in the Gospels* [New York: Macmillan, 1929], 229).

couplet in Matthew may well be an ancient doublet of one original saying, emerging out of the double meaning of the word *rav* in Hebrew (the language in which the proverb is attested in rabbinic literature) or Aramaic.

Similarly, it might be suggested that the *original* meaning of *rav* in Matt 23:8 was "master" rather than "teacher", i.e.: "do not be called *rabbi*, for you have one *master* [רב],"[37] and that the "one master" intended here is God.[38] The word καθηγητής, used in Matt 23:10, may well be another rendering of the word *rabbi*.[39] The same word, *rav*, in another sense ("great"), may be rendered by the words ὁ δὲ μείζων ὑμῶν, "he who is the greatest among you" in the next verse, Matt 23:11.[40]

4. In Matthew we read:[41]

> You have heard that it was said "You shall love your neighbor and hate your enemy", and I say to you: Love your enemies ... so that you may be sons of the father who is in heaven; for He makes his sun rise on the evil and on the good, and sends rain on the just and on the unjust. For if you love those who love you, what reward have you? Do not even the tax collectors do the same? And if you salute (ἐὰν ἀσπάσεσθε) only your brethren, what extraordinary thing are you doing (τί περισσὸν ποιεῖτε)? Do not even the gentiles do the same? You, therefore, must be

---

[37] Verse 9 continues by saying: "Call no man on earth your father, for you have one father, who is in heaven." Master/slave and father/son relations are the two basic similes for the relation between God and human beings.

[38] Thus D. FLUSSER, *Jesus*, 3rd ed. (Jerusalem: Magnes Press, 1997), 32.

[39] As suggested by DALMAN, *Words of Jesus*, 340. It should be noted that many MSS have the word καθηγητής in verse 8, instead of διδάσκαλος.

[40] Thus, albeit very hesitantly, W. D. DAVIES and D. C. ALLISON, *A Critical and Exegetical Commentary on the Gospel according to St. Matthew*, vol. 3 (Edinburgh: T & T Clark, 1997), 279 n. 94.

[41] For a detailed survey of the research concerning this passage see W. KLASSEN, "The Authenticity of the Command 'Love Your Enemy'," in B. CHILTON and C.A. EVANS (eds.), *Authenticating the Words of Jesus* (Leiden: Brill, 1999; NTTS 28,1), 385-407.

perfect (τέλειος) as your heavenly Father is perfect (τέλειος). (Matt 5:43-48)

Several details of this famous passage can be interpreted only against the background of Hebrew and Aramaic idioms.

First, the wording τὸν πλησίον σου, usually rendered into English as "your neighbor," is obviously a translation of the word לרעך (Lev 19:18), a word *basically* meaning "friend," which can also be employed in a more general sense; it can mean just any other person, or any other person of your community, as Jesus is indeed asked elsewhere "Who is my neighbor (probably רעי)?"[42] The choice of the word πλησίον in the Greek text of verse 43, following the rendering of Lev 19:18 in the Septuagint, has blurred the close relationship between it and the words ἀγαπῶντας ὑμᾶς, "those who love you," which are a translation of Hebrew אוהביכם or Aramaic רחמיכון. The Semitic words denote "friends,"[43] although the emotional meaning of "love" in friendly relations[44] is clearly present in them. These words are natural synonyms of Hebrew רע.

Moreover, a Palestinian Targum to Lev 19:18 translates the words ואהבת לרעך כמוך in this verse into Aramaic as ותרחמון לרחמיכון דכוותכון – i.e., "Love your friends (literally: those who love you) who are like you"![45] The Palestinian Targums as they have reached us should be dated several centuries later than the Gospels, but they certainly include some ancient exegetic and targumic traditions that go back to the Second Temple period. This case, where the Targum so strikingly matches Jesus' *objection* to the interpre-

---

[42] J. L. KUGEL, *Traditions of the Bible* (Cambridge, Mass.: Harvard University Press, 1998), 756-58; J. MILGROM, *Leviticus 17-22: A New Translation with Introduction and Commentary*, (New York: Doubleday, 2000) 1654-55; S. RUZER, "From 'Love your Neighbour' to 'Love Your Enemy'," *RB* 109 (2002), 371-89.

[43] The word אהוב is a common synonym for רע.

[44] Cf. Greek φίλος.

[45] A gloss of *Targum Neophyti* ad loc. (A. DIEZ MACHO, *Neophyti 1: Targum Palestinense MS de la biblioteca Vaticane*, vol. 3 [Madrid: Consejo Superior de Investigaciones Cientificas, 1971], 131).

tation of the biblical verse, is probably one of these cases. The words ותרחמון לרחמיכון in the Targum cited above are not far removed from other renderings of the words ואהבת לרעך in Palestinian translations, such as ותרחמון לחבריכון, the words חבר and רחם being synonyms.⁴⁶ The rendering דכוותכון interprets the word כמוך in the verse as an adjective (rather than an adverb)⁴⁷ – i.e., "your friends *who are like you*." A translation such as ותרחמון לרחמיכון דכוותכון might be read as a commandment that one should love only those who love him and are like him. (What does *that* mean? Does one have to love only Jews, like oneself?⁴⁸ or only righteous persons?⁴⁹ or all human beings?⁵⁰ persons of the same occupation? All these are legitimate interpretations of the single word דכוותכון.) Jesus' teaching is aimed primarily against such an interpretation.⁵¹

---

⁴⁶ This is the reading of the text of *Targum Neophyti*, ad loc.

⁴⁷ T. MURAOKA, "A Syntactic Problem in Lev. XIX 18b," *JSS* 23 (1978), 291-97. Milgrom rightly objects on the grounds of Lev 19:34, in which כמוך should be interpreted as an adverb (MILGROM, *Leviticus*, 1655).

⁴⁸ This is a possible interpretation to the word רע, especially since the preceding phrase in this verse applies to בני עמך, "members of your people." See *Sifra* to Lev 19:34: "As it was said concerning an Israelite, 'Love your neighbor as yourself', so it was said concerning a proselyte, 'Love him as yourself'."

⁴⁹ This would accord with the interpretation of בני עמך in *Sifra* to Lev 19:18; cf. also *Avot de-Rabbi Nathan*, Version A, ch. 16 (אם עושה מעשה עמך אתה אוהבו).

⁵⁰ Thus Sir 28:1-7, which alludes to Lev 19:18. In this text the interpretation "your fellow man who is like yourself" is taken as referring to other human beings, who are flesh and blood. See D. FLUSSER, "A New Sensitivity in Judaism and the Christian Message," *HTR* 61 (1968), 115-16 [=*Judaism and the Origins of Christianity* (Jerusalem: Magnes Press, 1988), 477-78]. Cf. also MURAOKA, "A Syntactic Problem."

⁵¹ There is no hint in Jesus' words that they are aimed against the Qumranic teaching, according to which one should love only the members of his community and hate those who are God's enemies (i.e., all those who are not members of one's sect), as suggested by (among others) K. SCHUBERT, "The Sermon on the Mount and the Qumran Texts," in K. STENDAHL (ed.), *The Scrolls and the New Testament* (London: SCM, 1957), 120-21; D. FLUSSER, "A New Sensitivity," 122-24 [=*Judaism*, 484-86]; KUGEL, *Traditions of the*

Second, we may note the parallelism between the phrases:

If you love those who love you, what reward have you?
If you salute only your brethren, what extraordinary thing are
 you doing?

This parallelism enables us to perceive the original Semitic wording.

The verb ἀσπάζομαι, translated as "salute" is related to "love" not only in Greek[52] but also in Semitic usage, where ש(ו)אל של(ו)ם stands in parallel to רחם or אוהב (=ἀγαπῶντας!) in Aramaic and Hebrew.[53] "Love," "friendship" and "salute" (שאל לשלום) are synonymous, and so are the words "those who love you" (אוהביכם or רחמיכון) and "your brethren" (אחיכון, אחיכם), or (according to other manuscripts) "your friends." What about the parallelism between

---

Bible, 1655; J. H. CHARLESWORTH, "The Dead Sea Scrolls and the Historical Jesus," in J. H. CHARLESWORTH (ed.), *Jesus and the Dead Sea Scrolls* (New York: Doubleday, 1992), 23-24; W. D. DAVIES and D. C. ALLISON, *St. Matthew*, vol. 1 (Edinburgh: T & T Clark, 1988), 549. It is more likely that Jesus reacted to the exegetical tradition reflected in the peculiar Palestinian Targum cited above, in which nothing indicates that it is non-rabbinic or of sectarian character.

[52] "ἀσπάζομαι certainly means more than 'greet', *be fond of, cherish* is better. w[ith] ἀγαπάω, of which it is almost a synonym" (for which Plutarch is cited) (W. BAUER, W. F. ARNDT and F. W. GINGRICH, *A Greek-English Lexicon of the New Testament*[4] [Chicago: University of Chicago, 1957], 116).

[53] אוהב // שואלי שלום (Sir 6:5); רחמוהי // שאלי שלמיה (Aramaic Levi Document); "His friends are many and his acquaintances great ones." Centuries later the people of a community living in a foreign city complain: לית לאילין עמא לא רחם ולא שאל שלם, "This (our) community has neither a friend nor an acquaintance" (*y. Shevi'it* 9:5 [39a]). The expression שאל שלום means "caring and inquiring about one's well-being"; as we read in Jeremiah: "Who will have pity on you ... who will bemoan you, who will turn aside to ask about your welfare?" (ומי יסור לשאול לשלום לך; Jer 15:5). See M. KISTER, "Some Notes on Biblical Expressions and Allusions and the Lexicography of Ben Sira," in T. MURAOKA and J. F. ELWODE (eds.), *Sirach, Scrolls, and Sages: Proceedings of a Second International Symposium on the Hebrew of the Dead Sea Scrolls, Ben Sira, and the Mishnah* (Leiden: Brill, 1999; STDJ 33), 173-75.

μισθός and περισσός? In Greek there is no parallel between the two words. In the LXX the word περισσός translates only words of the root יתר in the Hebrew Bible. Now this root has, both in Aramaic and in Hebrew, the meaning "superiority, excess" and also "profit, posession, gain."[54] In a verse of Ben Sira we even have the two words יתר ושכר juxtaposed (40:18) "gain and payment (שכר = μισθός in the Gospel)."[55] The original parallelism in Matthew's version of the saying was, therefore, mistranslated into Greek. The original should be translated: "If you love your friends (or: those who love you), what reward (or: payment) have you? ... and if you care for the well-being of your brethren (or: friends), what *gain* have you?"[56]

Third, a hitherto unnoticed parallel between this passage in Matthew and a midrash may be of importance for the reconstruction of this passage. The midrash reads:

'שיר השירים אשר לשלמה' מי אמרה? מי שהשלום שלו [ונוהג] שלום עם כל בריות. החמה זורחת על הצדיקים ועל הרשעים, ועושה שלום בין מלאכיו ...

---

[54] For Syriac ܟܘܬܪܐ, see R. PAYNE-SMITH, *Thesaurus Syriacus* (Oxford: Clarendon Press, 1879), 1650. In the Bible the word יתרון occurs only in Ecclesiastes; some verses seem to have the concrete sense, "profit, gain" (מה יתרון לאדם בכל עמלו, "what does one gain by all his work"; [Eccl 1:3; cf. also 2:11, 3:9]). "יתרון is probably a commercial term, the surplus of the balance sheet" (R. GORDIS, *Koheleth – The Man and His World: A Study of Ecclesiastes* [New York: Schocken, 1968], 205). In other verses in Ecclesiastes, the word has an abstract sense, "advantage" (2:13, 10:11; cf. מותר, 3:19).

[55] M. KISTER, "A Contribution to the Interpretation of Ben Sira," *Tarbiz* 59 (1990), 348-49 (in Hebrew). This usage illuminates the wording in a midrash: אם אי אני מוציא לך מעט רוח, יכול את לזרות? אפי' שכר אותו הרוח יכול את ליתן? הדא הוא דכתיב 'מה יתרון לו שיעמול לרוח' (*Lev. Rab.* 28:2 [ed. MARGULIES, 655]) "If I do not bring a bit of wind for you, will you be able to winnow? Can you pay me this wind's price? As it is written: מה יתרון לו שיעמול לרוח) Eccl. 5:15, here understood as: "What payment can a person give in order to toil for the wind?") The biblical word יתרון is explained by שכר. In Deliztsch's Hebrew translation, περισσός in Matt 5:47 is rendered יתרון.

[56] Admittedly, the Greek words τί περισσὸν ποιεῖτε cannot easily be literally reconstructed in either Hebrew or Aramaic; the employment of the Greek word ποιέω is still a riddle (it may be, of course, a free Greek rendering).

ושלום ביניהם ואוהבים זה לזה, "The Song of Songs of Solomon" – Who is the author of this (book)? The One to whom peace belongs, and who acts peacefully with all the creatures. The sun rises on the good and on the evil and he makes peace among his angels ... and there is peace between them and they are in peace and they love (or: are on friendly terms with) each other." (*Cant. Zuta* 1:1).[57]

The similarity between the sentence "The sun rises on the good and on the evil" and the passage in Matthew is striking. The emphasis on mutual "love" (i.e., friendship) between God's creatures that reflects the שלום, peaceful manner, in which God conducts the world is also remarkable and partly occurs elsewhere in rabbinic literature, most notably in *Cant. Rab.* 3:11 (interpreting the word שלמה). It is only in the passage in *Cant. Zuta*, however, that this peaceful manner is illustrated by making the sun rise for *all* creatures. Now it has already been noted that the wording of Matt 5:43-48 is rather similar to the wording of Matt 5:9:

Matt 5:45-48	Matt 5:9
ὅπως γένησθε υἱοὶ τοῦ πατρὸς ὑμῶν τοῦ ἐν οὐρανοῖς, ὅτι τὸν ἥλιον αὐτοῦ ἀνατέλλει ἐπὶ πονηροὺς καὶ ἀγαθοὺς ... ἔσεσθε οὖν ὑμεῖς τέλειοι ὡς ὁ πατὴρ ὑμῶν ὁ οὐράνιος τέλειός ἐστιν	μακάριοι οἱ εἰρηνοποιοί ὅτι υἱοὶ θεοῦ κληθήσονται
so that you may be sons of the Father who is in heaven; for he makes his sun rise on the evil and the good ... be, therefore, perfect, as your heavenly father is perfect	blessed are the peacemakers, for they shall be called sons of God

---

[57] *Cant. Zuta* in its present form is not an ancient composition, but it embodies many ancient traditions, sometimes significantly altered.

The word τέλειοι is paralleled by εἰρηνοποιοί; cf. in mishnaic Hebrew: 'אבנים שלמות' - אבנים שמטילות שלום (*Mekhilta de-R. Yishma'el*, Ba-ḥodesh §11 [ad Exod 20:22], ed. LAUTERBACH, p. 290). The internal and external parallel may lead us to the conclusion that the word τέλειος, "perfect," may well be an inadequate translation of the rare Hebrew word שָׁלֵם, in the sense of "have peaceful relations with, being friendly, acting peacefully." Thus the people of Shechem say concerning Jacob's family: האנשים האלה שלמים הם אתנו, "These people have peaceful relations with us (or: are friendly with us)" (Gen 34:21).[58] The Semitic root שלם, meaning relations of friendship, caring and peaceful forgiveness, would be, then, the dominant root in this passage, uniting the Greek words ἀσπάζομαι (שאל שלום), τέλειος (שלם) and εἰρηνοποιός (עושי שלום? מטילי שלום?) and the notion of God's care for the good and the evil.[59]

Lastly, we should discern the exegetical point of these verses and its relation to a rabbinic text. Jesus demonstrates, according to this passage, that the right interpretation of the words ואהבת לרעך כמוך is to love all human beings, including one's enemies, as God does, by interpreting the last words of Lev 19:18, 'אני ה ("I am the Lord") as indicating the divine love that should be imitated by human beings: קדשים תהיו כי קדוש אני ה' אלהיכם, "Be ye holy for I, the Lord your God, is holy" (Lev 19:2).[60] The words "If you love those who love you ... do not the tax collectors do the same?" has an interesting parallel in a midrash on the words כי חנון אני, "for I am merciful" (Exod 22:26):

---

[58] See also Ps 55:21. The original wording of Matt 5:9 may have been slightly different.

[59] Delitzsch translates תשאלו לשלום ... מה יתרון לכם ... שלמים ... שלם. This point was explicitly made by M. BLACK, *An Aramaic Approach to the Gospels and Acts* (Oxford: Oxford University Press, 1967), 181. We have dealt only with the Matthean version of this saying and ignored the parallel in Luke 6:27-36. In this case, every text has to be interpreted independently, and the relation of the two texts to Jesus' *ipsissima verba* is a matter of guesswork.

[60] M. KISTER, "The Sayings of Jesus and the Midrash," *Immanuel* 15 (1982/3), 46-47.

היה ר' שמעון אומר: אוהבי ממון אוהבין זה את זה והגזלנין אוהבין זה את
זה והחמסנין אוהבין זה את זה ומלוי רבית אוהבין זה את זה. למי נאה ליפרע
מכל אלו? אני הוא שאין בי אחת מכל המידות הללו "R. Shim'on used
to say: money-lovers love each other, robbers love each other
and usurers love each other. Who is the appropriate one to give
[the appropriate] reward [i.e., punishment] to all of these? It is
I, for none of these traits can be found in me" (*Mekhilta de-R.
Shim'on b. Yohai* [ed. EPSTEIN-MELAMED, pp. 212-13]).[61]

We encounter in this source a contrast between human beings, who
love those who are like them, and God, speaking in the first person (אני).[62] A similar contrast is found in Jesus' saying: "If you love
those who love you, what reward have you? Do not even the tax
collectors do the same?" The wording in Matthew might be related to sayings like the one preserved in this midrash.

5. In an anecdote found only in Luke we read:

As he said these things, a woman in the crowd raised her voice
and said to him, "Blessed is the womb that bore you and the
breasts that you sucked." And he said, "Blessed rather (μενοῦν)
are those who hear the word of God and keep it." (Luke 11:27-28)

Hebrew and Aramaic parallels to this formula have been cited for
more than three hundred years,[63] but modern scholarship is still at

---

[61] This source is preserved only in the medieval compilation *Midrash ha-Gadol*, but scholars have rightly discerned that it is probably derived from the *tannaitic* midrash *Mekhilta de-Rabbi Shim'on b. Yohai*.

[62] It is likely that Rabbi Shim'on's saying was not originally a comment on Exod 22:26. It cannot be excluded that the saying referred to Lev 19:18 "*Love your friend who is like you, I* am God" (cf. also the punishment deduced from the formula אני ה' in *Sifra* to Lev 18:5-6), but it is next to impossible to know the original context of R. Shim'on's saying. Be that as it may, the similarity between this saying and Matthew seems to be more than a coincidence.

[63] Many commentators cite some of the rabbinic parallels. One of the richest collections of rabbinic parallels to this saying is Schoettgen's book of Hebrew and rabbinic parallels to the New Testament, published in 1733. See C. SCHOETTGEN, *Horae Hebraicae et talmudicae in universum Novum Testa-*

loss to explain the saying. Opposite formulae occur in rabbinic literature as a popular negative exclamation: "Cursed be the breasts that have suckled this person" (*Gen. Rab.* 5:9, p. 39; *Tanhuma Ki-Tava* 1). A similar negative formula is "Cursed is he who caused to bear this [woman], cursed is he who reared this [woman], cursed is he of whose loins she did come" (*b. Sanhedrin* 52a). The blessing formula, very similar to the one in the Gospel, occurs in the Palestinian Targum to Gen 49:25 and in *Genesis Rabbah* to the same verse (*Gen. Rab.* 98:20 [p. 1270]), where it refers to Joseph, and also in a later addition to *Pesiqta de-Rav Kahana* (ed. MANDELBAUM, p. 470), where it refers to the Messiah, and in *Hekhalot* texts (mystical literature of Late Antiquity), where it refers to King David.[64] Similar blessings, such as "Blessed is she who bore you"[65] and "Blessed is Abraham our father of whose loins you have come forth,"[66] are often recorded as praise formulae, especially after a remarkable oration. The latter formula is certainly based on a more mundane one: "Blessed is your father, of whose loins you have came forth."[67] The interplay between the two formulae is one of the points of the story concerning Rabbi Eliezer in *Avot de-Rabbi Nathan* (*Version B*, ch. 13). It has been noted (but overlooked in many commentaries), that similar formulae occur in Greek and Roman literature: "Blessed be he who fathered you, and the mother who bore you. And very blessed be the womb which sheltered you" (ὄλβιος ὅς σε φύτευσε καὶ ὄλβιη ἡ τέκε μήτηρ. γαστήρ ἥ σε λόχευσε μακαρτάτη; Musaios grammaticus, *Hero et*

---

    mentum (Dresden and Leipzig: Christoph. Hekelii B. Filium, 1733), 282. A few rabbinic parallels to Jesus' saying were cited already in H. GROTIUS, *Annotationes in Novum Testamentum* (Amsterdam, 1650) 721.

[64] D. FLUSSER and B. YOUNG, "Messianic Blessings in Jewish and Christian Texts," in FLUSSER, *Judaism and the Origins of Christianity*, 280-300.

[65] *m. Avot* 2:8; *Mekhilta de-R. Shim'on b. Yohai* to Exod 21:1 (p. 159); *b. Hagiga* 14b; *Ex. Rab.* 51:6; *Tanhuma* ed. BUBER, *Pequde*, 4.

[66] *t. Hagiga* 2:1; *Mekhilta de-R. Shim'on b. Yohai* to Exod 21:1 (p. 159) and parallels; *Avot de-R. Nathan* Version B, ch. 13; *Mekhilta de-R. Yishma'el*, Pisha §16 (ad Exod 13:1, ed. LAUTERBACH, p. 132); *Sifre Num.* §75 (p. 70).

[67] Note *b. Sanhedrin* 52a, cited above.

Leander, lines 138-139); "Happy is your mother who bore such a son as you" (O felicem, inquit, matrem tuam, quae te talem peperit; Petronius, *Satyricon*, 94).[68]

Bearing all this in mind, it does *not* seem that the woman extolled Jesus "in a typically maternal way," as stated by several commentators,[69] since the formula is mostly employed by men in rabbinic literature; the claim that "it is ... very probable that the woman ... is merely citing a targumic paraphrase to Gen 49:25 which she heard in the synagogue"[70] is untenable, since the targum is merely employing a blessing that was very popular ("People say") among Jews and pagans alike. The hypothesis that this is a "Messianic blessing" also seems quite unlikely: although it refers to the Messiah in a late addition to *Pesiqta de-Rav Kahana*,[71] the same pattern appears in many other contexts (in which it is applied to different persons) and there is nothing necessarily "messianic" in the context. Neither is this praise of Mary, but rather of Jesus himself.[72] This is clearly the case in the two non-Jewish utterances cited above: the praise of one's parents is certainly no more than a

---

[68] The former was noted as a parallel already by Hugo Grotius (above, n. 63) in the 17th century; the latter is cited in Klostermann's commentary (E. KLOSTERMANN, *Das Lukasevangelium* [Tübingen: Mohr Siebeck, 1929] 127-28), without drawing the necessary conclusions.

[69] See, for example, J. A. FITZMYER, *The Gospel according to Luke*, vol. 2 (New York, Doubleday, 1981), 927.

[70] M. MCNAMARA, *The New Testament and the Palestinian Targum on the Pentateuch* (Rome: Biblical Institute Press, 1966), 131-33.

[71] Thus Flusser and Young ("Messianic Blessings," 280-300). Note especially, however, their reservation on p. 292.

[72] This apophthegm is sometimes entitled "The blessing of Mary." It is certainly not the original interpretation, and it is also questionable whether this was Luke's interpretation of these verses. Cf. F. MUSSNER, "Lk. 1, 48 f; 11, 27 f und die Anfänge der Marienverehrung in der Urkirche," *Catholica* 21 (1967), 291-94; H. ZIMMERMANN, "Selig, die das Wort Gottes Hören und es Bewahren", *Catholica* 29 (1975), 114-19. The possibility that "the primary object of the macarism is the son not the mother" is rejected in R. E. BROWN, K. P. DOUFRIED, J. A. FITZMYER and J. REUMANN (eds.), *Mary in the New Testament* (London: G. Chapman, 1978), 171-72.

rhetorical device for one's own praise. If Mary is not at the center of the praise formula in verse 27, then the interpretation of verse 28 as "asserting that physical kinship is of lesser importance" than the spiritual one,[73] seems rather forced, whatever the relation between this passage and Jesus' rejection of his mother in Mark 3:31-35.[74]

A close reading of this anecdote by itself yields the following: The woman extols Jesus personally, and Jesus retorts by shifting the praise to the audience. According to the setting of the anecdote in Luke, Jesus is praised for what he has just said. Jesus' *speaking* (v. 27) is opposed to "those who *hear* the word of God *and keep it*" (v. 28). This is a dialogue between the teacher and the audience. The teacher seems to be in the center: he is praised personally for his ability. He retorts by emphasizing the importance of the audience: his speech is valuable only if it leads the audience to observance of God's word; his value depends on the audience; the value of *his words* depends on the *audience's acts* in response.

In several stories in rabbinic literature a sage is described as praised by his teacher in similar formulae after finishing his oration. According to one of the rabbinic stories mentioned above, Rabbi Yohanan ben Zakkai exclaimed, after a remarkable oration by his student: אלעזר בן ערך נאה דורש ונאה מקיים. אשריך אברהם אבינו שאלעזר בן ערך יצא מחלציך, "El'azar ben 'Arakh nicely teaches and nicely observes. Blessed be you, Abraham our father, that El'azar

---

[73] Many scholars share this interpretation. See, for example, R. BULTMANN, *History of the Synoptic Tradition* (Oxford: Oxford University Press, 1963), 30-31; "To be the mother of Jesus implies no more than a share in His humanity. To hear and keep the word of God implies communion with what is divine" (A. PLUMMER, *A Critical and Exegetical Commentary on the Gospel according to St. Luke* [Edinburgh: T & T Clark, 1989], 306).

[74] It is not our task here to solve the complicated problem of Luke's source and of the relation between our verses in Luke and Mark 3:31-35. If these verses are related in any way to the verses in Luke, it might be more plausibly suggested that they are a misinterpretation of Luke's source rather than the other way around.

ben 'Arakh came out of your loins" (*t. Hagigah* 2:1).⁷⁵ A praise formula similar to the one in our anecdote is accompanied in this rabbinic story by the emphasis that keeping the word of God is no less important than uttering it. Thus a conventional exclamation of praise for the speaker is put into perspective in both stories: only observance of what has been heard is of importance (and in this the speaker is not necessarily better than his audience).

By noting the whole range of parallels to the blessing in rabbinic literature one can eliminate several possibilities of interpretation of the isolated anecdote preserved in Luke. Many Jewish parallels have been repeatedly cited in scholarship, but the consequences for the interpretation of this passage have not been fully realized. A close reading of the anecdote seems to suggest that the praise of the teacher was assessed in relation to two axes: "speaking/hearing", "saying/keeping." Rabbinic literature supplies a striking parallel to the latter axis.⁷⁶

6. The devil, when tempting Jesus, says, according to Luke:

> "To you I will give all this authority (ἐξουσία) and their (i.e., the kingdoms') glory, for it has been given to me and I give it to whom I wish (ὅτι ἐμοὶ παραδέδοται καὶ ᾧ ἐὰν θέλω δίδωμι αὐτήν)." (Luke 4:7).

It has been observed⁷⁷ that this text is based on a legal formula documented in the Elephantine archives; for instance: זך ביתא יהבתה

---

⁷⁵ This sentence is probably transferred from a tradition concerning an exoteric teaching of Rabbi El'azar Ben Arakh. See E. E. URBACH, "Traditions Concerning Mystical Teachings in the Tannaitic Period," in idem, *The World of the Sages: Collected Essays* (Jerusalem: Magnes Press, 1988), 488 (in Hebrew); M. KISTER, *Studies in Avot de-Rabbi Nathan: Text, Redaction and Interpretation*, Jerusalem 1998, 215-216 (in Hebrew).

⁷⁶ Contrast Bultmann's statement: "Lk. 11:27f was a section conceived as a unity, with its point in its opposition to the Jewish outlook of v. 27" (BULTMANN, *History*, 30).

⁷⁷ J. A. FITZMYER, *The Gospel according to Luke*, vol. 1 (New York: Doubleday, 1981; AB), 516.

לך ... ולמן זי תצבין הבהי, "That house – I have given it to you ... it is yours forever and give it to whomever you wish."⁷⁸ Similar legal formulae occur in religious contexts in the literature of the Second Temple period and in rabbinic literature.⁷⁹ The formula is also found in an Aramaic inscription written in Greek characters (the Negev, 6th century CE):⁸⁰ ΣΙΜΑΘΑ ΚΑΙΑΜΑ ΛΑΜΑΝ ΔΑΕΛΑΑ ΣΑΒΗ ΟΥ ΙΑΕΒ ΛΑΚ, transliterating the Aramaic words: סימתא קימא למן דאלהא צבא הוא יהב לך (לה?). The text of this inscription should be interpreted, according to the legal (and religious) formulae: "The treasure endures; to whomever God wishes, he gives it (or: he gives to you)."⁸¹

In contrast to the legal formula employed in Luke 4:7 that has been noted, it has not been noted that the same Semitic formula is echoed elsewhere in the Gospels, in Jesus' saying:

πάντα μοι παρεδόθη ὑπὸ τοῦ πατρός μου, καὶ οὐδεὶς ἐπιγνώσκει τὸν υἱὸν εἰ μὴ ὁ πατήρ, οὐδὲ τὸν πατέρα τις ἐπιγνώσκει εἰ μὴ ὁ υἱὸς καὶ ᾧ ἐὰν βούληται ὁ υἱὸς ἀποκαλύψαι, "All things

---

⁷⁸ A document from Elephantine (COWLEY 13, 15-16. 21; B. PORTEN and A. YARDENI, *Textbook of Aramaic Documents from Ancient Egypt*, vol. 2 [Jerusalem: Akademon, 1989], B2.7, 34).

⁷⁹ KISTER, "'Let Us Make a Man'" (anove, n. 30), 31-37.

⁸⁰ C. PETERS, "Ein aramäischen Graffito aus Südpalästinas," *OLZ* 43 (1940), 218-222. An inferior interpretation of this inscription is given by Milik (J. T. MILIK, "Notes d'éet de topography Jordanniennes," *Liber Annuus* 10 (1959/60), 154-55. I am grateful to my friend Prof. S. Naeh, for drawing my attention to the inscription and the attempts to decipher the Aramaic texts.

⁸¹ Peters translates: "ein Schatz besteht für den, den Gott will; er <sei> gebend <ihn> dir". There are two sentences in the inscription, according to this interpretation: (1) סימתא קימא למן דאלהא צבא (2) הו יהב לך. The legal formula discussed here renders such an interpretation highly unlikely. The word לך is not easily understood; one would expect at the end the word לה. The *kappa* at the end is either a mistake or a transliteration of [a] or [ah] at the end of a word; cf. D. ROSENTHAL, "Ἀκελδαμαχ – שדה בוכים," in M. BAR-ASHER and D. ROSENTHAL (eds.), *Mehqerei Talmud II: Talmudic Studies Dedicated to the Memory of Prof. E. S. Rosenthal* (Jerusalem: Magnes Press, 1993), 509-13, esp. 509 n. 97 [in Hebrew]).

have been delivered to me by my Father; and no one knows the Son except the Father, and no one knows the Father except the Son, and to whomever the Son wishes to reveal." (Matt 11:27 par. Luke 10:22)

This observation seems to have important exegetical consequences, for it means that the words "No one knows the Son except the Father, and no one knows the Father except the Son" were added to the basic legal formula: πάντα μοι παρεδόθη ὑπὸ τοῦ πατρός μου, καὶ ᾧ ἐὰν βούληται ὁ υἱὸς ἀποκαλύψαι (All things have been delivered to me by my Father; and to whomever the Son wishes to reveal.)[82] The infinitive "to reveal" may perhaps be explained by another, similar formula in the Elephantine papyri: יהבן לך ... אנת ... שליט בביתא זך ... ולמן די צבית למנתן, literally: "We gave it to you ... you ... have the right to that house ... and to whomever you wish *to give* it."[83] Two changes in the basic formula can best be explained as a result of adding the sentences concerning the Father and the Son: first, the shift from "to me" at the beginning of the verse to "to the Son" at its end; second, the verb "reveal" (instead of the verb "deliver" that is expected).[84] The background of the originally legal Aramaic formula is significant for the analysis of this saying – to establish its wording,[85] to assess

---

[82] For a discussion of this saying and its theological background see J. G. D. DUNN, *Jesus and the Spirit: A Study of the Religious and Charismatic Experience of Jesus and the First Christians as Reflected in the New Testament* (London: SCM, 1975), 26-34.

[83] KRAELING 3, 10-12 (PORTEN and YARDENI, *Textbook of Aramaic Documents*, vol. 2 (B3.4), pp. 64 [text], 67 [translation]).

[84] The word πάντα could originally refer not only to divine knowledge; compare A. HARNACK, *The Sayings of Jesus: The Second Source of St. Matthew and St. Luke* (London: Williams & Norgate, 1908), 298 n. 1.

[85] See P. WINTER, "Matthew XI 27 and Luke X 22 from the First to the Fifth Century: Reflections on the Development of a Text," *NT* 1 (1956), 112-48. See especially his discussion of the reading βούληται ἀποκαλύψαι as against the reading ἀποκαλύψῃ attested in early citations. The latter reading is preferred by WINTER (143-46), following A. HARNACK, *The Sayings of Jesus*, 281-310.

the originality of its various parts[86] and even to determine its correct translation.

7. On his way to Golgotha, Jesus called the daughters of Jerusalem to mourn themselves and their children. Jerusalem is not accused in this passage of killing Jesus or of any particular sin. The "daughters of Jerusalem" addressed by Jesus[87] are described as mourning his death.[88] The message is that a great catastrophe is expected to come after Jesus' death, as is expected after the death of righteous persons (*t. Sotah* 10:1: וכשנפטרין ‹הצדיקים› מן העולם פורענות באה לעולם, "When ‹the righteous› pass away from the world, calamity comes to the world"); similarly, after R. Aqiva's martyrdom two other sages said that his death was a sign of the future desolation of the whole nation: מכאן ועד ימים קלין לא ימצא מקום בארץ ישראל שלא יהיו שם הרוגים מושלכים בו, "In a few days there will not be a place in the Land of Israel in which bodies of the slain will not have been cast" (*Masekhet Semahot*, 8:9), a passage whose content is rather similar to Jesus' foretelling the calamity that would befall the whole nation after his death (Luke 23:28-30).

Jesus concludes with the proverb: ὅτι εἰ ἐν τῷ ὑγρῷ ξύλῳ ταῦτα ποιοῦσιν, ἐν τῷ ξηρῷ τί γένηται; "For if they do this to the green wood, what will happen when it is dry?" (Luke 23:31). As has been

---

[86] The sentence concerning the Father and the Son (see DUNN, above, n. 82) may well be an early interpolation in or extension of an established saying.

[87] Note that this address, "Daughters of Jerusalem, do not weep for me, but weep for yourselves," overturns the conventional address: "Daughters of Israel, weep for Saul" (2 Sam 1:24). A similar reverse of conventions is found in a eulogy cited in rabbinic literature: instead of the conventional address to mourn the deceased one, it was said: בכו לאבלים ולא לאבדה שהיא למנוחה ואנו לאנחה "Weep for the mourners and not for their loss, for the departed goes to his rest, and we to our sighing" (*b. Mo'ed Qatan* 25b).

[88] D. FLUSSER and B. YOUNG, "Messianic Blessings in Jewish and Christian Texts," in FLUSSER, *Judaism and the Origins of Christianity*, 291 n. 26.

observed,[89] a perfect parallel to this sentence occurs in the midrash *Tanna de-be Eliyahu*: אמרו חכמים: אם אש אחזה בלחים, מה יעשו יבשים, "The Sages said: if wet (wood can) catch fire, how much more so dry (wood) (more literally: what will dry [wood] do?)" (ch. 14; ed. FRIEDMANN, p. 65). This sentence is also attested in early Palestinian *piyyutim* of the Byzantine period.[90] It has been noted[91] that a similar formula is used in a eulogy of the late Amoraic period: אם בארזים נפלה שלהבת מה יעשו אזובי הקיר, "If cedars can catch fire, how much more so the hyssop that grows on walls (more literally: what will the hyssop that grows on walls do?)" (*b. Mo'ed Qatan* 25b).[92] The context is similar in all these sources: the death of those who are most righteous indicates that all others should be concerned about *their own* fates.[93] This is expressed by the expression מה יעשו, literally "What will [X]s do?" Such utterances are especially appropriate regarding the death of a righteous person, in a eulogy for a great sage (in the Talmud) or regarding Jesus' death.[94]

The formula in Luke is most similar to the Hebrew proverb in *Tanna de-be Eliyahu*. Unlike the Hebrew, however, the Greek text has nouns in dative singular in the *two* stichoi. In a literal translation of the Hebrew formula, we would expect the *second* stich to read מה יעשו, in a literal translation: τί ποιοῦσιν (or: ποιήσουσιν). It seems, then, that the word ποιοῦσιν in the first stich in Luke is a remnant of the word יעשו, which should occur in the second stich

---

[89] BILLERBECK–STRACK, *Kommentar zum Neuen Testament aus Talmud und Midrasch*, vol. 2 (Munich: Beck, 1924), 263-64.

[90] Y. ADLER, "If a Flame among the Cedars has Fallen," *Tarbiz* 53 (1984), 296-303 (in Hebrew).

[91] See above, n. 89.

[92] The eulogy cited here continues in the same stylistic pattern: לויתן בחכה הועלה, מה יעשו דגי רקק; בנחל שוטף נפלה הרבה, מה יעשו מי גבים.

[93] The interpretation closest to this is the one suggested by FITZMYER, *Luke*, vol. 2, 1489.

[94] We may add that the formula מה יעשו is used to express an argument *a minori ad maius* in other contexts as well; see *y. Ta'aniyyot* 1,3 [64b]; *Exod. Rab.* 29:9.

according to the Hebrew formula.⁹⁵ This observation helps to solve some exegetical queries concerning the verb ποιοῦσιν and its antecedents.⁹⁶

It should be noted that a somewhat similar formula occurs also in a passage of the *Testament of Levi* in the *Testaments of the Twelve Patriarchs*:

ὑμεῖς οἱ φωστῆρες τοῦ οὐρανοῦ (or: Ισραηλ) ὡς ὁ ἥλιος καὶ ἡ σελήνη. τί ποιήσουσι πάντα τὰ ἔθνη ἐὰν ὑμεῖς σκοτισθῆτε ἐν ἀσεβείᾳ, "You are the lights of Israel as the sun and the moon. For what will all the nations do if you become darkened by impiety?" (14:3-4)⁹⁷

A reading that fits even better the literary formula discussed above is preserved in MS *d* of the *Testament of Levi* (similarly MS *c*): καὶ ἐὰν ὑμεῖς σκοτισθῆτε, τί ποιήσουσι πάντα τὰ ἔθνη, "And if you become darkened, what will all the nations do?"⁹⁸ Being aware of the rhetorical formula, a free translation of the sentence would be: "and if you [=the lights] become darkened, how much more so all the nations."

8. Comparing the verse in the *Testament of Levi* (14:3-4) with two verses in Matthew is instructive:

---

⁹⁵ It may be the the verbs γίγνομαι and ποιέω were transposed because the idiom מה יעשו was not understood. The plural form of the word ποιοῦσιν may still retain the original Hebrew wording using always plural in the second stich.

⁹⁶ See J. NOLLAND, *Luke 18:35–24:53* (Dallas: Word Books, 1993), 1138.

⁹⁷ M. DE JONGE, *The Testament of the Twelve Patriarchs: A Critical Edition of the Greek Text* (Leiden: Brill, 1978), 41-42.

⁹⁸ See *variae lectiones*, ad loc., in De Jonge's edition. Milik suggested that this passage is preseved in a tiny fragment from Qumran (J. T. MILIK, *The Books of Enoch* [Oxford: Oxford University Press, 1976], 23.). Stone doubts this suggestion (M. E. STONE, *Qumran Cave 4.XVII: Parabiblical Texts, Part 3*, DJD 22 [Oxford: Oxford University Press, 1996], 20-22).

Testament of Levi 14:3-4	Matthew
ὑμεῖς οἱ φωστῆρες τοῦ Ισραηλ ... τί ποιήσουσι πάντα τὰ ἔθνη ἐὰν ὑμεῖς σκοτισθῆτε ἐν ἀσεβείᾳ	Matt 5:13-14: ὑμεῖς ἐστε τὸ ἅλας τῆς γῆς· ἐαν δὲ τὸ ἅλας μωρανθῇ, ἐν τίνι ἁλισθήσεται; ὑμεῖς ἐστε τὸ φῶς τοῦ κόσμου Matt 6:23: εἰ οὖν τὸ φῶς ἐν σοὶ σκότος ἐστίν, τὸ σκότος πόσον
You are the lights of Israel as the sun and the moon. For if you become darkened, what will all the nations do?	5:13-14: You are the salt of the earth; but if salt has lost its taste, how will it be salted? You are the light of the world 6:23: If the light in you is darkness, how much is the darkness!

The similarity of Matt 6:23 to the *Testament of Levi* is clear, but the passages seem to deal with two very distinct topics. The *stylistic* similarity between Matt 6:23 and 5:13 is evident, but is it more than a coincidence? The passage in Matt 6:22-23 reads: "The eye is the lamp of the body. So if your eye is sound (ἁπλοῦς),[99] your whole body is full of light. But if your eye is sick (πονηρός), your whole body is full of darkness. If then the light in you is darkness,[100] how much is the darkness!"

One may hypothesize that the eye metaphor could have applied originally to the disciples in relation to the others (cf. 5:13). Concerning the members of the Sanhedrin, it is said in *Cant. Zuta*: מה העינים מאירים לגוף, אף דבריהם מאירים לכל ישראל, "As eyes give light the body, so their words enlighten all Israel" (*Cant. Zuta*

---

[99] For the interpretation of this word see DAVIES and ALLISON, *St. Matthew*, vol. 1, 638.
[100] The Hebrew/Aramaic original could be "darkens" (חשך נהרא or חשך האור; cf. Delitzsch's translation).

according to the reading in *Yalqut Shim'oni*, 2:988).[101] In a rabbinic story, the two metaphors, "light of the world" (=φῶς τοῦ κόσμου, Matt 5:14) and "eye of the world" (cf. Matt 6:22), are applied to the sages (*b. Bava Bathra* 4a):[102] They enlighten Israel and the whole world and thus are compared to the eyes that give light to the body or to the light of the world (cf. *Testament of Levi* cited above). Possibly, the subject of Jesus' saying concerning eye and body was not originally the eyes and body of an individual,[103] but rather the relation between his disciples (or Jewish leadership?) and the people.[104] Read along these lines, Jesus' saying may be closely related to Matt 5:13-14 and to the *Testament of Levi*, not only in style but also in content.

---

[101] For an interpretation of Jesus' saying against the background of ancient (Greek and non-Greek) conceptions of vision, see D. C. ALLISON, "The Eye Is the Lamp of the Body," *NTS* 33 (1987), 66-83. The wording in *Cant. Zuta* is the closest parallel to it in Hebrew/Aramaic sources. On the other hand, understanding conceptions of vision in the Gospels is instructive for a correct interpretation of some rabbinic sources, whose relevance to Jesus' saying has not hitherto been noticed.

[102] *Stylistically*, the wording of Matt 6:22-23 par. Luke 11:34 is reminiscent of another saying in rabbinic literature referring to the leadership (especially the Patriarch) in relation to the people:

ἐὰν (Luke: ὅταν) ὁ ὀφθαλμὸς ἁπλοῦς, ὅλον τὸ σῶμα σοῦ ... · ἐὰν (Luke: ἐπὰν) δὲ πονηρός ᾖ, ὅλον τὸ σῶμα σου ...

(משל לכלה) כל זמן שעיניה יפות אין כל גופה צריך בדיקה, עיניה טרוטות כל גופה צריך בדיקה (*b. Ta'anit* 24a, ed. MALTER, p. 105).

This passage, as well as *b. Bava Batra* 4a, cites Num. 15:24, interpreting the word עיני in this verse as referring to the leaders of the people (cf. Arabic *a'yān*, chiefs) – i.e., the sages, who enlighten all the people by their teaching.

[103] According to this hypothesis, the addition of the personal pronouns "*you*" and "*yours*" changed the meaning of the saying and transferred it to any individual.

[104] In this second stage the term ὀφθαλμὸς πονηρός was understood as referring to greed. See DAVIES and ALLISON, *St. Matthew*, vol. 1, 635; D. A. HANGER, *Matthew 1–13* (Dallas: Word Books, 1993), 158.

9. Literal parallels to passages in rabbinic literature are sometimes important for both sources. Thus we read in the Sermon on the Mount:

Οὐδὲ καίουσιν λύχνος καὶ τιθέασιν αὐτὸν ὑπὸ τὸν μόδιον ἀλλ' ἐπὶ τὴν λυχνίαν καὶ λάμπει πᾶσιν τοῖς ἐν τῇ οἰκίᾳ. Οὕτως λαμψάτω τὸ φῶς ὑμῶν ἔμπροσθεν τῶν ἀνθρώπων, ὅπως ἴδωσιν ὑμῶν τὰ καλὰ ἔργα ... "Nor do men light a lamp and put it under a bushel, but on a stand, and *it gives light to all in the house*. Even so, *let your light shine before men*, that they may see your good works ..." (Matt 5:15-16)

In the late midrashic compilation, *Midrash ha-Gadol*, in which ancient midrashic sources have been preserved, we read:

'הנה אנכי שלח מלאך לפניך' – זה נביא ... 'לפניך' שיהא מאיר לפניך כנר שהוא מאיר לכל הבית. 'לשמרך בדרך' – להזהירך על דברי תורה, "'Behold, I send an angel before you' – refers to a prophet, 'before you' – that *he may shine before you as a candle that gives light to all the house*; 'to guard you in the way' – to warn you concerning (the observance) of the words of the Torah" (ad Exod 23:20 [ed. MARGULIES, p. 545]).

The medieval compilation does not name the midrashim from which its exegetical comments were derived. Quite often early sources can be reconstructed only on the basis of this compilation. The source just cited as a parallel to Matthew may be a tannaitic saying, although this is by no means certain.[105]

This striking parallel demonstrates the antiquity of the rabbinic source. It seems that Matt 5:16b is an elaboration of an earlier Jewish sentence.[106] In the parallel to our verse, Luke 11:33, the

---

[105] E. Z. Melamed included it (albeit with some hesitation, see his note to line 16) in his edition (together with J. N. Epstein) of *Mekhilta de-Rabbi Shim'on ben Yohai*, 219, which is reconstructed at this point solely on *Midrash ha-Gadol*.

[106] Contrast DAVIES and ALLISON, *St. Matthew*, vol. 1, 478. We have also to

lamp metaphor seems to refer to Jesus' ministry.[107] The Christological context in Luke is much closer to the context in the Jewish source, where the lamp metaphor is applied to "a prophet"; the wording of the saying in Luke, however, has little in common with our midrash. It is plausible, then, that there was a pre-Matthean source whose *context* was different from the existing redaction of the Sermon on the Mount, but whose *wording* was similar to the wording in Matthew.

CONCLUSIONS

I have tried to elucidate the Semitic words and expressions behind some passages in the Gospels. A full reconstruction is impossible (it is often even difficult to decide whether the saying should be reconstructed into Hebrew or Aramaic), but in some cases Hebrew and Aramaic words, expressions and formulae shed light on the meaning and wording of Jesus' sayings and their background. Usually, reading the Gospel passages as reflecting a Semitic original (frequently culturally charged) is related to reading them as Jewish. Linguistic and midrashic links between words and sentences that cannot be discerned in Greek may be discerned in the reconstructed Semitic original. The contribution of such an approach to the elucidation of passages in the Gospels is evident. On the other hand, Gospel passages are important as evidence of the Semitic usage or of early midrashim. I hope this essay illustrates how different corpora (the Gospels, rabbinic literature, Dead Sea scrolls, Pseudepigrapha, epigraphic material) may illuminate one another.

---

reconsider whether the saying is necessarily as universalistic as assumed by New Testament commentators, for the Jewish saying apparently applies only to Jews.

[107] See, for example, FITZMYER, *Luke*, vol. 2, 938; NOLLAD, *Luke 9:21–18:34*, 657.

PART TWO

Serge RUZER and Mila GINSBURSKAYA

MATT 6:1-18: COLLATION OF TWO AVENUES
TO GOD'S FORGIVENESS*

1. GENERAL REMARKS

Unlike the discussion that precedes them in Matthew 5, Jesus' words in the continuation of the Sermon on the Mount (SM) in Matthew 6 are presented as detached from Torah exegesis. This additional deliberation is absent in Luke's version of the Sermon.[1] Opinions vary regarding the provenance of Matt 6:1-18: most scholars believe that at least Matt 6:9-13 goes back to Jesus himself and should be seen as composed by a particular Jewish teacher from existing religious patterns.[2] Matt 6:1-6 and 16-18 are generally perceived as a piece of tradition, rooted in Jewish thought, that

---

* The authors are grateful to Shmuel Ben Or, Eliashiv Frenkel, and Maoz Kahana, who collected relevant material from rabbinic sources and Qumran. All relevant texts referred to in the footnotes, but for the New Testament passages, are quoted in the Sources section appended at the end of the discussion. All Scriptural quotations are according to the *Revised Standard Version*. We are grateful to Zeev Elizur and Sergey Minov, whose contribution was crucial for preparing that section.

[1] See Luke 6:17-49.
[2] DAVIES (309-313); BETZ (349, 372-373, 377); LUZ (369-372), DAVIES-ALLISON (590-597). See below, n. 30 and the discussion there.

had been handed down to Matthew (or to the redactor of Matthew).[3] It was also suggested that this section mainly reflected the *Sitz im Leben* of the Matthean community.[4] Since this community is generally perceived as a Jewish-Christian one engaged in polemics with other first-century Jewish groups,[5] all appraisals presuppose a Jewish setting for Matt 6:1-18.

The link to the Jewish setting does not have to find expression in a uniformity of *opinion* on the issues under discussion – after all, the period was one of great fluidity and a variety of opinions – but rather in an inherited agenda as well as the technical or structural characteristics of religious discourse. The agenda of that discourse might also have been influenced by general patterns of Hellenistic thought, an issue that has been discussed in research.[6]

---

[3] Betz calls the tripartite Matt 6:1-8 the "cultic didache" and suggests that for its composition "the author of the SM has ... taken over and integrated texts already in existence" (330). He further observes that Matt 6:1-18 is not harmonized theologically, which, according to him, points to the multiple authorship of the pericope (338-339, 347-348). Luz (354-356) singles out v.1 as Matthean (cf. Betz, 351), while suggesting that for vv. 2-6 and 16-18 "a written source is probable, one that Matthew changed relatively little." Since no trace of Christology could be found in the text, Luz agrees with Betz about its possible pre-Easter origin. An alternative suggestion is that the author was a Jewish-Christian from the time when "the followers of Jesus within the synagogue community had to come to terms with Jewish practices of piety." Davies-Allison's commentary advances arguments in favor of post-Easter but pre-Matthean Jewish-Christian provenance of the text. It also distinguishes between two different pieces of Matt 6:1-8 and indicates that it is impossible to know "whether or not 6:7-13 was attracted to 6:1-6, 16-18 before Matthew took up his pen or whether the evangelist himself is responsible for inserting the Lord's Prayer into its present context" (573-575).

There are also various suggestions regarding the provenance and history of the composition of 6:7-8 (instruction preceding the *PN*) and 6:14-15 (commentary on the *PN*) – see discussion in Betz 347-349, 363; Luz 364-366.

[4] Syreeni (537-539).

[5] Betz (373, 419); Davies; Saldarini; Overman; Repschinski; Sim et al.

[6] For a discussion of Greco-Roman parallels, see Betz, 339-340 (hiddenness / omniscience of God), 341-343 (theorizing about prayer), 343-346; and Luz, 358 (inconspicuous piety).

This study, however, will focus on a narrower, more properly Jewish, setting of Matt 6:1-18 and on the importance of the pericope as a first-century CE witness to a certain topic in Jewish religious thought discussed both in the Second Temple period and in later rabbinic sources.

Discussion of the proper performance and importance of such religious practices as almsgiving, prayer and fasting was prominent in Second Temple Judaism, where its various configurations are attested.[7] In the New Testament a tripartite configuration is found only in Matthew, while the *Pater Noster* (*PN*) prayer (6:9-13) belongs to the tradition shared by Matthew and Luke.[8] Suggestions have been raised of the *PN* being an interpolation into the tripartite discussion;[9] if accepted, they may provide a clue regarding the compiler's perception of the core theme of the whole pericope.[10] There are close structural affinities among the sections

---

[7] See Sir 34:25-35:3, 35:11-36:8; Tob 12:8-10. Cf. *Gos. Thom.* 6, 14; *2 Clem.* 16. See also BETZ (337-338); LACHS (338); DAVIES-ALLISON (575). For a discussion of different configurations of tripartite structure, see DAVIES (305-308).

[8] See Luke 11:1-4. Cf. Did. 8:2. For a discussion of the relation between the two versions and different models suggested to explain their developing (most scholars see Matthew's version as closer to the original with regard to the wording and Lukan with regard to the form), see BETZ (370-375); LUZ (369-371); JEREMIAS (1980, 9-14). According to BETZ (372), BROWN (220), JEREMIAS (1980, 9-10), Lukan tradition is under the influence of Gentile churches, and the wording might have been adapted to their use. For a discussion on the *PN*'s authenticity, see, for example, DAVIES-ALLISON (590-593). For a discussion on the *PN*'s literary structure and its character (group or personal), see BETZ (373-374, 376); MCCAUGHEY (32); DAVIES-ALLISON (617, 620). Some scholars believe that the *PN* was not tailored to the narrow circle of disciples but was intended for everyone. See, for example, LUZ (383, 387); BETZ (382). Cf. FRIEDLANDER (148); BROWN (223); JEREMIAS (1980, 16).

[9] BETZ (350-351, 363, 369-370); DAVIES-ALLISON (575, 590-592); LUZ (352); GERHARDSSON (1996, 85); O'HARA (5).

[10] According to HAGNER (145): "The fact that it interrupts the flow of the larger passage (vv. 1-18) suggests that the evangelist regarded its content as of great importance."

dealing with the three practices in Matthew (6:2-4; 6:5-6; 6:16-18);[11] one of the keynote motifs uniting the three is the recurrent promise of God's reward "and your Father ... will reward you" (ὁ πατήρ σου ... ἀποδώσει σοι) that concludes the exposition on each one of the practices: almsgiving (6:4), prayer (6:6) and fasting (6:18).

However, within that initial tripartite structure (before the insertion of the *PN*) the particular nature of God's recompense remained obscure; the Second Temple period book of Tobit, which combines prayer with fasting and almsgiving (and righteousness – cf. Matt 6:1) as preconditions for God's reward, testifies to possible differing aspects of that reward:

> Prayer is good when accompanied by fasting, almsgiving, and righteousness.
> A little with righteousness is better than much with wrongdoing.
> It is better to give alms than to treasure up gold.
> For almsgiving delivers from death (ἐκ θανάτου ῥύεται),
> and it will purge away every sin (καὶ αὐτὴ ἀποκαθαριεῖ πᾶσαν ἁμαρτίαν).
> Those who perform deeds of charity and of righteousness
> will have fullness of life (πλησθήσονται ζωῆς);
> but those who commit sin are the enemies of their own lives.[12]

Later tannaitic sources in their turn attest to a distinction made between reward meted out in this world and that meant for the world to come.[13]

---

[11] DAVIES-ALLISON (572-573); LUZ (354); BETZ (349-350).
[12] Tob 12:8-10 (*RSV*). See also the discussion below.
[13] For example, *m. Avot* 2:16; *m. Peah* 1:1. For further discussion, see BONSIRVEN (108-109). For non-eschatological notions of reward in rabbinic sources, see URBACH (1975, 349-351, 417, 439-441 and corresponding footnotes). GEORGE (597) is of the opinion (not substantiated by the *immediate context* of the Sermon) that Jesus' concept of reward in the *PN* is based on the doctrine of life after death.

To our mind, the interpolation of the *PN* not only provides a "model prayer pattern" but also indicates the kind of reward the compiler believed to be primarily at stake in the tripartite discussion of Matt 6:1-18: the interpretation added by the compiler in Matt 6:14-15 highlights forgiveness of sins out of the various possible kinds of recompense. The forgiveness of sins – undeniably a most prominent issue in first-century Judaism[14] – is presented here as the core supplication, virtually *the topic* of the *PN*.[15]

No explicit mention of the forgiveness of sins is to be found in the tripartite discussion itself; likewise, the word "recompense" does not appear in the *PN*. It may be suggested, however, that the collation of these two instances of tradition with the emphasis on the forgiveness of sins established by the interpolation of the *PN*[16]

---

[14] BETZ (400 and note 478, also 416); LUZ (383 and note 94). There are important Jewish liturgical parallels containing supplication for forgiveness of sins – for example, the Sixth Benediction of the *Amidah*, *Avinu Malkenu* and *Havinenu*. See STRACK-BILLERBECK (I:421).

[15] Cf. Luke 11:5-12, where the author of the Gospel, having presented the Lord's Prayer, elaborates on the motif of "daily bread" instead of forgiveness of sins. For discussion of the possible meanings of the "daily bread" supplication (6:11) and comparison with the Lukan version, see, for example, LUZ (380-383); FRIEDLANDER (153-155); SCHWEIZER (153-154); JEREMIAS (1980, 23-26); BETZ (379). For a detailed analysis and history of interpretation, see CARMIGNAC (118-221). Another peculiarity of Luke's version is its emphasis on the gift of the Holy Spirit (Luke 11:13). This may indicate notions of the kind – attested, for example, in Qumran – according to which one cannot get cleansed of sins, cannot even understand them, without the help of the Holy Spirit granted by God to his chosen ones. See 1QH^a IV 17-28; XII 28-33. Cf. Ps 51:9-11; Ezek 36:25-27. The gift of the Holy Spirit is bestowed only on the repentant, those who "shunned" sin according to *m. Sota* 9:15. See FRIEDLANDER (152). An interesting variant reading is attested for Luke 11:2, substituting ελθ. το πνευμα σου το αγιον εφ ημας και καθαρισατω ημας for ἐλθέτω ἡ βασιλεία σου. For discussion of the possible backgrounds for the insertion of Matt 6:14-15, see BETZ (415-417).

[16] Scholars differ in their appreciation of the character – eschatological or non-eschatological – of the *PN*, and one's stance on the issue influences the interpretation of the nature of forgiveness mentioned in Matt 6:12. See discussion in section 4, below.

informs our understanding of recompense mentioned in connection with all three of the religious practices referred to in Matt 6:1-18.[17] Thus unlike Tobit, who mentions a spectrum of rewards, *including* the forgiveness of sins, related to the triad of almsgiving–prayer–fasting, the compiler of Matthew 6 emphasizes the forgiveness of sins as the core topic of our pericope. A number of Second Temple and later rabbinic sources seem to go in a similar direction, establishing the "three practices" (in different modifications of the triad) as instrumental in bringing about the abolition of punishment for sins committed.[18]

Matt 6:1-18 may thus be seen as an appendix to Matthew 5: Matthew 5, which has put forward very high demands of religious perfection and the notion of harsh punishment (*Gehenna*) for not living up to those demands, is complemented in Matthew 6 with the notion of forgiveness of sins, here presented as the ultimate religious *desideratum*.[19]

Second Temple Jewish sources bear witness to different notions of the avenues leading to the forgiveness of sins. In addition to the traditional biblical idea of atoning sacrifice, also mentioned in this context as early as the second century BCE, are ethical conduct,[20]

---

[17] Cf. *m. Avot* 1:3, where anticipation of a recompense whose nature remains unclear is prohibited.

[18] For example, Sir 7:8-10 (sin-offering, prayer and alms); *y. Ta'an.* 2,1 [65a]; *y. Sanh.* 10,2 [28b–28c] (prayer, charity and repentance). The triad pattern in general (disconnected from the issue of forgiveness) was widespread in sayings of a proverbial nature; see, for example, *T. Jos.* 10:1-2. It could also be expanded into a four-component structure, as in Tobit 12:8. Cf. *m. Peah* 1:1. It is notable that the overall scheme of Matt 6:1-18 contains the same four elements as the passage from Tobit: righteousness (Matt 6:1), almsgiving, prayer and fasting. See also BETZ (335-338). For a "negative triad," the three things that "put a man out of the world," see, for example, *m. Avot* 2:11. Characteristically, "hatred of mankind" is one of them.

[19] Cf. BETZ (417). On structural parallels between Matt 5:17-48 and 6:1-18, see DAVIES-ALLISON (577-578, 621 [actions versus intentions]).

[20] The avenues of almsgiving, sin offering and ethical conduct (with the addition of repentance!) are related to in Ben Sira: Sir 3:1-4:14, 45:15-16. See MURPHY (265).

suffering as a consequence of sin, and death itself[21] – all these avenues for the expiation of sin seem to have been perceived as conditional upon sincere repentance.[22] Of course, the motif of repentance characterizes many parts of the Gospel tradition.[23] Matthew 5 also relates positively to the Temple offering as atonement for sins. We have seen, however, that in Matt 6:1-18 other avenues are emphasized. In rabbinic sources, reflecting the reality after the destruction of the Temple, prayer (and sometimes almsgiving) are presented as substitutes for sacrificial worship and therefore as ways leading to forgiveness of sins.[24] But as early as in Psalms, prayer assumes expiatory significance; certain Second Temple traditions ascribe such significance also to almsgiving.[25] The stance of Matthew 6, then, does not necessarily reflect later, post-destruction layers of redaction; it may be seen instead as bearing witness – together with Matthew 5 and other relevant passages – to the *plurality* of opinion that infiltrated the New Testament: In the context of discussing the inherited Jewish theme of forgiveness, various notions, solutions and emphases are probed.

---

[21] 2 Macc 7:18, 32. It should be noted that unlike traditions attested in such later sources as *Mekhilta* mas. Bachodesh par. 7 on Exod 20:7, *Mekhilta* mas. Nezikin. par. 18 on Exod 22:22, *b. Yoma* 86a (see MOORE, 534, BONSIRVEN, 114-115), in 2 Macc 7:30-38 the death of the just is presented as bringing forgiveness not only for their own sins but also for those of others. It may be noted that these motifs are completely absent in Matt 6:1-18. Cf. discussion in *b. Sanh.* 47a.

[22] Sir 5:5-7, 34:25-26, 17:22-29; *T. Jos.* 4:3-6. See MURPHY (265-269). For tannaitic sources, see *m. Yoma* 8:8; *t. Yoma* 5:9. See RUZER (1999, 151-165). Cf. Matt 3:5-9 and parallels. See also MOORE (518-519, 530-534).

[23] For example, Matt 3:1-2, 8 and parallels; Matt 4:13, 9:13, 11:10-11, 12:41; Mark 2:17, 6:12; Luke 5:32, 10:13, 11:32, 13:3-5, 15:7-10, 16:30. Cf. Luke 17:3-4. The centrality of *metanoia* is especially emphasized by the author of Luke-Acts at crucial points of the two-part narrative (Luke 24:47, Acts 2:37-38, 3:19): see MOORE (518-519).

[24] *Sifre Deut.* 41. See MOORE (14-15, 504-506); ABRAHAMS (1:128); DAVIES (305-308). See below, note 29 and discussion there.

[25] Ps 141:1; Sir 3:30, 35:1-7; Tob 4:7-11; 12:9, 14:11; 1QS IX 3-6, X 5-8; CD-A XI 17-21. Cf. Sir 7:8-10; 12:3; 16:14; 17:22; 29:8-13; 34(31):11; 40:17, 24, etc. See BETZ (337-338); MURPHY (268).

The interpolation of the *PN* gives the discourse in Matt 6:1-18 its peculiar twofold structure: two complementing avenues to acquiring God's forgiveness are collated in the pericope. On the one hand, the imperative to forgive others (Matt 6:12 highlighted in the interpretation provided by Matt 6:14-15) and, on the other, proper performance of certain acts of *ritual piety*: prayer (Matt 6:5-13/Luke 11:1-4; Matt 7:7-11/Luke 11:9-13),[26] fasting (Matt 6:16-18),[27] and deeds of charity/compassion (Matt 6:1-4). This collation of two avenues to forgiveness as God's reward may be seen as the characteristic feature of Matt 6:1-18. It is worth noting that the terminology of reward in connection with both forgiveness of and punishment for sins is used in a Second Temple period Qumranic psalm:

> ... bend your ear and grant my plea,
> and what I ask, do not deny me;
> build up my soul and do not demolish it;
> and do not forsake it in the presence of wicked people.
> May the judge of truth turn away from me the recompenses of evil (גמולי הרע).
> O YHWH, do not judge me by my sin ... (11QPs^a XXIV 4-7)

2. THE *PATER NOSTER* AS A SUPPLICATION FOR THE FORGIVENESS OF SINS

The *PN* seems to reflect a pre-destruction stage in the development of a proto-rabbinic Jewish tradition, when the process of establishing a standard set of prayers was far from having been completed.[28] Unlike the Qumran covenanters, who already then – as a compen-

---

[26] Cf. Mark 11:22-26.
[27] Appears nowhere else in the NT. But cf. Matt 9:14-15; Mark 2:18-20; Luke 5:33-35, 18:12; Acts 13:2-3.
[28] Even according to FLEISCHER (426-441), who argues for an early fixation of basic Jewish liturgical texts, no fixed obligatory prayers existed in pre-70 proto-rabbinic Judaism. Cf. GOSHEN-GOTTSTEIN (40-52), who suggests that in the wake of the destruction those were Torah and acts of loving-kindness that had first been presented as substitutes for the defunct Temple service and it was only gradually that prayer came to take the place of deeds of mercy.

sation for the loss of the sacrificial cult and an expression of their community-centered outlook – developed stereotyped patterns of prayer,[29] the milieu of the sages was characterized by creative suggestions put forward by various teachers.[30] Matt 6:9-13 may be considered as one such suggestion, using existing motifs and formulas[31] – those that would eventually be absorbed also into *Kaddish* and *Shmoneh-Esreh*.[32] Some scholars interpret the textual variations between the *PN* in Matthew (cf. *Didache*)[33] and Luke as reflecting the relative freedom of the initial suggestion made by Jesus – a suggestion that might have been of a somewhat general character, rather than a fixed formula.[34] A number of language peculiarities have been interpreted by some scholars as indicating that Aramaic, not Hebrew, should be assumed to have been the original language of the *PN*.[35] It is worth noting that the demand

---

[29] See TALMON (273-284). For a study of literary prayer patterns in Qumran, see NITZAN (1994).

[30] See Luke 11:1. Even later traditions bear witness to the existence of the phenomenon. See *t. Ber.* 3:7. See also *m. Ber.* 4:2; *b. Ber.* 29b (prayer recommended by Rabbi Eliezer for use in the hour of danger). See discussion in FRIEDLANDER (147-150); PETUCHOWSKY (21-44); VIVIANO (431-435). TALMON (271-272) suggests there was a conscious resistance on the part of early rabbis to the prayers attaining fixity of wording and/or committing them to writing. See also above, nn. 2 and 8, and below, n. 34.

[31] CHARLESWORTH (1998, 48-53) places the "Prayer of Jesus" (Matt 6; Luke 11; Did. 8) in the category of *Early Nonrabbinic Jewish Prayers*. According to BROWN (220), Matthean tradition represents a prayer to whose original petitions have been joined other sayings of Jesus (just as the Matthean beatitudes and SM are longer than the Lukan).

[32] DAVIES-ALLISON (595-597); FRIEDLANDER (137); JEREMIAS (1967, 76); SCHWEIZER (151); VÖGTLE (95-97). FLUSSER (1992, 85-86) is of the opinion that the three "You" petitions of Matt 6:9-10 depend on an older version of the *Kaddish*. Cf. VIVIANO (449).

[33] Did. 8:2; see also above, n. 8.

[34] Cf. Mark 11:25. See BROWN (222-223, 234); BETZ (370-373); CHARLESWORTH (1994, 5). Cf. SCHWEIZER (158).

[35] See LUZ (371-372); JEREMIAS (1968, 76-77). Cf. CARMIGNAC (29-52), arguing in favor of Hebrew. For further discussion and additional bibliography, see BETZ (374-375).

for brevity in prayer (Matt 6:7-8) is well attested in Second Temple and later rabbinic sources.[36] Alternative opinions are represented in rabbinic tradition as well.[37] It is telling that in the Gospel of Luke, instead of the call for brevity, an alternative emphasis on *insistence and importunity* in prayer is propounded in connection with the *PN*[38] – here again the New Testament seems to provide early evidence for a variety of opinions on an acute, and undecided, issue of Jewish religious discourse.

According to Matthew 6:14-15, it is forgiveness toward others that will bring forgiveness from God. This is the interpretation (a summary) suggested by the Gospel writer for the *PN*, an interpretation that, as noted, turns Matt 6:12 ("And forgive us our debts, as we also have forgiven our debtors")[39] into the *PN* core supplication.[40]

---

[36] See, for example, Sir 7:14; *b. Ber.* 61a ("A man's words should always be few towards God"). For biblical precedents, see Eccl 5:1-2; Isa 1:15, 65:24. For Hellenistic sources, see DAVIES-ALLISON (586-588); BETZ (366-367).

[37] For example, *y. Ber.* 4,1 [7b-7c]. Cf. *b. Ber.* 5b. See also *Mekhilta* mas. Vayassa par. 1 (there is a time to prolong and a time to shorten prayer). For a further discussion of, inter alia, talmudic sources, see ABRAHAMS (2:86-88, 102-103); FRIEDLANDER (113-118).

[38] Luke 11:5-10.

[39] According to the interpretation suggested in Matt 6:14-15, God's forgiveness in Matt 6:12 should be understood as conditional upon one's readiness to forgive others. This precondition was recognized as theologically problematic (CARMIGNAC, 231-235). For a discussion on possible meanings of the clause, see, for example, ABRAHAMS (2:95-96); CARMIGNAC (222-235). Cf. Matt 18:23-35 (parable of the unforgiving servant); Luke 7:41-42. The language of "debts" (ὀφειλήματα) used in Matt 6:12 and interpreted in Matt 6:14-15 (in harmony with Mark 11:25, cf. Luke 11:4) as "trespasses" (παραπτώματα) has drawn the attention of scholars. An Aramaic background for the expression has been suggested: see JEREMIAS (1980, 13); LUZ (371); FRIEDLANDER (155); BEAR (177). For Hebrew/biblical background see CARMIGNAC (222-225). In a forthcoming study ANDERSON discusses transformations in the Jewish notion of the sin-appeasement mechanism – inter alia, adoption of the "business vocabulary" that might have been behind the Matthean terminology.

[40] See also Matthew 7:1-5; Luke 6:36-42; Mark 11:25-26. Cf. Mark 4:24. For a rabbinic discussion on the effectiveness of prayer as compared with that of repentance for the forgiveness of sins, see *Lev. R.* 10,5.

A similar move characterizes Mark 11:24-25 – possibly evidence for a pre-Matthean tradition.[41] Markan discourse on prayer also presupposes a variety of prayerful petitions (Mark 11:24: "whatever you ask in prayer..."); but further on Jesus highlights only a single supplication – namely, forgiveness of sins conditional upon one's readiness to forgive others (Mark 11:25: "And whenever you stand praying, forgive, if you have anything against anyone; so that your Father also who is in heaven may forgive you your trespasses"). Mark therefore provides one more indication of the importance ascribed to this particular motif in Jesus' tradition.[42]

This avenue to acquiring God's forgiveness was propagated in Second Temple Judaism – although not in the context of a prayerful supplication – at least from the beginning of the second century BCE.[43] It was presented also in *T. 12 Patr.*[44] and later in the *Two Ways* as an exegesis of Lev 19:18.[45] So the Gospel seems to

---

[41] DAVIES-ALLISON (616); SCHWEIZER (157). CARMIGNAC (226, 362) calls Mark 11:25 a "summary" of the Lord's Prayer.

[42] The negative component (Matt 6:15/Mark 11:26) is absent in the earliest manuscripts of Mark. Cf. the parable of the unforgiving servant in Matt 18:23-35. The passage in Mark may also bear witness to the initial lack of a fixed formula in the tradition of Jesus' teaching on prayer. See SCHWEIZER (147) and also above, n. 30 and the discussion there. SCHWEIZER (155) also suggests that the Matthean community was so concerned with the issue of forgiveness that a call for forgiveness was incorporated into the *PN*, of which it did not initially form a part.

[43] Sir 27:30-28:7, cf. Sir 8:5; Philo, *Ex Antonio* (MANGEY, II 670-672). See FLUSSER (1988, 469-489; 2001, 84-86). See also MOULE (279-280); LUZ (383-384); MURPHY (269).

[44] See *T. Zeb.* 5:3, 8:1, 2; *T. Jos.* 18:2. Cf. *T. Gad* 6:1-7. Some scholars – for example, MOULE and LUZ – ascribe importance to the observation that this conditionality of God's forgiveness did not find its way into rabbinic liturgical texts.

[45] See RUZER (2002 ["The Double Love Precept"], 363). Tannaitic *Sifre Deut.* 323 on Deut 32:29 (which belongs to the tradition stemming from the school of R. Aqiva, who found in Lev 19:18 the core principle of Torah) promotes loving-kindness (*gemilut hasadim*) as the basic principle of all human intercourse.

make use here of a rather established trend with exegetical overtones, a stance that may be described as less radical than the one in Matt 5:43-48, where a demand to *love* one's enemies was put forward.[46]

This notion of God's forgiveness being conditional upon one's readiness to forgive one's wrongdoers is also well attested in later rabbinic sources.[47] Some traditions were ready to go as far as claiming that the forgiving inclination was a trademark feature of the "chosen people".[48] Thus Matt 6:12, 14-15 may be seen as bearing witness to a middle stage in the long history of this pattern of Jewish thought, starting at least two centuries earlier and going all

---

[46] Cf. Prov 24:17-18 (quoted in *m. Avot* 4:19); 25:21-22 (quoted in Rom 12:20); Job 31:29-30; 1QS I 9-11, X 17-20. See CHARLES (492-505); RUZER (2002 ["From 'Love Your Neighbor'"], 371-389; 2004, 193-208). As noted above, the difference in the ultimate objective to which one should aspire is rather telling: in Matt 5 it was perfection, whereas in Matt 6 (a complementing move!) it is forgiveness of one's sins.

[47] E.g., *m. B. Qama* 8:7; *b. Yoma* 22b–23a; *b. Ta'an.* 25b; *Pesiqta Rab.* 38 (cf. Matt 18:15-18, 21). Cf., *b. B. Qama* 92a, where the reward for Abraham's readiness to forgive Abimelech is Sarah's pregnancy; *b. Meg.* 28a, where the reward for readiness to forgive is a "good old age." Cf. *b. Ber.* 10a, where Beruriah, the wife of R. Meir, explained Ps 104:35 as a prayer that sin not sinners should be made an end of and urged R. Meir to pray for the repentance of sinners. See MOULE (279-280); FRIEDLANDER (156-157); MOORE (152f.).

[48] "He who is merciful towards all men (הבריות) thereby shows himself of the seed of Abraham" (*b. Beza* 32b). In *T. Jos.* and *T. Benj.*, Joseph is presented as one who shows mercy and forgiveness toward all, see *T. Jos.* 17, 18; *T. Benj.* 3:1-6; 4; 5. An extreme expression of the same sentiment may be found in such sayings as: "Be of the persecuted not of the persecutors" (*b. B. Qam.* 93a and elsewhere), and even "To whom 'hiding of the face' does not apply [i.e., he who is not persecuted] is not one of them [people of Israel]" (*b. Hag.* 5a). Cf. *b. Yeb.* 79a, where it is claimed that the Holy One distinguished Israel by three gifts, making them "merciful, bashful and benevolent." At least in some instances, the basis seems to be *imitatio Dei* (for example, *Mekhilta* mas. Shira par. 3; *b. Sabb.* 133b, et al.). See discussion in SCHECHTER (199-218); ABRAHAMS (2:166).

the way to the classical rabbinic tradition.[49] It should be noted that the general idea of God's forgiveness being conditional upon the nature of one's relations with one's fellow men developed also in the opposite direction – namely, that receiving forgiveness *from* a fellow man is a precondition for God's forgiveness. It seems that this latter pattern, well attested in tannaitic sources,[50] may be discerned already in the Sermon on the Mount (Matt 5:23-26). We should note again the existence of a variety of opinions on a core issue (here it is the parallel between one's obligations vis-à-vis God and vis-à-vis one's fellow men) – a phenomenon that characterizes Jewish religious discourse in general and is also discerned in the Gospels. One may surmise, therefore, that the particular notion expressed in the *PN* may be either in harmony or in tension with alternative emphases belonging to that variety and attested elsewhere in the New Testament.

3. MATT 6:13

It has been shown above that the compiler of Matthew 6 presented Matt 6:12 (by means of his redactional remark in Matt 6:14-15) as the core supplication of the *PN*. The *PN*, however, contains two more "we-petitions": 6:11 and 6:13 (as distinguished from the first three "You" petitions of the *PN*). The "daily bread" supplication constitutes a separate issue and lacks immediate connection to

---

[49] This means, of course, that the tradition attested in Matthew might have been only one expression of the variety of religious patterns that were in existence in the late Second Temple period. In research there have been numerous attempts to assess the relation of this tradition to the whole range – in other words, its "measure of peculiarity." See, e.g., MOULE (285-286). A connection between forgiveness and healing (sin and illness) is suggested by such Second Temple period sources as Sir 38:9-15; 4QPr Nab (cf. Matt 9:2-7; Mark 2:3-11; Luke 5:20-24). For a mishnaic evidence, see, for example, *m. B. Qama* 8:7. See MURPHY (265).

[50] *m. Yoma* 8:9; *m. B. Qama* 8:7; *Sifra* Acharei Mot 8 on Lev 16:30. See also *m. B. Metz.* 4:7; *b. Rosh Hashanah* 17b. Cf. *b. Yoma* 87a.

Matt 6:12.[51] Alternatively, the possibility of Matt 6:13 ("And lead us not into temptation, but deliver us from evil") being linked to Matt 6:12 should be considered.

Although the so-called doxology at the end of Matt 6:13 (ὅτι σου ἐστιν ἡ βασιλεία καὶ ἡ δύναμις καὶ ἡ δόξα) seems to represent a traditional element and is attested in different modifications, both in Jewish liturgical sources outside of the New Testament and elsewhere in the New Testament itself,[52] a number of early Matthew manuscripts and the Lukan parallel indicate that it might not originally have been part of the prayer.[53] If so, the Matt 6:13 petition was located between what was defined as the core supplication of the *PN* in Matt 6:12 and its interpretation / summary in Matt 6:14-15. The petition to be delivered from "temptation" might therefore have been perceived by the compiler as relating to the situation presupposed in the previous verse – namely, the situation when one is tempted by the behavior of others to judge them according to their sinful deeds and bear a grudge against them,

---

[51] See above, n. 15. Cf. BETZ (379-380), who attempts to establish a connection between the "bread petition" and the following one (on forgiveness), surmising that although the ingredients for making bread are provided by God, these are people who produce and provide "our bread"; our daily sustenance therefore depends on their willingness to share. BETZ interprets the petition as an appeal to God to influence the human heart toward generosity and benevolence.

[52] 1 Chr 29:10-11 and Targum, ad loc.; 2 Tim 4:18. See also *t. Ber.* 3:7 and *b. Ber.* 29b (the prayer is ascribed there to R. Eliezer, who recommends it for use in an hour of danger). For more examples, see CARMIGNAC (327-328).

[53] BETZ (376); ALBRIGHT-MANN (77). LUZ (385) believes Jewish prayer without concluding doxology would be unthinkable; but this very fact may explain why there was no immediate need to write it down. A doxology might have been added by later copyists, who understood from their own practice that such was the customary way to end a prayer. It has been suggested, moreover, that doxology – even for the same prayer – was not fixed but, being an expression of personal piety, might have varied from one occasion to another: thus JEREMIAS (1980, 31-32). For a thorough discussion, see BLACK (327-332); CARMIGNAC (320-333).

which (according to the notion reflected in Matt 6:12) may lead to evil consequences, such as God being unforgiving.[54]

The suggestion of an immediate thematic connection between Matt 6:12 and Matt 6:13 is also supported by early Qumranic evidence, where petitions for forgiveness of sins are paired with a plea for preservation from future temptations:

> Remember me and do not forget me
> or lead me into difficulties too great for me.
> Remove the sin of my childhood from me (Vermes: Put away from me the sin of my youth),
> and may my offences (Vermes: my sins) not be remembered against me.[55]

Traditionally, the "evil" (τοῦ πονηροῦ) of Matt 6:13 has tended to be rendered as the "Evil One" (Satan), and some scholars still support this understanding.[56] However, weighty arguments have late-

---

[54] Cf. Matt 5:22-23, where it is claimed that being angry with others entails the risk of being punished in Gehenna. Cf. also Matt 5:26, where the language of repaying debts is employed. CARMIGNAC too (316-317) regards Matt 6:13 as a logical continuation of the fifth petition.

[55] 11QPs^a XXIV, 10-11 (in GARCÍA MARTÍNEZ and TIGCHELAAR's translation). For a broader context, see 11QPs^a XXIV 3-14. See also 11QPs^a XIX. A wording similar to 11QPs^a XIX 13-16 and XXIV 10-13 – and Matt 6:13! – is also attested in *b. Ber.* 60b. It seems clear that the motifs attested in the *PN* are but one expression of a long trajectory of the underlying religious sentiment. See discussion in PHILONENKO (150-151); VÖGTLE (95-98).

[56] See DENIS (333-336); PHILONENKO (152-155); BROWN (250-252); DAVIES-ALLISON (614-615); CARMIGNAC (306-319). See also discussion in VÖGTLE (100-101); BLACK (333-338). The following fragments from Qumran have been regarded as supporting this interpretation, for in them *Belial* (Satan) is alternatively called *rasha'* (רשע, the wicked one) or *Melkhiresha'* (מלכירשע), which could be rendered in Greek as *poneros*: 4Q286 7 II; 4Q Amram^b (4Q544 Frgs. 1-3) vis-à-vis 4Q280 1; 11QPsa XIX:15-16. See also *Ap. Jas.* 4:28-31 and *b. Ber.* 16b.

ly been put forward – mainly on the basis of biblical and post-biblical Jewish evidence, including internal NT parallels, – for τοῦ πονηροῦ to be understood in a neutral sense – namely, as the evil/pain/sorrow, to which one asks God not to be exposed.[57] What temptation and what resulting evil are meant in this supplication? Does this petition refer to the eschatological tribulation or to the everyday predicament of sin? A range of solutions has been put forward in research;[58] the suggestion we now raise ties Matt 6:13 more closely to its immediate context.[59]

4. Eschatological or pre-eschatological?

Opinions differ with regard to the nature of the *PN*. Some scholars see the *PN* and Matt 6:1-18 in general as reflecting a clearly eschatological outlook. According to this approach, the first three "You" petitions in Matt 6:9-10, with their language of Kingdom (ἐλθέτω ἡ βασιλεία σου), provide a clear indication of the eschatological

---

[57] See Luz (385). The petition in Matt 6:13 agrees verbatim with *Did.* 8:2, whereas Luke 11:4 is a parallel only to 13a (cf. also Mark 14:38). Luke's shorter version is probably earlier than Matthew's explanatory expansion: see Friedlander (157). Cf. Gal 1:4f; 2 Tim 4:18. See also *Did.* 10:5. Mostly later rabbinic examples are referred to in Strack–Billerbeck: *Shemoneh-Esreh* Seventh Benediction, *b. Ber.* 60b, *b. Ber.* 16b. Afflictions one asks to be saved from in these sources are mainly those of everyday experience: illness, poverty, evil encounters, suffering, bad dreams, evil people, evil companions and neighbors, evil impulses and evil thoughts. For earlier evidence (not in the context of prayer of supplication) on distinguishing between good and evil where evil definitely does not represent Satan, see, for example, *T. Ash.* 1:3,5. The notion of a personal devil is likewise foreign to Philo. For internal NT evidence, see, for example, Matt 5:39; Luke 6:45; Gal 1:4f.; Rom 12:9; 1 Thes 5:22; 2 Tim 4:18.

[58] Jeremias (1980, 29); Brown (249-253); Davies-Allison (614-615) – eschatological; Luz (385) – everyday; Schweizer (156), Hagner (151) – both.

[59] The suggestion that follows was treated in detail by Ginsburskaya in her MA thesis.

stance of the prayer as a whole,[60] so that Matt 6:12 should be understood as relating to the Last Judgment.

However, already in tannaitic sources an important polemical shift is attested in the notion of the Kingdom of God: the Kingdom stands in these sources not so much for the general *eschaton* but for the acceptance of God's exclusive kingship "here and now" by the individual.[61] The use, then, of "Kingdom language" in the opening petitions of the *PN* does not automatically mean that the forgiveness of sins presented further on as one's ultimate reward is purely eschatological in character.[62] It should be emphasized that the motif of God's forgiveness of one's sins as conditional upon

---

[60] DAVIES-ALLISON (593-594); ALBRIGHT-MANN (75); JEREMIAS (1980, 28); BROWN (217-253). Another opinion sees the first three "You" petitions as explicitly eschatological (GERHARDSSON, 1996, 88-91) – with reference to Ezek 36:23 (cf. also Tg. Isa 24:23, 31:4-5, 40:9, 52:7 and Mic 4:7). On the other hand, the following "we" petitions are perceived as relating to the present (pre-eschatological) experience (GERHARDSSON, 1996, 91-94). BROWN (239) distinguishes between the eschatologically flavored Matthean aorist of δός and the Lukan present imperative of δίδου coupled with non-eschatological distributive of καθ' ἡμέραν. See also VIVIANO (447-450). For a detailed exposition see also LUZ (377-385), discussing the *PN* and its nature; CARMIGNAC (337-347), emphasizing the "here and now" in the *PN*; BRAUN (I, 12-12), who discerns an eschatological background in Matthew 5 and Matt 6:19, 24-25, in comparison with Qumranic texts, does not discuss the *PN* at all.

[61] See, for example, *m. Ber.* 2:2; 2:5 (see also *b. Ber.* 14b–15a); cf. *m. Avot* 2:4, *Mekhilta* mas. Shira 10 on Exod 15:18, *b. Ber.* 29b. See FLUSSER (2001, 110-112, 258-275); LUZ (378-380); FRIEDLANDER (144-145); BONSIRVEN (105). Cf. BEARE (173-175); HAGNER (148).

[62] CARMIGNAC (339-340); VÖGTLE (100); HAGNER (150); GERHARDSSON (1996, 92-93). See also BONSIRVEN (110). It is worth noting that the appellation *avi* (my Father, in relation to God) is employed in a non-eschatological prayerful context in 4Q 372 (*4QApocryphon of Joseph*) Frag. 1 16 ("my Father and my God") and 4Q 460 Frag. 9 I 6 ("my Father and my Lord"): see ALLISON (5). On the collation of historical and eschatological notions of Kingdom linked to Deut 6:4f (*Shma Israel*) in rabbinic sources, see BECKER (62-65).

one's readiness to forgive others appears both in Ben Sira and in later rabbinic sources in the context of an individual's religious predicament[63] – and not in the context of the Last Judgment. In general, the notion of reward in Jewish sources is a multifaceted one, and even in later rabbinic sources it may reflect both eschatological and non-eschatological concerns.[64] This fact considerably strengthens the possibility of Matt 6:12 having additional aspects of meaning derived from its non-eschatological background.[65]

5. A COMPLEMENTING TRACK TO FORGIVENESS

As observed, Matt 6:1-18 is characterized by propagating two parallel, complementing avenues to acquiring the reward of God's forgiveness; on the one hand, forgiving others, and on the other, proper performance of certain acts of piety: prayer (Matt 6:5-13; 7:7-11/Luke 11:1-3),[66] fasting (Matt 6:16-18),[67] deeds of chari-

---

[63] Sir 27:30-28:7. For rabbinic sources, see above, n. 47.
[64] See above, note 13.
[65] Cf. FREY, who, relying inter alia on Qumran parallels, shows that Matt 5:25-26 should be considered as originally representing a piece of sapiental instruction for everyday life rather than relating to the Last Judgment.
[66] See above, n. 26.
[67] Appears nowhere outside the pericope under discussion. But cf. Matthew 9:14-15; Mark 2:18-20; Luke 5:33-35; 18:12; Acts 13:2-3 (see above, n. 27). See O'HARA (3-18). Seems to represent here a non-eschatological pattern of religious thought – in contradistinction to, for example, Mark 2:18-22, where Jesus speaks about the abolition of fasting in messianic times. Cf. *Gos. Thom.* 6, 14; *b. Rosh Hashana* 18b. Fasting is coupled with prayer in an explicitly non-eschatological context in *T. Jos.* 4:7-8; *T. Benj.* 1:2-6. The practice of fasting is very ancient in Israel; it was exercised in times of mourning (1 Sam 31:11-13; 2 Sam 3:30-35; etc.) and of supplication – both communal (1 Sam 14:24) and private (2 Sam 12:16-17, etc.) – and included abstention from food, and a prohibition on washing and the wearing of special clothes. Some of these practices are related to and criticized in Matt 6. See GEORGE (594). In Jonah 3:5-10 fasting is explicitly connected with repentance and pleading with God for compassion and forgiveness of sins. See MOORE (67-69).

ty/compassion (Matt 6:1-4).⁶⁸ A number of instances appear in early Jewish tradition where one or another issue (prayer, fasting, or charity) is separately discussed.⁶⁹ We, however, will focus on similar general (tripartite) lines. As noted earlier, the Second Temple period book of Tobit (12:8-10) contains a summary of Jewish piety in a didactic form, including references to almsgiving, prayer and fasting – acts that lead, inter alia, to forgiveness of sins.⁷⁰ In rabbinic sources of Palestinian provenance, three acts that are claimed to "nullify the harsh decree" and bring forgiveness are: prayer, charity and repentance.⁷¹ Fasting, too, was often presented, both in biblical and, later, in rabbinic tradition, as a means – combined with true repentance – to obtain God's forgiveness and/or ameliorate calamities.⁷² Institutionalized fasting seems not to have exist-

---

Criticism of the undue emphasis on the external expressions and/or excesses of fasting was voiced by the biblical prophets (Isa 58:3-7; Jer 14:10-12; Zech 7:5-7) and appeared also in Second Temple literature (Sir 34:25-26; *T. Asher* 2:8; *Apoc. Elijah* 1:18-19) and rabbinic sources (*m. Ta'an.* 2:1; *t. Ta'an.* 1:8; *b. Ta'an.* 16a; cf. *b. Ta'an.* 22b; *b. B. Bath.* 60b). See DAVIES-ALLISON (617-620); LUZ (361). On the link between fasting and other penitential practices, see O'HARA (10); on the criticism of excesses, see, for example, BONSIRVEN (159).

⁶⁸ Cf. *Gos. Thom.* 6, 14 (BETZ, 335). The latter logion, representing a radical (later) development, underlines the "conservative character" of Matt 6. GERHARDSSON (1972, 69-77, esp. 74) connects almsgiving, prayer and fasting with an interpretation of Deut 6:4-5 (*Shema*): almsgiving corresponds to "all your might" understood as mammon (cf. *m. Ber.* 9:5), prayer to "all your heart" and fasting to "all your soul" (cf. *Sifre Deut.* 41 on Deut 11:13; *b. Sukk.* 49b).

⁶⁹ For example, the importance of charity is stressed in *t. Peah* 4:19; *Mekhilta mas. Amalek* 4 on Exod 18:27. For a later talmudic discussion, see *b. B. Bathra* 9a–11a. For further references, see STRACK–BILLERBECK (I: 386-406).

⁷⁰ See discussion above.

⁷¹ E.g., *y. Sanh.* 10, 2 [28b–28c]. The triadic structure appears also in other contexts, both similar and quite different. See, for example, *T. Jos.* 10:1-2; *m. Avot* 1:2, 18. See also above, n. 18.

⁷² For a thorough discussion, see ABRAHAMS (1:122-127). Fasting is preferred to almsgiving in *b. Ber.* 32b, while their joint value is stressed in *b. Ber.* 6b. For additional references to the practice and importance of fasting, see above, n. 67.

ed in Qumran, but fasting is mentioned in clear connection to repentance in at least one Qumranic text.[73]

As noted, in Matthew 6 the notion of God's forgiveness as conditional upon one's forgiving attitude toward others seems to have been inherited (by Jesus? by the compiler of the Sermon?) from the contemporary Jewish tradition. How, then, should the evidence on the alternative avenue to acquiring God's forgiveness – namely, the tripartite option of right ritual behavior – be interpreted? It would be far-fetched to suggest that the tripartite structure was invented by the compiler of the Sermon and reinvented later by the transmitters of the rabbinic tradition. It seems much more plausible (and Tobit provides clear evidence in this direction) that the tripartite pattern as such was already traditional in the days of Jesus, whereas its details might have been disputed. The Matthean tradition may thus be seen as an important early witness to the development of the tripartite avenue to forgiveness of sins attested later in rabbinic sources.

The call to perform deeds of charity, to fast and to pray in secret is undoubtedly the most characteristic feature of the Gospel stance here. In tannaitic tradition, acts of secret charity are discussed in connection with the Temple.[74] Even in later texts, performing charitable and merciful deeds (צדקה וגמילות חסדים) secretly is still recommended.[75] However, a strong emphasis on public prayer in the synagogue is also attested.[76] In rabbinic tradition we find a notion of

---

[73] See 4Q266 Frag. 11.
[74] See, for example, *m. Sheq.* 5:6; see BETZ (338).
[75] For example, *b. B. Bath.* 9b. Cf. SYREENI (529-531), who sees Matt 6:1-8 as reflecting the stance of a closed community whose observances are different from those of outsiders – hence the fear of disclosure and the need for concealment.
[76] See *y. Ber.* 4,4 [8c]; 5,1 [8d–9a]; *b. Ber.* 7b–8a. Cf. Isa 26:20. FRIEDLANDER (109-110) sees in the Matthean emphasis on secrecy a connection to Isaiah and thus an additional indication of the eschatological character of Jesus' teaching. BETZ (360) suggests that "the reason for the secrecy is to protect one's eschatological reward." He also notes (374) that the *PN* itself does not contain a polemic against the synagogue. The emphasis on public prayer in the synagogue was complemented by rabbinic exhortations to be sincere in prayer: see *Sifre Deut.* 41 on Deut 11:13; *m. Ber.* 5:1; *t. Ber.* 3:18. See also *b. Taan.* 8a; *b. Ber.* 30b; *Midr. Ps.* on Ps 108:1.

the synagogue as the only place where one's prayers are readily heard because God is present there (as earlier in the Temple).[77] The stance of Matthew 6 is clearly different: it seems to reflect a transitional situation (prior to the destruction of the Temple?), where the practice of prayer in the synagogue already existed but did not attain an indisputable status and thus might have been perceived as a sign of outward piety only – on a par with prayer "on street corners"![78] Thus the Matthean evidence may again be seen as providing important data for a better understanding of proto-rabbinic developments in appraising synagogue prayer as a substitute for Temple worship.[79]

However, it is worth noting that if the suggestion of the *PN* having been interpolated into the discourse in Matt 6:1-18 is accepted, Jesus' general exhortation to pray in secret (Matt 6:5-6) did not necessarily apply to the Lord's Prayer – parallels in Luke and Mark, devoid of any mention of secrecy, also seem to point in this direction.[80]

CONCLUSION

It turns out that each of the two avenues to forgiveness collated in Matthew 6 represents inherited topics of Jewish thought that will

---

[77] *y. Ber.* 5,1 [8d–9a]; *b. Ber.* 6b.

[78] On the instances where prayer at crossroads might have occurred, see GEORGE (593); LUZ (358-359). A polemical note is clearly discernible in Matthew 6:5-6: καὶ ὁ πατήρ σου ὁ βλέπων ἐν τῷ κρυπτῷ ἀποδώσει σοι (some mss add ἐν τῷ φανερῷ) – "your Father ... will reward *you*" (and not *them*!). The Synoptic tradition (e.g., Matt 14:23, 26:39, 42, 44 and parallels) does portray Jesus as one who is inclined to pray in solitude (cf. 2 Kgs 4:32-35, *T. Jos.* 3:3, *T. Jacob* 1:9, *b. Taan.* 23b); but this is a far cry from outright condemnation of public prayer as such – according to the Gospels' narrative, Jesus himself prayed in synagogues and in the Temple, and there is therefore absolutely no reason to suppose that he totally opposed common liturgical practices. See VIVIANO (434); ALBRIGHT-MANN (75); BETZ (361, 373-374); DAVIES-ALLISON (584-586). HEINEMANN (86-87) sees the *PN* as comprising in a peculiar way the features of both public and private Jewish prayers.

[79] See discussion in TALMON (273-284).

[80] Luke 11:1-10; Mark 11:24-26.

later be addressed, *mutatis mutandis*, in rabbinic sources. Thus the Gospel account may be perceived as witness to a first-century offshoot in this long trajectory. The above discussion has aimed, inter alia, at demonstrating the relevance of the New Testament evidence for a clearer appraisal of overall developments in Jewish tradition.

We have seen that a number of different suggestions as to how one should act to attain forgiveness of sins were attested in the Second Temple period sources. The coexistence of various (not necessarily harmonized) suggestions on this issue constitutes here an important characteristic of the religious agenda inherited by the compiler of Matthew 6. This situation engendered a variety of responses – from both within and outside the New Testament. For example, disparate avenues to forgiveness were addressed independently in different parts of Ben Sira,[81] whereas in Matt 6:1-18 a *collation* of the "two ways" to forgiveness was employed. Such tight collation is nowhere attested in other surviving texts from the Second Temple and early rabbinic period, constituting a distinctive editorial feature of the Sermon on the Mount.[82]

BIBLIOGRAPHY

ABRAHAMS, I. *Studies in Pharisaism and the Gospels*, 2 vols. London: Cambridge University Press, 1917/1924.

ALBRIGHT, W. F., and C. S. MANN, introd., transl., and notes. *Matthew*. The Anchor Bible. New York / London: Doubleday, 1971.

ALLISON, D. C. *Jesus of Nazareth: Millenarian Prophet*. Minneapolis: Fortress Press, 1998.

ANDERSON, G. "From Israel's Burden to Israel's Debt: Towards a Theology of Sin in Biblical and Early Second Temple Sources." In E. G. CHAZON and D. DIMANT, eds. *Reworking the Bible at*

---

[81] See discussion above.

[82] A looser collation of the same "two ways" reappears later in the traditional Jewish Yom Kippur liturgy.

Qumran in the Context of Second Temple Judaism. Forthcoming.

BEARE, F. W. *The Gospel according to Matthew: A Commentary.* Oxford: Basil Blackwell, 1981.

BECKER, H.-J. "Matthew, the Rabbis and Billerbeck on the Kingdom of Heaven." In this volume, pp. 57-69.

BETZ, H. D. *The Sermon on the Mount: A Commentary on the Sermon on the Mount, Including the Sermon on the Plain (Matthew 5:3-7:27 and Luke 6:20-49).* Minneapolis: Fortress Press, 1995.

BLACK, M. "The Doxology to the *Pater Noster* with a Note on Matthew 6:13b." In P. R. DAVIES and R. T. WHITE, eds. *A Tribute to Geza Vermes*, pp. 327-338. JSOTSS 100, 1990.

BONSIRVEN, J. *Palestinian Judaism in the Time of Jesus Christ.* New York: Holt, Rinehart and Winston, 1964.

BRAUN, H. *Qumran und das Neue Testament*, 2 vols. Tübingen: Mohr, 1966.

BROWN, R. E. "The Pater Noster as an Eschatological Prayer." In *New Testament Essays,* pp. 217-253. Milwaukee: Bruce Publishing Company, 1965.

CARMIGNAC, J. *Recherches sur le "Nôtre Père."* Paris: Letouzey et Ané, 1969.

CHARLES, R. H. "Man's Forgiveness of his Neighbour – A Study in Religious Development." *The Expositor* 6 (1908), pp. 492-505.

CHARLESWORTH, J. H. "A Caveat on Textual Transmission and the Meaning of *Abba*: A Study of the Lord's Prayer." In IDEM, M. HARDING and M. KILEY, eds. *The Lord's Prayer and Other Prayer Texts from the Greco-Roman Era*, pp. 1-14. Valley Forge, Pa: Trinity Press International, 1994.

———. *Critical Reflections on the Odes of Solomon. Vol. 1: Literary Setting, Textual Studies, Gnosticism, the Dead Sea Scrolls and the Gospel of John,* JSPSS 22. Sheffield: Sheffield Academic Press, 1998.

DAVIES, W. D. *The Setting of the Sermon on the Mount.* Cambridge: Cambridge University Press, 1964.

DAVIES, W. D., and D. C. ALLISON. *A Critical and Exegetical Commentary on the Gospel according to Saint Matthew.* Edinburgh: T.&T. Clark, 1988.

FLEISCHER, E. "On the Beginnings of Obligatory Jewish Prayer." *Tarbiz* 59 (1990), pp. 397-441 (in Hebrew).
FLUSSER, D. "A New Sensitivity in Judaism and the Christian Message." In IDEM, *Judaism and the Origins of Christianity*, pp. 469-489. Jerusalem: Magnes Press, 1988.
——. *Jesus.* Jerusalem: Magnes Press, 2001.
——. "Jesus and Judaism: Jewish Perspectives." In H. W. ATTRIDGE and G. HATA, eds. *Eusebius, Christianity, and Judaism*, pp. 80-109. Leiden / New York / Cologne: Brill, 1992.
FREY, J. "The Character and Background of Mt 5:25-26: A Case Study for the Value of Qumran Literature in New Testament Interpretation." In this volume, pp. 3-39.
FRIEDLANDER, G. *The Jewish Sources of the Sermon on the Mount.* London: Routledge & Sons, 1911.
GEORGE, A. "La justice à faire dans le secret: Matthieu 6, 1-6 et 16-18." *Biblica* 40 (1959), pp. 590-598.
GERHARDSSON, B. "Geistiger Opferdienst nach Matth 6,1-6, 16-21." In H. BALTENSWEILER and B. REICKE, eds., *Neues Testament und Geschichte. Oscar Cullman zum 70. Geburtstag*, pp. 69-77. Tübingen: J. C. B. Mohr and Paul Siebeck, 1972.
——. "The Matthaean Version of the Lord's Prayer (Matt. 6:9b-13): Some Observations." In IDEM, *The Shema in the New Testament*, pp. 84-97. Lund: Novapress, 1996.
GINSBURSKAYA, M. "The Enigma of the Lord's Prayer Petition for Preservation (Matthew 6:13): Between This-worldly and Eschatological Woes." Master's thesis, The Hebrew University of Jerusalem, 2003.
GOSHEN-GOTTSTEIN, A. "Hillel and Jesus: Are Comparisons Possible?" In J. H. CHARLESWORTH and L. L. JOHNS eds., *Hillel and Jesus: Comparative Studies of Two Major Religious Leaders*, pp. 31-55. Minneapolis: Fortress Press, 1997.
HAGNER, D. A. *World Biblical Commentary: Matthew 1-13.* Vol. 33A. Dallas, Tex.: Word Books, 1993.
HEINEMANN, J. "The Background of Jesus' Prayer in the Jewish Liturgical Tradition." In J. J. PETUCHOWSKI and M. BROCKE, eds., *The Lord's Prayer*, pp. 81-89. London: Burns & Oates, 1978.

JEREMIAS, J. *The Lord's Prayer.* Philadelphia: Fortress Press, 1980.
——. *The Prayers of Jesus.* Norwich: Fletcher & Son, SCM Press, 1967.
LACHS, S. T. *A Rabbinic Commentary on the New Testament: The Gospels of Matthew, Mark and Luke.* Hoboken, N.J.: Ktav, 1987
LUZ, U. *Matthew 1–7: A Continental Commentary.* Minneapolis: Fortress Press, 1989.
MCCAUGHEY, D. "Matt 6.13A. The Sixth Petition in the Lord's Prayer." *Australian Biblical Review* 33 (1985), pp. 31-36.
MOORE, G. F. *Judaism in the First Century of the Christian Era: The Age of the Tannaim.* New York: Schocken Books, 1971.
MOULE, C. F. D. "… As we forgive …: A Note on the Distinction between Deserts and Capacity in the Understanding of Forgiveness." In IDEM, *Essays in New Testament Interpretation*, pp. 278-286. Cambridge: Cambridge University Press, 1982.
MURPHY, R. E. "Sin, Repentance, and Forgiveness in Sirach." In *Der Einzelne und sein Gemeinschft bei Ben Sira*, pp. 261-269. Beihefte zur Zeitschrift für die alttestamentliche Wissenschaft 270. Berlin and New York: Walter de Gruyter, 1998.
NITZAN, B. *Qumran Prayer and Religious Poetry.* Leiden: Brill, 1994.
O'HARA, J. "Christian Fasting: Mt. 6, 16-18." *Scripture* 19 (1967), pp. 3-18.
OVERMAN, J. A. *Matthew's Gospel and Formative Judaism: The Social World of the Matthean Community.* Minneapolis: Fortress Press, 1990.
PETUCHOWSKI, J. J., ed. and trans. "Jewish Prayer Texts of the Rabbinic Period." In J. J. PETUCHOWSKI and M. BROCKE, eds. *The Lord's Prayer*, pp. 21-44. London: Burns & Oates, 1978.
PHILONENKO, M. *Le Nôtre Père: De la Prière de Jésus la prière des disciples.* Paris: Gallimard, 2001.
REPSCHINSKI, B. *The Controversy Stories in the Gospel of Matthew: Their Redaction, Form and Relevance for the Relationship between the Matthean Community and Formative Judaism.* Göttingen: Vandenhoeck & Ruprecht, 2000.
RUZER, S. "The Death Motif in Late Antique Jewish *Teshuva* Narrative Patterns and in Paul's Thought." In J. ASSMAN and

G. STROUMSA, eds., *Transforming the Inner Self in Ancient Religions*, pp. 151-165. Leiden: Brill, 1999.

——. "From 'Love Your Neighbor' to 'Love Your Enemy': Trajectories in Early Jewish Exegesis." *Revue Biblique* 109, no. 3 (2002), pp. 371-389.

——. "'Love Your Enemy' Precept in the Sermon on the Mount in the Context of Early Jewish Exegesis: A New Perspective." *Revue Biblique* 111, no. 2 (2004), pp. 193-208.

——. "The Double Love Precept in the New Testament and the *Rule of the Community*." *Tarbiz* 71 (2002), pp. 353-370 (in Hebrew).

SALDARINI, A. J. *Matthew's Christian-Jewish Community*. Chicago and London: University of Chicago Press, 1994.

SCHECHTER, S. *Aspects of Rabbinic Theology.* London: Adam and Charles Black, 1909.

SCHWEIZER, E. *The Good News according to Matthew.* Atlanta: John Knox Press, 1975.

SIM, D. *The Gospel of Matthew and Christian Judaism: The History and Social Setting of the Matthean Community.* Edinburgh: T. & T. Clark, 1998.

STRACK, H. L., and P. BILLERBECK *Kommentar zum Neuen Testament aus Talmud und Midrash*, 5 vols. Munich: C. H. Beck, 1922.

SYREENI, K. "Separation and Identity: Aspects of the Symbolic World of Matt. 6:1-18." *New Testament Studdies* 40 (1994), pp. 522-541.

TALMON, S. "The Emergence of Institutionalized Prayer in Israel in the Light of the Qumran Literature." In M. DELCOR, ed. *Qumran: sa piété, sa théologie et son milieu*, pp. 265-284. BETL 46. Louvain: Peeters, 1978.

URBACH, E. E. *The Sages: Their Concepts and Beliefs.* Jerusalem: Magnes Press, 1975.

——. "Religious and Social Aspects of the Sages' Notion of Zedaka." In IDEM, *The World of the Sages*, pp. 97-124. Jerusalem: Magnes Press, 1988 (in Hebrew).

VIVIANO, B. T. "Hillel and Jesus on Prayer." In J. H. CHARLESWORTH and L. L. JOHNS eds., *Hillel and Jesus: Compa-*

rative Studies of Two Major Religious Leaders, pp. 427-459. Minneapolis, Fortress Press, 1997.

VÖGTLE, A. "The Lord's Prayer: A Prayer for Jews and Christians?" In J. J. PETUCHOWSKI and M. BROCKE, eds. *The Lord's Prayer*, pp. 94-117. London: Burns & Oates, 1978.

Appendix: SOURCES

⇨ N. 7

SIRACH 34:25–35:3, 35:11–36:8

34:25 If a man washes after touching a dead body, and touches it again, what has he gained by his washing? 26 So if a man fasts for his sins, and goes again and does the same things, who will listen to his prayer? And what has he gained by humbling himself? 35:1 He who keeps the law makes many offerings; he who heeds the commandments sacrifices a peace offering. 2 He who returns a kindness offers fine flour, and he who gives alms sacrifices a thank offering. 3 To keep from wickedness is pleasing to the Lord, and to forsake unrighteousness is atonement.

35:11 For the Lord is the one who repays, and he will repay you sevenfold. 12 Do not offer him a bribe, for he will not accept it; and do not trust to an unrighteous sacrifice; for the Lord is the judge, and with him is no partiality. 13 He will not show partiality in the case of a poor man; and he will listen to the prayer of one who is wronged. 14 He will not ignore the supplication of the fatherless, nor the widow when she pours out her story. 15 Do not the tears of the widow run down her cheek as she cries out against him who has caused them to fall? 16 He whose service is pleasing to the Lord will be accepted, and his prayer will reach to the clouds. 17 The prayer of the humble pierces the clouds, and he will not be consoled until it reaches the Lord; he will not desist until the Most High visits him, and does justice for the righteous, and executes judgment. 18 And the Lord will not delay, neither will he be patient with them, till he crushes the loins of the unmerciful and repays vengeance on the nations; till he takes away the multitude of the insolent, and breaks the scepters of the unrighteous; 19 till he repays the man according to his deed, and the works of men according to their devices; till he judges the case of his people and makes them rejoice in his mercy. 20 Mercy is as welcome when he afflicts them as clouds of rain in the time of drought. 36:1 Have mercy upon us, O Lord, the God of all, and look upon us, 2 and cause the fear of thee to fall upon all the nations. 3 Lift up thy hand against foreign nations and let them see thy might. 4 As in us thou hast been sanctified before them, so in them be thou magnified before us; 5 and let them know thee, as we have known that there is not God but thee, O Lord. 6 Show signs anew, and work further wonders;

make thy hand and thy right arm glorious. 7 Rouse thy anger and pour out thy wrath; destroy the adversary and wipe out the enemy. 8 Hasten the day, and remember the appointed time, and let people recount thy mighty deeds.

TOBIT 12:8-10

8 Prayer is good when accompanied by fasting, almsgiving, and righteousness. A little with righteousness is better than much with wrongdoing. It is better to give alms than to treasure up gold. 9 For almsgiving delivers from death, and it will purge away every sin. Those who perform deeds of charity and of righteousness will have fulness of life; 10 but those who commit sin are the enemies of their own lives.

Gospel of Thomas 6 (Layton, p. 55; tr. T.O. Lambdin)

His disciples questioned him and said to him, "Do you want us to fast? How shall we pray? Shall we give alms? What diet shall we observe?" Jesus said, "Do not tell lies, and do not do what you hate, for all things are plain in the sight of heaven. For nothing hidden will not become manifest, and nothing covered will remain without being uncovered."

Gospel of Thomas 14 (Layton, p. 59; tr. T.O. Lambdin)

Jesus said to them, "If you fast, you will give rise to sin for yourselves; and if you pray, you will be condemned; and if you give alms, you will do harm to your spirits. <...>"

2 Clement 16 (Holmes, p. 123)

Therefore, brothers, inasmuch as we have received no small opportunity to repent, let us, while we still have time, turn again to God who has called us, while we still have one who accepts us. For if we renounce these pleasures and conquer our soul by refusing to fulfill its evil desires, we will share in Jesus' mercy. But you know that "the day" of judgment is already "coming as blazing furnace", and "some of the heavens will dissolve", and the whole earth will be like lead melting in a fire, and then the works of men, the secret and the public, will appear. Charitable giving, therefore, is good, as is repentance from sin. Fasting is better than prayer, while charitable giving is better than both, and "love covers a multitude of sins", while prayer arising from a good conscience delivers one from death. Blessed is everyone who is found full of these, for charitable giving relieves the burden of sin.

⇨ N. 8

***Didache* 8:2** (Lake, p. 321)

And do not pray as the hypocrites, but as the Lord commanded in his Gospel, pray thus: "Our Father, who art in Heaven, hallowed be thy Name, thy Kingdom come, thy will be done, as in Heaven so also upon earth; give us to-day our daily bread, and forgive us our debt as we forgive our debtors, and lead us not into trial, but deliver us from the Evil One,[1] for thine is the power and the glory for ever."

⇨ N. 13

***m. Avot* 2:16** (Danby, p. 449)

He (i.e. R. Tarfon) used to say: It is not thy part to finish the task, yet thou art not free to desist from it. If thou hast studied much in the Law much reward will be given thee, and faithful is thy taskmaster who shall pay thee the reward of thy labour. And know that the recompense of the reward of the righteous is for the time to come.

***m. Peah* 1:1** (Danby, pp. 10-11)

These are things for which no measure is prescribed: Peah, First-fruits, the Festal Offerings, deeds of loving-kindness and the study of the Law. These are things whose fruits a man enjoys in this world while the capital is laid up for him in the world to come: honouring father and mother, deeds of loving-kindness, making peace between a man and his fellow; and the study of the Law is equal to them all.

⇨ N. 14

Sixth benediction of *Amidah* (Birnbaum, p. 164)

Forgive us, our Father, for we have sinned; pardon us, our King, for we have transgressed; for thou dost pardon and forgive. Blessed art thou, O Lord, who art gracious and ever forgiving.

---

[1] Or: "the evil".

Avinu Malkenu (Birnbaum, pp. 98-102)

Our father, our King, we have sinned before thee.
Our father, our King, we have no king except thee.
Our father, our King, deal with us kindly for the sake of thy name.
Our father, our King, renew for us a good year.
Our father, our King, abolish all evil decrees against us...

Our father, our King, forgive and pardon all our sins.
Our father, our King, blot out and remove our transgressions and sins from thy sight.
Our father, our King, cancel in thy abundant mercy all the records of our sins.
Our father, our King, bring us back in perfect repentance to thee.
Our father, our King, send a perfect healing to the sick among thy people.
Our father, our King, tear up the evil sentence decreed against us.
Our father, our King, remember us favorably.
Our father, our King, inscribe us in the book of happy life.
Our father, our King, inscribe us in the book of redemption and salvation.
Our father, our King, inscribe us in the book of maintenance and sustenance.
Our father, our King, inscribe us in the book of merit.
Our father, our King, inscribe us in the book of pardon and forgiveness...

Our father, our King, hear our voice, spare us and have mercy on us.
Our father, our King, receive our prayer with mercy and favor.
Our father, our King, open the gates of heaven to our prayer.
Our father, our King, dismiss us not empty-handed from thy presence.
Our father, our King, remember that we are but dust.
Our father, our King, may this hour be an hour of mercy and a time of grace with thee.
Our father, our King, have compassion on us, on our children and our infants.
Our father, our King, act for the sake of those who were slain for thy holy name.
Our father, our King, act for the sake of those who were slaughtered for proclaiming thy Oneness.
Our father, our King, act for the sake of those who went through fire and water for the sanctification of thy name.
Our father, our King, avenge the spilt blood of thy servants.

Our father, our King, do it for thy sake, if not for ours.
Our father, our King, do it for thy sake and save us.
Our father, our King, do it for the sake of thy abundant mercy.
Our father, our King, do it for the sake of thy great, mighty and revered name by which we are called.
Our father, our King, be gracious to us and answer us, though we have no merits, deal charitably with us and save us.

Havinenu (Birnbaum, p. 98)

Grant us, Lord our God, wisdom to learn thy ways; subject out heart to thy worship; forgive us so that we may be redeemed; keep us from suffering; satisfy us with the products of thy earth; gather our dispersed people from the four corners of the earth. Judge those who stray from thy faith; punish the wicked; may the righteous rejoice over the rebuilding of thy city, the reconstruction of thy Temple, the flourishing dynasty of thy servant David and the continuance of the offspring of thy anointed, the son of Jesse. Answer us before we call. Blessed art thou, O Lord, who hearest prayer.

⇨ N. 15

1QHodayot **IV 17-28** (García Martínez–Tigchelaar, v. 1, p. 149)

17 [I give] you [thanks] for the spirits which you placed in me. I want to find a reply on (my) tongue to recount your acts of justice, the patience 18 [of] your [judgments,] the deeds of your mighty right hand, the [pardon]ing of my former offences, to [bow] low and beg favour for 19 ... [...] of my deeds and the depravity of my heart. Because I defiled myself with impurity, I [separated myself] from the foundation [of truth] and I was not allied with [...] 20 [...] ... To you does justice belong, blessing belongs to your Name for ever! [Act according to] your justice, free 21 [your servant,] the wicked should come to an end! However, I have understood that [you smoothen] the path of the one whom you choose and by the insight 22 [of your knowledge you pre]vent him from sinning against you, you [re]store his humility through your punishments, and by [...] you [...] his heart. *Blank* 23 [Prevent] your servant from sinning against you, from tripping over all the things of your will. Strengthen [...] against [fiendish] spirits, 24 [so that] he can walk in all that you love, and loathe all that [you] hate, [so he can do] what is good in your eyes 25 [...]

in my vitals, for your servant is a spirit of flesh. *Blank*
26 [I give you thanks, because] you have spread [your] holy spirit upon your servant [...] ... [...] his heart 27 [...] and I will consider every human treaty [...] they shall find it 28 [..] ... and those who love it [...] for ever and ever.

1QHodayot **XII 28-33** (García Martínez–Tigchelaar, v. 1, pp. 169-171)

28 <...> and to show 29 your powerful acts to all living things. What is flesh compared to this? What creature of clay can do wonders? He is in iniquity 30 from his maternal womb, and in guilt of unfaithfulness right to old age. But I know that justice does not belong to man nor to a son of Adam a perfect 31 path. To God Most High belong all the acts of justice, and the path of man is not secure except by the spirit which God creates for him 32 to perfect the path of the sons of Adam so that all his creatures come to know the strength of his power and the abundance of his compassion with all the sons of 33 his approval.

Ps 51:9-11

9 Hide your face from my sins, and blot out all my iniquities. 10 Create in me a clean heart, O God, and put a new and right spirit within me. 11 Do not cast me away from your presence, and do not take your holy Spirit from me.

Ezek 36:25-27

25 I will sprinkle clean water upon you, and you shall be clean from all your uncleannesses, and from all your idols I will cleanse you. 26 A new heart I will give you, and a new spirit I will put within you; and I will take out of your flesh the heart of stone and give you a heart of flesh. 27 And I will put my spirit within you, and cause you to walk in my statutes and be careful to observe my ordinances.

m. Sotah **9:15** (Danby, pp. 306-307)

R. Phineas b. Jair says: Heedfulness leads to cleanliness, and cleanliness leads to purity, and purity leads to abstinence, and abstinence leads to holiness, and holiness leads to humility, and humility leads to the shunning of sin, and the shunning of sin leads to saintliness, and saintliness leads to [the gift of] the Holy Spirit, and the Holy Spirit leads to the resurrection of the dead. And the resurrection of the dead shall come through Elijah of blessed memory. Amen.

⇨ N. 17

m. Avot 1:3 (Danby, p. 446)

Antigonus of Soko received [the Law] from Simeon the Just. He used to say: Be not like slaves that minister to the master for the sake of receiving a bounty, but be like slaves that minister to the master not for the sake of receiving a bounty; and let the fear of Heaven be upon you.

⇨ N. 18

SIRACH 7:8-10

8 Do not commit a sin twice; even for one you will not go unpunished. 9 Do not say, "He will consider the multitude of my gifts, and when I make an offering to the Most High God he will accept it." 10 Do not be fainthearted in your prayer, nor neglect to give alms.

y. Ta'anit 2,1 [65a] (Neusner 1982-1991, v. 18, p. 178)

Said R. Eleazar, "Three acts nullify the harsh decree, and these are they: prayer, charity, and repentance." And all of them are to be derived from a single verse of Scripture: "If my people who are called by my name humble themselves, [pray and seek my face, and turn from their wicked ways, then I will hear from heaven and will forgive their sin and heal their land]" (2Chr 7:14). "Pray" – this refers to prayer. "And seek my face" – this refers to charity, as you say, "As for me, I shall behold thy face in righteousness; when I awake, I shall be satisfied with beholding thy form" (Ps 17:15). "And turn from their wicked ways" – this refers to repentance. Now if they do these things, what is written concerning them there? "Then I will hear from heaven and will forgive their sin and heal their land." R. Haggai preached this lesson of R. Eleazar every time there was a fast.

y. Sanhedrin 10,2 [28b-28c] (Neusner 1982-1991, v. 31, pp. 331-332)

Now what did Manasseh so? It is written, "In those days Hezekia became sick and was at the point of death. [And Isaiah the prophet and son of Amoz came to him, and said to him, 'Thus says the Lord: Set your house in order; for you shall die, you shall not recover]'" (Is 38:1). "For you shall die and you shall not recover" – "You shall die" in this world, "And you shall not recover" in the world to come. He said to him, "Why?" He said to him, "Because you did not want to raise up children." He said to him, "And why did you not want to raise up children?" He said to him, "Because I saw that I would produce an evil son. On that account, I did not want to raise up children." He said to him, "Take my daughter. Perhaps on my account and your account she will produce a good man." Even so, only a bad person came forth. That is in line with the following verse of Scripture: "The knaveries of the knave are evil; [he devises wicked devices to ruin the poor with lying words, even when the plea of the needy is right]" (Is 32:7). He said to him, "I am not going to listen to you. I am going to follow only that which my elder said to me, ' If you see bad dreams or bad visions, seek three things and you will be saved, and these are they: prayer, charity, and repentance,'" And three of them are to be derived from a single verse of Scripture: "If my people who are called by my name humble themselves, and pray and seek my face, and turn from their wicked ways, then I will hear from heaven and will forgive their sin and heal their land" (2Chr. 7:14). "Pray" – this refers to prayer. "And seek my face" – this refers to charity, as you say, "As for me, I shall behold thy face in righteousness; when I awake, I shall be satisfied with beholding thy form" (Ps 17:15). "And turn from their wicked ways" – this refers to repentance. Now if they do these things, what is written concerning them there? "Then I will hear from heaven and will forgive their sin and heal their land." Forthwith, "And he turned...", as it is written, "Then Hezekiah turned his face to the wall, and prayed to the Lord" (Is 38:2).

Testament of Joseph **10:1-2** (Charlesworth, v. 1, p. 821)

1 So you see, my children, how great are the things that patience and prayer with fasting accomplish. 2 You also, if you pursue self-control and purity with patience and prayer with fasting in humility of heart, the Lord will dwell among you, because he loves self-control.

TOBIT 12:8

See above, n. 7.

m. Peah **1:1**

See above, n. 13.

***m. Avot* 2:11** (Danby, p. 449)

R. Joshua said: The evil eye and the evil nature and hatred of mankind put a man out of the world.

⇨ N. 20

SIRACH 3:1–4:14

3:1 Listen to me your father, O children; and act accordingly, that you may be kept in safety. 2 For the Lord honored the father above the children, and he confirmed the right of the mother over her sons. 3 Whoever honors his father atones for sins, 4 and whoever glorifies his mother is like one who lays up treasure. 5 Whoever honors his father will be gladdened by his own children, and when he prays he will be heard. 6 Whoever glorifies his father will have long life, and whoever obeys the Lord will refresh his mother; 7 he will serve his parents as his masters. 8 Honor your father by word and deed, that a blessing from him may come upon you. 9 For a father's blessing strengthens the houses of the children, but a mother's curse uproots their foundations. 10 Do not glorify yourself by dishonoring your father, for your father's dishonor is no glory to you. 11 For a man's glory comes from honoring his father, and it is a disgrace for children not to respect their mother. 12 O son, help your father in his old age, and do not grieve him as long as he lives; 13 even if he is lacking in understanding, show forbearance; in all your strength do not despise him. 14 For kindness to a father will not be forgotten, and against your sins it will be credited to you; 15 in the day of your affliction it will be remembered in your favor; as frost in fair weather, your sins will melt away <...>
30 Water extinguishes a blazing fire: so almsgiving atones for sin. 31 Whoever requites favors gives thought to the future; at the moment of his falling he will find support. 4:1 My son, deprive not the poor of his living, and do not keep needy eyes waiting. 2 Do not grieve the one who is hungry, nor anger a man in want. 3 Do not add to the troubles of an angry mind, nor delay your gift to a beggar. 4 Do not reject an afflicted suppliant, nor turn your face away from the poor. 5 Do not avert your eye from the needy, nor give a man occasion to curse you; 6 for if in bitterness of soul he calls down a curse upon you, his Creator will hear his prayer. 7 Make yourself beloved in the congregation; bow your head

low to a great man. 8 Incline your ear to the poor, and answer him peaceably and gently. 9 Deliver him who is wronged from the hand of the wrongdoer; and do not be fainthearted in judging a case. 10 Be like a father to orphans, and instead of a husband to their mother; you will then be like a son of the Most High, and he will love you more than does your mother.

SIRACH 45:15-16

15 Moses ordained him, and anointed him with holy oil; it was an everlasting covenant for him and for his descendants all the days of heaven, to minister to the Lord and serve as priest and bless his people in his name. 16 He chose him out of all the living to offer sacrifice to the Lord, incense and a pleasing odor as a memorial portion, to make atonement for the people.

⇨ N. 21

2 MACC 7:18, 30-38

18 After him they brought forward the sixth. And when he was about to die, he said, "Do not deceive yourself in vain. For we are suffering these things on our own account, because of our sins against our own God. Therefore astounding things have happened."

30 <...> The young man said, "What are you waiting for? I will not obey the king's command, but I obey the command of the law that was given to our ancestors through Moses. 31 But you, who have contrived all sorts of evil against the Hebrews, will certainly not escape the hands of God. 32 For we are suffering because of our own sins. 33 And if our living Lord is angry for a little while, to rebuke and discipline us, he will again be reconciled with his own servants. 34 But you, unholy wretch, you most defiled of all mortals, do not be elated in vain and puffed up by uncertain hopes, when you raise your hand against the children of heaven. 35 You have not yet escaped the judgment of the almighty, all-seeing God. 36 For our brothers after enduring a brief suffering have drunk of ever-flowing life, under God's covenant; but you, by the judgment of God, will receive just punishment for your arrogance. 37 I, like my brothers, give up body and life for the laws of our ancestors, appealing to God to show mercy soon to our nation and by trials and plagues to

make you confess that he alone is God, 38 and through me and my brothers to bring to an end the wrath of the Almighty that has justly fallen on our whole nation."

Mekhilta de-Rabbi Ishmael, **Bachodesh 7** [on Exod. 20:7] (Lauterbach, v. 2, pp. 249-251)

For four things did R. Matia b. Heresh go to r. Eleazar ha-Kapar to Laodicea. He said to him: Master! Have you heard the four distinctions in atonement which R. Ishmael used to explain? He said to him: Yes. One scriptural passage says: "Return, O backsliding children" (Jer 3:14), from which we learn that repentance brings forgiveness. And another scriptural passage says: "For on this day shall atonement be made for you" (Lev 16:30), from which we learn that the Day of Atonement brings forgiveness. Still another scriptural passage says: "Surely this iniquity shall not be expiated by you till you die" (Is 22:14), from which we learn that death brings forgiveness. And still another scriptural passage says: "Then will I visit their transgressions with the rod, and their iniquity with strokes" (Ps 89:33), from which we learn that chastisements bring forgiveness. How are all these four passages to be maintained? If one has transgressed a positive commandment and repents on it, he is forgiven on the spot. Concerning this it is said: "Return, O backsliding children." If one has violated a negative commandment and repents, repentance alone has not the power of atonement. It merely leaves the matter pending and the Day of Atonement brings forgiveness. Concerning this it is said: "For on this day shall atonement be made for you." If one willfully commits transgressions punishable by extinction or by death at the hands of the court and repents, repentance cannot leave the matter pending nor can the Day of Atonement bring forgiveness. But both repentance and the Day of Atonement together bring him half a pardon. And chastisements secure him half a pardon. Concerning this it is said: " Then will I visit their transgressions with the rod, and their iniquity with strokes." However, if one has profaned the name of God and repents, his repentance cannot make the case pending, neither can the Day of Atonement bring him forgiveness, nor can sufferings cleanse him of his guilt. But repentance and the Day of Atonement both can merely make the matter pend. And the day of death with the suffering preceding it completes the atonement. To this applies: "Surely this iniquity shall not be expiated by you till ye die." And so also when it says: "that the iniquity of Eli's house shall not be expiated with sacrifice nor offering" (1Sam 3:14) it means: With sacrifice and offering it cannot be expiated, but it will be expiated by the day of death. Rabbi says: I might have thought that the day of death does not bring forgiveness. But when it says: "When I have opened your graves" etc. (Ezek 37:13), behold we learn that the day of death does bring atonement.

Mekhilta de-Rabbi Ishmael, **Nezikin 18** [on Exod. 22:22] (Lauterbach, v. 3, pp. 141-142)

If thou afflict in any wise, whether by a severe affliction or a light affliction... At the time when R. Simon and R. Ishmael were led out to be killed, R. Simon said to R. Ishmael: Master, my heart fails me, for I do not know why I am to be killed. R. Ishmael said to him: Did it never happen in your life that a man came to you for judgment or with a question and you let him wait until you had sipped your cup, or had tied your sandals, or had put on your cloak? And the Torah had said: "If thou afflict in any wise" – whether it be a severe affliction or a light affliction. Whereupon R. Simon said to him: "You have comforted me, master."

b. **Yoma 86a**[2]

R. Matthia b. Heresh asked R. Eleazar b. Azariah in Rome: have you heard about the four kinds of sins, concerning which R. Ishmael has lectured? He answered: They are three, and with each is repentance connected <...> But if he has been guilty of the profanation of the Name, then penitence has no power to suspend punishment, nor the Day of Atonement to procure atonement, nor suffering to finish it, but all of them together suspend the punishment and only death finishes it, as it is said: *And the Lord of hosts revealed Himself in my ears; surely this iniquity shall not be expiated by you till ye die* (Isa. 22:14).

b. **Sanhedrin 47a-b**

R. Joseph said: We too have learnt similarly: If there are holy objects therein, that which is dedicated to the altar [i.e. sacrifices] must die; to

---

[2] All fragments from the Babylonian Talmud are according to the Soncino translation and are taken from the JUDAIC CLASSICS LIBRARY CD-ROM edition.

the Temple repair, must be redeemed. Now we pondered thereon, Why should they die? Since they [the inhabitants of the condemned city] are executed, they obtain forgiveness: should they [the sacrifices] not then be offered to Heaven! Surely then is it not so because we hold that once invalidated, they remain so? Abaye retorted; Do you then think that he who dies in his wickedness obtains forgiveness [by his death]? Nay, he who dies in his wickedness does not obtain forgiveness, for R. Shemaiah learnt: One might have thought that even if his [the priest's] parents had dissociated themselves from the practices of the congregation, he [the priest] may defile himself: but Scripture states, *among his people* (Lev. 21:1-2) teaching, that it is so provided he [the parent] has followed the practices of his people. Said Raba to him: Dost thou compare one who was executed in his wickedness to one who died in his wickedness? In the latter case, since he dies a natural death, he attains no forgiveness; but in the former, since he does not die a natural death, he obtains forgiveness [by the mere execution]. In proof thereof, it is written, *A Psalm of Asaph, O God, the heathen are come into Thine inheritance; they have defiled Thy Holy Temple... They have given the dead bodies of Thy servants to be food unto the fowls of the heaven; the flesh of Thy saints onto the beasts of the earth* (Ps. 79:1-2). Who are meant by 'Thy servants,' and who by 'Thy saints'? Surely 'thy saints' means literally, saints, whereas, 'thy servants' means those who were at first liable to sentence [of death], but having been slain, are designated 'servants'. Abaye retorted: Would you compare those who are slain by a [Gentile] Government, to those who are executed by the Beth din? The former, since their death is not in accordance with [Jewish] law, obtain forgiveness; but the latter, whose death is justly merited, are not [thereby] forgiven. This can also he proved from what we learnt: THEY DID NOT BURY HIM IN HIS ANCESTRAL TOMB. And if you should imagine that having been executed, he attains forgiveness: he should be buried [with his fathers]! – Both death and [shameful] burial are necessary [for forgiveness].

R. Adda b. Ahabah objected: THEY OBSERVED NO MOURNING RITES, BUT GRIEVED FOR HIM FOR GRIEF IS BORNE ONLY IN THE HEART. But should you think that having been [shamefully] buried, he attains forgiveness, they should observe mourning rites! – The decay of the flesh too is necessary. This also follows from what he [the Tanna] teaches: WHEN THE FLESH WAS COMPLETELY DECOMPOSED, THE BONES WERE GATHERED AND BURIED IN THEIR PROPER PLACE. This proves it.

⇨ N. 22

SIRACH 5:5-7

5 Do not be so confident of atonement that you add sin to sin. 6 Do not say, "His mercy is great, he will forgive the multitude of my sins," for both mercy and wrath are with him, and his anger rests on sinners. 7 Do not delay to turn to the Lord, nor postpone it from day to day; for suddenly the wrath of the Lord will go forth, and at the time of punishment you will perish.

SIRACH 34:25-26

See above, n. 7.

SIRACH 17:22-29

22 A man's almsgiving is like a signet with the Lord and he will keep a person's kindness like the apple of his eye. 23 Afterward he will arise and requite them, and he will bring their recompense on their heads. 24 Yet to those who repent he grants a return, and he encourages those whose endurance is failing. 25 Turn to the Lord and forsake your sins; pray in his presence and lessen your offenses. 26 Return to the Most High and turn away from iniquity, and hate abominations intensely. 27 Who will sing praises to the Most High in Hades, as do those who are alive and give thanks? 28 From the dead, as from one who does not exist, thanksgiving has ceased; he who is alive and well sings the Lord's praises. 29 How great is the mercy of the Lord, and his forgiveness for those who turn to him!

Testament of Joseph 4:3-6 (Charlesworth, v. 1, p. 820)

3 During all these affairs I stretched out on the ground praying God to rescue me from her treachery. 4 When she achieved nothing by means of it, she began to approach me for instruction, so that she might learn the Word of God. 5 And she kept saying to me, 'If you want me to abandon the idols, have intercourse with me, and I shall persuade to put away the idols, and we shall live in the presence of your Lord.' 6 But I kept telling her that the Lord did not want worshipers who come by means of uncleanness, nor would he be pleased with adulterers, but with those who were pure in heart and undefiled in speech.

***m. Yoma* 8:8** (Danby, p. 172)

The Sin-offering and the unconditional Guilt-offering effect atonement; death and the Day of Atonement effect atonement if there is repentance. Repentance affects atonement for lesser transgressions against both positive and negative commands in the Law; while for graver transgressions it suspends punishment until the Day of Atonement comes and effects atonement.

***t. Yoma* 5:9** (Neusner 2002, v. 1, p. 564)

The sin-offering, guilt-offering, and Day of Atonement all effect atonement only along with repentance, since it says, *But on the tenth day of the seventh month [is a Day of Atonement]* (Lev. 23:27). If [the sinner] repents, atonement is effected for him, and if not, it is not effected for him. R. Eleazar says, "*Forgiving [iniquity, transgression, and sin]* (Ex. 34:7) – He forgives iniquity to penitents, but he does not forgive iniquity to those who do not repent." R. Judah says: "Death and the Day of Atonement effect atonement along with repentance. Repentance effects atonement with death. And the day of death – lo, it is tantamount to an act of repentance."

⇨ N. 24

Sifre on Deuteronomy 41 [on Deut 11:13] (Hammer, pp. 85-86)

And to serve Him: This refers here to study. You might say, "This refers to study [according to you], but might it not refer to actual work?" [The answer is, No,] since Scripture says, *And the Lord God took the man, and put him into the Garden of Eden to work it and to guard it* (Gen 2:15) – what kind of work or guarding was there at the time? Thus you learn that *to work it* refers to study, and *to guard it* refers to the commandments. Just as serving at the altar is called "service," so is study called "service." Another interpretation of *and to serve Him*: This refers to prayer. You might say, "This refers to prayer [according to you], but might it not refer to [Temple] service?" [The answer is, No,] since Scripture says, *With all your heart and with all your soul* – is there such a thing as [Temple] service in one's heart? Therefore what does the verse mean by *and to serve Him*? It refers to prayer. Similarly David says, *Let my prayer be set forth as incense before Thee, the lifting up of my hands as the evening sacrifice* (Ps 141:2), and it is said, *and when Daniel knew that the writing was signed, he went into his house – now his windows were open in his upper chamber toward Jerusalem – and he kneeled upon his knees three times a day, and prayed* (Dan 6:11), and *O Daniel, servant of the living God, is thy God, whom thou servest continually, able to deliver thee from the lions?* (Dan 6:21). And is there [Temple] worship in Babylon? Therefore what does Scripture mean by *and to serve Him*? It means prayer, and just as the service of the altar is called "service," so is prayer called "service."

R. Eliezer ben Jacob says: *And to serve Him with all your heart and with all your soul* – this is a warning to the priests not to be of two minds when serving [in the Temple]. Another interpretation: What does [the repetition of] *with all your heart and with all your soul* mean? Does not Scripture say elsewhere, *With all thy heart and with all thy soul* (Deut 6:5)? [The answer is,] the latter refers to the individual, while the former refers to the entire community; the latter refers to study, while the former refers to performance. Since, having heard, you performed what you were to perform, I too will perform what I promised to perform – *I will give the rain of your land in its season.*

⇨ N. 25

Ps 141:1-2

1 A Psalm of David. I call upon thee, O Lord; make haste to me! Give ear to my voice, when I call to thee! 2 Let my prayer be counted as incense before thee, and the lifting up of my hands as an evening sacrifice!

Sirach 3:30

Water extinguishes a blazing fire: so almsgiving atones for sin.

Sirach 35:1-7

1 He who keeps the law makes many offerings; he who heeds the commandments sacrifices a peace offering. 2 He who returns a kindness offers fine flour, and he who gives alms sacrifices a thank offering. 3 To keep from wickedness is pleasing to the Lord, and to forsake unrighteousness is atonement. 4 Do not appear before the Lord empty-handed, 5 for all these things are to be done because of the commandment. 6 The offering of a righteous man anoints the altar, and its pleasing odor rises

before the Most High. 7 The sacrifice of a righteous man is acceptable, and the memory of it will not be forgotten.

TOBIT 4:7-11

7 Give alms from your possessions to all who live uprightly, and do not let your eye begrudge the gift when you make it. Do not turn your face away from any poor man, and the face of God will not be turned away from you. 8 If you have many possessions, make your gift from them in proportion; if few, do not be afraid to give according to the little you have. 9 So you will be laying up a good treasure for yourself against the day of necessity. 10 For charity delivers from death and keeps you from entering the darkness; 11 and for all who practice it charity is an excellent offering in the presence of the Most High.

TOBIT 12:9

See above, n. 7.

TOBIT 14:11

"So now, my children, consider what almsgiving accomplishes and how righteousness delivers." As he said this he died in his bed. He was a hundred and fifty-eight years old; and Tobias gave him a magnificent funeral.

1QS IX 3-6 (García Martínez–Tigchelaar, v. 1, p. 91)

3 When these exist in Israel in accordance with these rules in order to establish the spirit of holiness in truth 4 eternal, in order to atone for the guilt of iniquity and for the unfaithfulness of sin, and for approval for the earth, without the flesh of burnt offerings and without the fats of sacrifice – the offering of 5 the lips in compliance with the decree will be like the pleasant aroma of justice and the perfectness of behaviour will be acceptable like a freewill offering – at that moment the men of 6 the Community shall set apart a holy house for Aaron, in order to form a most holy community, and a house of the Community for Israel, those who walk in perfection.

1QS X 5-8 (García Martínez–Tigchelaar, v. 1, p. 95)

5 <...> At the commencement of the months in their seasons, and of the holy days in their sequence, as a reminder in their seasons. 6 With the

offering of lips I shall bless him, in accordance with the decree recorded for ever. At the commencement of the years and in the turning of their seasons, when the decree of 7 their disposition is carried out, on its prescribed day, one after another; the season of the harvest up to summer, the season of seed-time up to the season of the grass, the seasons of the years up to their seven-year periods. 8 At the commencement of the seven-year periods up to the moment decided for deliverance. And in all my existence the precept will be engraved on my tongue to be a fruit of eulogy, and a portion (of offering) of my lips.

CD-A XI, 17-21 (García Martínez–Tigchelaar, v. 1, p. 569)

<...> 17 no-one should take him out with a ladder or a rope or a utensil. *Blank* No-one should offer anything upon the altar on the sabbath, 18 except the sacrifice of the sabbath, for thus is it written: "except your offerings of the sabbath" (Lev. 23:38). *Blank* No-one should send 19 to the altar a sacrifice, or an offering, or incense, or wood, by the hand of a man impure from any 20 of the impurities, so allowing him to defile the altar, for it is written: "the sacrifice 21 of the wicked is an abomination, but the prayer of the just is like an agreeable offering" (Prov. 15:8).

SIRACH 7:8-10

See above, n. 18.

SIRACH 12:3

No good will come to the man who persists in evil or to him who does not give alms.

SIRACH 16:14

He will make room for every act of mercy; every one will receive in accordance with his deeds.

SIRACH 17:22

See above, n. 22.

SIRACH 29:8-13

8 Nevertheless, be patient with a man in humble circumstances, and do not make him wait for your alms. 9 Help a poor man for the command-

ment's sake, and because of his need do not send him away empty. 10 Lose your silver for the sake of a brother or a friend, and do not let it rust under a stone and be lost. 11 Lay up your treasure according to the commandments of the Most High, and it will profit you more than gold. 12 Store up almsgiving in your treasury, and it will rescue you from all affliction; 13 more than a mighty shield and more than a heavy spear, it will fight on your behalf against your enemy.

SIRACH 34(31):11

His prosperity will be established, and the assembly will relate his acts of charity.

SIRACH 40:17

Kindness is like a garden of blessings, and almsgiving endures for ever.

SIRACH 40:24

Brothers and help are for a time of trouble, but almsgiving rescues better than both.

⇨ N. 30

t. Berakhot 3:7 (Neusner 2002, v. 1, p. 16; tr. T. Zahavy)

One who was walking in a place of danger and of bandits *recites a brief prayer* [*m.Ber*. 4:4B]. What is this brief prayer? R. Eliezer says, "May thy will be done in the heavens above, and grant ease to those who fear you, and do what is good in thine own eyes. Praised [be Thou, O Lord,] who hearkens to prayer." [*ed. princ.*: R. Eleazar b. R. Sadok says, "Hearken to the sound of the cries of your people Israel and quickly fulfill their requests. Praised (be Thou, O Lord,) who hearkens to prayer."] Others say, "The needs of thy people are many and they are impatient. May it be thy will, Lord our God, to give to each and every one according to his needs, and to each and every creature that which he lacks. Praised [be Thou, O Lord,] who hearkens to prayer." Said R. Eleazar b. R. Sadok, "My father used to recite a short prayer on the eve of the Sabbath: 'And on account of the love, Lord our God, with which Thou hast loved thy people Israel, and on account of the compassion, our King, which Thou hast bestowed on the members of thy covenant, Thou hast given us, Lord our God, this great and holy seventh day with love.' Over the cup [of wine] he would say, 'who sanctified the Sabbath day,' and he would not conclude [the benediction with a closing benedictory formula]."

***m. Berakhot* 4:2** (Danby, p. 5)

R. Nehunya b. ha-Kanah used to pray a short prayer when he entered the House of Study and when he came forth. They said to him, 'What is the nature of this prayer?' He replied, 'When I enter I pray that no offence shall happen through me, and when I come forth I give thanks for my lot.'

***b. Berakhot* 29b**

Our Rabbis taught: One who passes through a place infested with beasts or bands of robbers says a short Tefillah. What is a short Tefillah? – R. Eliezer says: Do Thy will in heaven above, and grant relief to them that fear Thee below and do that which is good in Thine eyes. Blessed art Thou, O Lord, who hearest prayer. R. Joshua says: Hear the supplication of Thy people Israel and speedily fulfil their request. Blessed art Thou, O Lord, who hearest prayer. R. Eleazar son of R. Zadok says: Hear the cry of thy people Israel and speedily fulfil their request. Blessed art Thou, O Lord, who hearkenest unto prayer. Others say: The needs of Thy people Israel are many and their wit is small. May it be Thy will, O Lord our God, to give to each one his sustenance and to each body what it lacks. Blessed art Thou, O Lord, who hearkenest unto prayer. R. Huna said: The halachah follows the 'Others'.

⇨ N. 32

Kaddish (Petuchowski, p. 37)

Exalted and hallowed be His great Name
in the world which He created
according to His will.
May He establish His kingdom
    (*Some rites add:* and cause His salvation to sprout,
                    and hasten the coming of His messiah,)
in your lifetime and in your days,
and in the lifetime of the whole household of Israel,
speedily and at a near time.
And say: Amen.

⇨ N. 33

Didache 8:2

See above, n. 8.

⇨ N. 36

SIRACH 7:14

Do not prattle in the assembly of the elders, nor repeat yourself in your prayer.

b. Berakhot 61a

R. Huna further said in the name of R. Meir: A man's words should always be few in addressing the Holy One, blessed be He, since it says, *Be not rash with thy mouth and let not thy heart be hasty to utter a word before God, for God is in heaven and thou upon earth; therefore let thy words be few* (Eccl. 5:1).

ECCL 5:1-2

1 Guard your steps when you go to the house of God; to draw near to listen is better than to offer the sacrifice of fools; for they do not know that they are doing evil. 2 Be not rash with your mouth, nor let your heart be hasty to utter a word before God, for God is in heaven, and you upon earth; therefore let your words be few.

ISA 1:15

When you spread forth your hands, I will hide my eyes from you; even though you make many prayers, I will not listen; your hands are full of blood.

ISA 65:24

Before they call I will answer, while they are yet speaking I will hear.

⇨ N. 37

y. Berakhot 4,1 [7b–7c] (Neusner 1982-1991, v. 1, pp. 157-158; tr. T. Zahavy)

Whence [do we derive the obligation to recite] the Closing service [*Ne'ilah*, on the Day of Atonement and other public fast days]? Said R. Levi, "'Even though you make many prayers I will not listen' (Is. 1:15). [Only in that instance will he not listen. Ordinarily he would listen.] From here we learn that all those who add more prayers, are answered." [The Closing Prayer is an instance of an added prayer.] [It appears that] R. Levi holds the opposite view elsewhere [i.e., that adding prayers may be detrimental]. There said R. Abba son of R. Pappi, R. Joshua of Sakhnin in the name of R. Levi, "'In all toil there is profit, but mere talk tends only to want' (Prov. 14:23). By adding to her prayers, Hannah shortened Samuel's life. [She asked that he live for fifty years. How so?] For she said, ['As soon as the child is weaned, I will bring him, that he may appear in the presence of the Lord,] and abide there forever' (1Sam. 1:22). 'Forever' for a Levite means for fifty years. As it is written, 'From the age of fifty years they shall withdraw from the work of the service and serve no more' (Num. 8:25)." But [Samuel] lived fifty-two years! Said R. Yose b. R. Bun, "[Add] two years [before] he was weaned." [In any case, Hannah's added prayers were heared, and her son Samuel's life was shortened accordingly.] Does [Levi] then say [that increasing Prayer may be detrimental]? If he does, it is only regarding the Prayer of an individual [such as Hannah]. But regarding communal Prayer [Levi holds the view that adding to it is beneficial]. R. Hiyya in the name of R. Yohanan, R. Simeon b. Halafta in the name of R. Meir, "As she continued praying before the Lord' (1Sam. 1:12) – *from this we learn that all who add to their prayers are answered. [Even an individual benefits by adding prayers, contrary to Levi's view.]*"

b. Berakhot 5b

It has been taught: Abba Benjamin says, When two people enter [a Synagogue] to pray, and one of them finishes his prayer first and does not wait for the other but leaves, his prayer is torn up before his face. For it is written: *Thou that tearest thyself in thine anger, shall the earth be forsaken for thee?* (Job 18:4) And more than that, he causes the Divine Presence to remove itself from Israel. For it says: *Or shall the rock be removed out of its place?* (Ibid.) And 'rock' is nothing else than the Holy

One, blessed be He, as it says: *Of the Rock that begot thee thou wast unmindful* (Deut. 32:18). And if he does wait, what is his reward?

Mekhilta de-Rabbi Ishmael, Vayassa 1 [on Exod. 15:25] (Lauterbach, v. 2, pp. 91-92)

And he cried unto the Lord etc. <...> By the way, you also learn that the prayer of the righteous is short. It happened once that a disciple, in the presence of R. Eliezer, went up to read the service, and made his prayers short. The other disciples remarked to R. Eliezer: "You notice how so and so made his prayers short." – and they used to say about him: "This one is a scholar who makes short prayers." – But R. Eliezer said to them: He did not make it shorter than Moses did, as it is said: "Heal her now, O God, I beseech Thee" (Num. 12:13). Again it happened once that a disciple in the presence of R. Eliezer went up to read the service and made his prayers long. The other disciples remarked to R. Eliezer: "You notice that so and so made his prayers long." – And they used to say about him: "This one is a scholar who makes long prayers." – But R. Eliezer said to them: He did not make them longer than Moses did, as it is said: "so I fell down before the Lord the forty days," etc. (Deut. 9:25). For R. Eliezer used to say: There is a time to be brief in prayer and a time to be lengthy.

⇨ N. 40

Leviticus Rabbah 10:5 (Freedman-Simon, p. 126)

R. Judah and R. Joshua b. Levi expressed differing views. R. Judah said: Repentance effects half [atonement], but prayer effects a complete [atonement]. R. Joshua b. Levi said: Repentance effects a whole, but prayer only a half. Whence is derived the view of R. Judah b. Rabbi that repentance effects only half? – From the case of Cain, against whom a decree was pronounced. When he repented, half of the decree was withheld. Whence do we know that Cain repented? – It is said, *And Cain said unto the Lord: Mine iniquity is too great to be forgiven* (Gen. 4:13). And whence do we know that half of the sentence was withheld? It is written, *And Cain went out from the presence of the Lord, and dwelt in the land of Nod* [i.e. wandering] *on the east of Eden* (ib. 16). Here is written not fugitive and wandering [as originally decreed], but '*The land of Wandering, eastward of Eden*'.

Another interpretation: '*And Cain went out.*' In what manner did he go out? R. Judan said in the name of r. Aibu: He bundled up his clothes and threw them over his back, and went off like one who had tried to impose upon Heaven. R. Berekiah said in the name of r. Ila'i b. Shemaiah: He went forth like one who had cheated and deceived his Creator. R. Huna said, in the name of r. Hanina b. Isaac: '*He went forth*' means, in a glad mood, the sense in which the expression is used in [the passage], *And also, behold, he cometh forth to meet thee; and when he seeth thee, he will be glad in his heart* (Exod. 4:14). As Cain went forth, Adam, the first man, met him and asked him: 'What happened at your trial?' He answered: 'I repented and I was pardoned'. When Adam heard this, he gave himself a slap on the face, and said to Cain: 'So great is the power of repentance, and I did not know!' On that occasion, Adam, the first man, composed *The Psalm, the song for the Sabbath day* (Ps. 92:1). R. Levi said: Adam composed this Psalm.

Whence is derived the view of r. Judah b. Rabbi that prayer effects complete pardon? – From the case of Hezekiah. The original term of Hezekiah's kingship was only fourteen years, as it is written, *Now it came to pass in the fourteenth year of King Hezekiah*, etc. *In those days was Hezekiah sick unto death* (Isa. 36:1, 38:1), but after he prayed, fifteen years more were given him, as it is said, *Then came the word of the Lord...behold I will add unto thy days fifteen years* (ib. 5).

Whence is derived the view of r. Joshua b. Levi, who said that repentance effects complete atonement? – From the men of Anathoth, of whom it is said, *The young men shall die by the sword* (Jer. 11:22), but because they repented, they were privileged to be mentioned in the genealogical record, as it is said, *The men of Anathoth, a hundred and twenty and eight* (Neh. 7:27).

⇨ **N. 43**

SIRACH 27:30–28:7

27:30 Anger and wrath, these also are abominations, and the sinful man will possess them. 28:1 He that takes vengeance will suffer vengeance from the Lord, and he will firmly establish his sins. 2 Forgive your neighbor the wrong he has done, and then your sins will be pardoned when you pray. 3 Does a man harbor anger against another, and yet seek for healing from the Lord? 4 Does he have no mercy toward a man like himself, and yet pray for his own sins? 5 If he himself, being flesh, maintains wrath, who will make expiation for his sins? 6 Remember the end of your life, and cease from enmity, remember destruction and death, and be true to the commandments. 7 Remember the commandments, and do not be angry with your neighbor; remember the covenant of the Most High, and overlook ignorance.

SIRACH 8:5

Do not reproach a man who is turning away from sin; remember that we all deserve punishment.

Philo, fragments from *Ex Antonio* (Mangey, v. 2, pp. 670-672) [translated by M. Ginsburskaya]

Ser. VIII (p. 670)
If you are seeking forgiveness of your sins, do yourself forgive those who sinned against you, because absolution is balanced by absolution, and reconciliation with our fellow-slaves is liberation from the divine wrath.

Ser. IX (p. 670)
A civilized and kind person, inclined to forgive, does not remember at all any injury but desires to conquer (an adversary) by doing good rather than by harming.

Ser. LVII (p. 672)
Be the kind of person towards your servants that you wish God will be towards you. Since just as we listen we will be heard, and just as we see (others), we will be seen by Him. Let us show mercy for the sake of obtaining mercy, so that we may receive like for like.

Ser. LXXIV (p. 672)
Forgiveness usually generates repentance.

Ser. LXXXVII (p. 672)
God, merciful by nature, will not absolve from his sin the one who swears falsely for the sake of injustice, since such a person is hard to purify and defiled, even though he may escape human punishment.

⇨ N. 44

Testament of Zebulon 5:3 (Charlesworth, v. 1, p. 806)

Have mercy in your inner being, my children, because whatever anyone does to his neighbor, the Lord will do to him.

Testament of Zebulon 8:1-2 (Charlesworth, v. 1, p. 807)

1 You also, my children, have compassion toward every person with mercy, in order that the lord may be compassionate and merciful to you. 2 In the last days God will send his compassion on the earth, and whenever he finds compassionate mercy, in that person he will dwell.

Testament of Joseph 18:2 (Charlesworth, v. 1, p. 823)

And if anyone wishes to do you harm, you should pray for him, along with doing good, and you will be rescued by the Lord from every evil.

Testament of Gad 6:1-7 (Charlesworth, v. 1, p. 816)

1 Now, my children, each of you love his brother. Drive hatred out of your hearts. Love one another in deed and word and inward thoughts. 2 For when I stood before my father I would speak peaceably about Joseph, but when I went out, the spirit of hatred darkened my mind and aroused my soul to kill him. 3 Love one another from the heart, therefore, and if anyone sins against you, speak to him in peace. Expel the venom of hatred, and do not harbor deceit in your heart. If anyone confesses and repents, forgive him. 4 If anyone denies his guilt, do not be contentious with him, otherwise he may start cursing, and you would be sinning doubly. 5 In a dispute do not let an outsider hear your secrets, since out of hatred for you may become your enemy, and commit a great sin against you. He may talk to you frequently but treacherously, or be much concerned with you, but for an evil end, having absorbed from you the venom. 6 Even if he denies it and acts disgracefully out of a sense of guilt, be quiet and do not become upset. For he who denies will repent, and avoid offending you again; indeed he will honor you, will respect you and be at peace. 7 But even if he is devoid of shame and persists in his wickedness, forgive him from the heart and leave vengeance to God.

⇨ N. 45

***Sifre on Deuteronomy* 323** [on Deut 32:29] (Hammer, pp. 334-335)

If they were wise, they would understand this, (they would discern their latter end) (32:29): If Israel would but look closely at the words of Torah which I have given them, no nation or kingdom could dominate them. (The word) *this* always means Torah, as it is said, *And this is the Torah which Moses set (before the children of Israel)* (Deut 4:44). Another interpretation: *If they were wise, they would understand this*: If Israel would but look closely at what their father Jacob had said to them, no nation or kingdom could dominate them. What did he say to them? Accept upon yourselves the kingdom of heaven, vie with each other in fear of heaven, and act toward each other with loving-kindness.

⇨ N. 46

PROV 24:17-18

17 Do not rejoice when your enemy falls, and let not your heart be glad when he stumbles; 18 lest the Lord see it, and be displeased, and turn away his anger from him.

***m. Avot* 4:19** (Danby, p. 455)

Samuel the Younger said: *Rejoice not when thine enemy falleth, and let not thine heart be glad when he is overthrown, lest the Lord see it and it displease him, and he turn away his wrath from him* (Prov. 24:17-18).

PROV 25:21-22

21 If your enemy is hungry, give him bread to eat; and if he is thirsty, give him water to drink; 22 for you will heap coals of fire on his head, and the Lord will reward you.

JOB 31:29-30

29 "If I have rejoiced at the ruin of him that hated me, or exulted when evil overtook him 30 I have not let my mouth sin by asking for his life with a curse."

1QS I 9-11 (García Martínez–Tigchelaar, v. 1, p. 71)

9 <...> in order to love all the sons of light, each one 10 according to his lot in God's plan, and to detest all the sons of darkness, each one in accordance with his guilt 11 in God's vindication.

1QS X 17-20 (García Martínez–Tigchelaar, v. 1, pp. 95-97)

17 <...> I shall not repay anyone with an evil reward; 18 with goodness I shall pursue man. For to God (belongs) the judgement of every living being, and it is he who pays man his wages. I shall not be jealous with a wicked 19 spirit, and my soul shall not crave with violence; I {shall not sustain angry resentment for those who convert} /shall not be involved/ in any dispute with the men of the pit /until the day/ of vengeance. However, my anger I shall not 20 remove from unjust men, not I shall be appeased, until he carries out his judgement.

⇨ N. 47

m. Baba Qama 8:7 (Danby, p. 343)

Even though a man pays [him that suffers the indignity], it is not forgiven him until he seeks forgiveness from him, for it is written, *Now, therefore, restore the man's wife ... [and he shall pray for thee]* (Gen. 20:7). And whence do we learn that if he did not forgive him he would be accounted merciless? Because it is written, *And Abraham prayed unto God and God healed Abimelech ...* (Gen. 20:17).

b. Yoma 22b–23a

R. Johanan further said in the name of R. Simeon b. Jehozadak: Any scholar, who does not avenge himself and retain anger like a serpent, is no [real] scholar. But is it not written: *Thou shalt not take vengeance nor bear any grudge* (Lev. 19:18)? – That refers to monetary affairs, for it has been taught: What is revenge and what is bearing a grudge? If one said to his fellow: 'Lend me your sickle', and he replied 'No', and tomorrow the second comes [to the first] and says: 'Lend me your axe'! and he replies: 'I will not lend it to you, just as you would not lend me your sickle' – that is revenge. And what is bearing a grudge? If one says to his fellow: 'Lend me your axe, he replies 'No', and on the morrow the second asks: 'Lend me your garment', and he answers: 'Here it is. I am not like you who would not lend me [what I asked for]' – that is bearing a grudge. But [does] not [this prohibition apply to] personal affliction? Has it not been taught: Concerning those who are insulted but do not insult others [in revenge], who hear themselves reproached without replying, who [perform good] work out of love of the Lord and rejoice in their sufferings, Scripture says: *But they that love Him be as the sun when he goeth forth in his might* (Judg. 5:31)? – [That means,] indeed, that he keeps it in his heart [though without taking action]. Rut Raba said: He who passes over his retaliations has all his transgressions passed over? – [That speaks of the case] that an endeavour was made to obtain his reconciliation, and his consent is obtained.

b. Ta'anit 25b

It is further related of R. Eliezer that once he stepped down before the Ark and recited the twenty-four benedictions [for fast days] and his prayer was not answered. R. Akiba stepped down after him and exclaimed: Our Father, our King, we have no King but Thee; our Father, our King, for Thy sake have mercy upon us; and rain fell. The Rabbis present suspected [R. Eliezer], whereupon a Heavenly Voice was heard proclaiming.[The prayer of] this man [R. Akiba] was answered not because he is greater than the other man, but because he is ever forbearing and the other is not.

Pesiqta Rabbati 38 [ed. Buber 165b] (Braude 1968, v. 2, pp. 691-693)

Midrash Harninu

Let our master teach us: If there has been a quarrel between a man and his fellow, how may he obtain forgiveness on the Day of Atonement? Our Masters, using the style and method of the Mishnah, taught as follows: "The Day of Atonement atones for transgression of those things that are between man and God. As for the transgression of those things that are between man and his fellow man, the Day of Atonement does not bring atonement to a man unless he makes peace with his fellow man".

But if he goes to make peace with him, and his fellow man refuses to accept his offer of peace, what is he to do? R. Samuel bar Nahman said: Let him fetch ten men, have them draw up in a line, and in their presence say: "Between me and So-and-so there was a quarrel. I have sought to make peace with him, but he will not listen. Since he remains obdurate, I [in your presence] ask his pardon." And the source of this procedure?

Scripture, which says: Let him draw up a line of men and say: I have sinned, and perverted that which was right, etc. (Job 33:27). When the Holy One, blessed be He, sees that a man humbles himself, He forgives his sins. As long as a man holds on to his arrogance, no remission will be granted him. And if it is your wish to have proof of this statement, then consider the following: As long as Job stood obdurate against his friends and his friends against him, the measure of God's justice was ready to be discharged against them both, for we find Job saying to them: They that are younger than I have me in derision (Job 30:1), and find them replying: With us are both the gray-headed and the very aged men (Job 15:10). But as soon as Job made peace with them and besought mercy for them, in that very instant the Holy One, blessed be He, returned to him, as is said And the Lord returned at the return of Job (Job 42:10). When? When he prayed for his friends (ibid.). Scripture says further, When thou art endued with mercy, He has mercy upon thee (Deut. 13:18). R. Jose, son of a woman of Damascus, said: You may regard your compassion as a sign that God's compassion will follow – whenever you show compassion for your fellow man, the Lord will show compassion for other mortals as well as for you. Abraham is an example: because he procured mercy for Abimelech, having prayed for him, Abraham received his reward at once. Scripture tells us And Abraham prayed unto God; and God healed Abimelech and his wife (Gen. 20:17). And what reward did Abraham receive? Abraham's wife was remembered and she bore him a son, as the verse immediately following tells us: And the Lord remembered Sarah as He had said, and the Lord did unto Sarah as He had spoken (Gen. 21:1).

b. *Baba Qama* 92a

Raba said to Rabbah b. Mari: Whence can be derived the lesson taught by our Rabbis that one who solicits mercy for his fellow while he himself is in need of the same thing, [will be answered first]? – He replied: As it is written: *And the Lord changed the fortune of Job when he prayed for his friends* (Job 42:10). He said to him: You say it is from that text, but I say it is from this text: '*And Abraham prayed unto God and God healed Abimelech and his wife and his maidservants*' (Gen. 20:17), and immediately after it says: *And the Lord remembered Sarah as he had said*, etc. (Gen. 21:1), [i.e.] as Abraham had [prayed and] said regarding Abimelech.

b. Megillah 28a

R. Nehunia b. ha-Kaneh was asked by his disciples: In virtue of what have you reached such a good old age? He replied: Never in my life have I sought respect through the degradation of my fellow, nor has the curse of my fellow gone up with me upon my bed, and I have been generous with my money. 'I have not sought respect through the degradation of my fellow', as illustrated by R. Huna who once was carrying a spade on his shoulder when R. Hana b. Hanilai wanted to take it from him, but he said to him, If you are accustomed to carry in your own town, take it, but if not, I do not want to be paid respect through your degradation. 'Nor did the curse of my fellow go up on my bed with me'. This is illustrated by Mar Zutra, who, when he climbed into his bed said, I forgive all who have vexed me. 'I have been generous with my money', as a Master has said, 'Job was generous with his money; he used to leave with the shopkeeper a perutah of his change'.

b. Berakhot 10a

There were once some highwaymen in the neighbourhood of R. Meir who caused him a great deal of trouble. R. Meir accordingly prayed that they should die. His wife Beruria said to him: How do you make out [that such a prayer should be permitted]? Because it is written *Let hatta'im [sins] cease* (Ps. 104:35)? Is it written *hot'im [sinners]*? It is written *hatta'im*! Further, look at the end of the verse: *and let the wicked men be no more*. Since the sins will cease, there will be no more wicked men! Rather pray for them that they should repent, and there will be no more wicked. He did pray for them, and they repented.

⇨ N. 48

b. Bezah 32b

R. Nathan b. Abba further said in the name of Rab: The rich men of Babylon will go down to Gehenna; for once Shabthai b. Marinus came to Babylon and entreated them to provide him with facilities for trading and they refused this to him; neither did they give him any food. He said: These are the descendants of the 'mixed multitude', for it is written, *And [He will] show thee mercy and have compassion upon thee* (Deut. 13:18), [teaching that] whoever is merciful to his fellow-men is certainly of the children of our father Abraham, and whosoever is not merciful to his fellow-men is certainly not of the children of our father Abraham.

Testament of Joseph 17:1-8 (Charlesworth, v. 1, p. 823)

1 So you see, my children, how many things I endured in order not to bring my brothers into disgrace. 2 You, therefore, love one another and in patient endurance conceal one another's shortcomings. 3 God is delighted by harmony among brothers and by the intention of a kind heart that takes pleasure in goodness. 4 When my brothers came to Egypt they learned that I had returned their money to them, that I did not scorn them, and that I sought to console them. 5 After the death of Jacob, my father, I loved them beyond measure, and everything he had wanted for them I did abundantly in their behalf. 6 I did not permit them to be troubled by the slightest matter, and everything I had under my control I gave to them. 7 Their sons were mine, and mine were as their servants; their life was as my life, and every pain of theirs was my pain; every ailment of theirs was my sickness; their wish was my wish. 8 I did not exalt myself above them arrogantly because of my worldly position of glory, but I was among them as one of the least.

Testament of Joseph 18:1-4 (Charlesworth, v. 1, p. 823)

1 If you live in accord with the Lord's commands, God will exalt you with good things forever. And if anyone wishes to do you harm, you should pray for him, along with doing good, and you will be rescued by the Lord from every evil. 3 Indeed you can see that on account on my humility and patient endurance I took to myself a wife, the daughter of the priest of Heliopolis; a hundred talents of gold were given to me along with her, and my Lord caused them to be my servants. 4 And he also gave me mature beauty, more than those of mature beauty in Israel; he preserved me until old age with strength and beauty. In every way I was like Jacob.

Testament of Benjamin 3:1-6 (Charlesworth, v. 1, pp. 825-6)

1 Now, my children, love the Lord God of heaven and earth; keep his commandments; pattern your life after the good and pious man Joseph. 2 Let your thoughts incline to the good, as you know to be so with me, because he who has the right set of mind sees everything rightly. 3 Fear

the Lord and love your neighbor. Even if the spirits of Beliar seek to derange you with all sorts of wicked oppression, they will not dominate you, any more than they dominated Joseph, my brother. 4 How many men wanted to destroy him, and God looked out for him! For the person who fears God and loves his neighbor cannot be plagued by the spirit of Beliar since he is sheltered by the fear of God. 5 Neither man's schemes not those of animals can prevail over him, for he is aided in living by this; by the love which he has toward his neighbor. 6 Joseph also urged our father to pray for his brothers, that the Lord would not hold them accountable for their sin which they so wickedly committed against him.

Testament of Benjamin **4:1-5** (Charlesworth, v. 1, pp. 826)

1 See then, my children, what is the goal of the good man. Be imitators of him in his goodness because of his compassion, in order that you may wear crowns of glory. 2 For a good man does not have a blind eye, but he is merciful to all, even though they may be sinners. 3 And even if persons plot against him for evil ends, by doing good this man conquers evil, being watched over by God. He loves those who wrong him as he loves his own life. If anyone glorifies himself, he holds no envy. 4 If anyone becomes rich, he is not jealous. If anyone is brave, he praises him. He loves the moderate person; he shows mercy to the impoverished; to the ill he shows compassion; he fears God. 5 He loves the person who has gift of a good spirit as he loves his own life.

Testament of Benjamin **5:1-4** (Charlesworth, v. 1, pp. 826)

1 If your mind is set toward good, even evil men will be at peace with you; the dissolute will respect you and will turn back to the good. The greedy will not only abstain from their passion but will give to the oppressed the things which they covetously hold. 2 If you continue to do good, even the unclean spirits will flee from you and wild animals will fear you. 3 For where someone has within himself respect for good works and has light in the understanding, darkness will slink away from that person. 4 For if anyone wantonly attacks a pious man, he repents, since the pious man shows mercy to the one who abused him, and maintains silence. And if anyone betrays a righteous man, the righteous man prays. Even though for a brief time he may be humbled, later he will appear far more illustrious, as happened with Joseph, my brother.

b. Baba Qama 93a

R. Abbahu said: A man should always strive to be rather of the persecuted than of the persecutors as there is none among the birds more persecuted than doves and pigeons, and yet Scripture made them [alone] eligible for the altar.

b. Hagigah 5a

Then My anger shall be kindled against them in that day, and I will forsake them, and I will hide My face from them (Deut. 31:17). R. Bardela b. Tabyumi said that Rab said: To whomever 'hiding of the face' does not apply is not one of them (People of Israel) to whomever [the words] and they shall be devoured does not apply is not one of them.

b. Yebamoth 79a

This nation is distinguished by three characteristics: They are merciful, bashful and benevolent. 'Merciful', for it is written, *And shew thee mercy, and have compassion upon thee, and multiply thee* (Deut. 13:18). 'Bashful', for it is written, *That His fear may be before you* (Ex. 20:17). 'Benevolent', for it is written, *That he may command his children and his household* etc. (Gen. 18:19). Only he who cultivates these three characteristics is fit to join this nation.

Mekhilta de-Rabbi Ishmael, Shira 3 [on Exod. 15:2] (Lauterbach, v. 2, p. 25)

And I will glorify him. <...> Abba Saul says: O be like Him! Just as he is gracious and merciful, so be thou also gracious and merciful.

b. Shabbath 133b

Abba Saul interpreted, *and I will be like him* (cf. Ex. 15:2): be thou like Him: just as He is gracious and compassionate, so be thou gracious and compassionate.

⇨ N. 49

SIRACH 38:9-15

9 My son, when you are sick do not be negligent, but pray to the Lord, and he will heal you. 10 Give up your faults and direct your hands aright,

and cleanse your heart from all sin. 11 Offer a sweet-smelling sacrifice, and a memorial portion of fine flour, and pour oil on your offering, as much as you can afford. 12 And give the physician his place, for the Lord created him; let him not leave you, for there is need of him. 13 There is a time when success lies in the hands of physicians, 14 for they too will pray to the Lord that he should grant them success in diagnosis and in healing, for the sake of preserving life. 15 He who sins before his Maker, may he fall into the care of a physician.

4QPrayer of Nabonidus, **frags. 1-3** [4Q242] (García Martínez– Tigchelaar, v. 1, p. 487)

1 Words of the pr[ay]er which Nabonidus, king of [the] la[nd of Baby]lon, the [great] king, prayed [when he was afflicted] 2 by a malignant inflammation, by decree of the G[od Most Hi]gh, in Teiman. [I, Nabonidus,] was afflicted [by a malignant inflammation] 3 for seven years, and was banished far [from men, until I prayed to the God Most High] 4 and an exorcist forgave my sin. He was a Je[w] fr[om the exiles, who said to me:] 5 "Make a proclamation in writing, so that glory, exal[tation and hono]ur be given to the name of [the] G[od Most High". And I wrote as follows: "When] 6 I was afflicted by a ma[lignant] inflammation [...] in Teiman, [by decree of the God Most High,] 7 [I] prayed for seven years [to all] the gods of silver and gold, [of bronze and iron,] 8 of wood, of stone and of clay, because [I thoug]ht that t[hey were] gods [...]

m. Baba Qama **8:7**

See above, n. 47.

⇨ N. **50**

m. Yoma **8:9** (Danby, p. 172)

If a man said, 'I will sin and repent, and sin again and repent', he will be given no chance to repent. [If he said,] 'I will sin and the Day of Atonement will effect atonement', then the Day of Atonement effects no atonement. For transgressions that are between man and God the Day of Atonement effects atonement, but for transgressions that are between a man and his fellow the Day of Atonement effects atonement only if he has appeased his fellow. This did R. Eleazar b. Azariah expound: *From all your sins shall ye be clean before the Lord* (Lev. 16:30) – for transgressions that are between man and God the Day of Atonement effects atonement; but for transgressions that are between a man and his fellow the Day of Atonement effects atonement only if he has appeased his fellow.

***m. Baba Qama* 8:7**

See above, n. 47.

***Sifra*, Acharei Mot 8** [on Lev. 16:30] (Neusner 1988, p. 45)

For transgressions done between a person and the Omnipresent, the Day of Atonement atones. For transgressions between one person and another, the Day of Atonement atones only if the person will regain the good will of the friend. This exegesis did R. Eleazar b. Azaria present, "From all your sins shall you be clean before the Lord" (Lev. 16:30): For transgressions done between a person and the Omnipresent, the Day of Atonement atones. For transgressions between one person and another, the Day of Atonement atones only if the person will regain the good will of the friend.

***m. Baba Metzia* 4:7** (Danby, p. 354)

Four pieces of silver count as defrauding; two pieces of silver suffice in a claim [for repayment] and one *perutah*'s worth in an admission of indebtedness. In five cases is a *perutah* prescribed: in an admission of indebtedness the admission must be to [no less than] a *perutah*'s worth; a woman may be betrothed with a *perutah*'s worth; he that derives a *perutah*'s worth of benefit from what belongs to the Temple is subject to the law of Sacrilege; if a man found lost property of a *perutah*'s worth he must proclaim it; if a man robbed his fellow of a *perutah*'s worth and swore [falsely] to him [and would make restitution] he must take it and give it to him even [if his fellow had gone] as far as Media.

***b. Rosh Hashanah* 17b**

Come and hear [again]: 'Bluria the proselyte put this question to Rabban Gamaliel: It is written in your Law, [she said], *who lifteth not up the countenance* (Deut. 10:17), and it is also written, *The Lord shall lift up his countenance upon thee* (Num. 6:26). R. Jose the priest joined the conversation and said to her: I will give you a parable which will illustrate the matter. A man lent his neighbour a maneh and fixed a time for payment in the presence of the king, while the other swore to pay him by the life of the king. When the time arrived he did not pay him, and he went to excuse himself to the king. The king, however, said to him: The wrong done to me I excuse you, but go and obtain forgiveness from your neighbour. So here: one text speaks of offences committed by a man against God, the other of offences committed by a man against his fellow man.

b. Yoma 87a

R. Abba had a complaint against R. Jeremiah. He [R. Jeremiah] went and sat down at the door of R. Abba and as the maid poured out water, some drops fell upon his head. Then he said: They have made a dung-heap of me, and he cited this passage about himself: *He raiseth up the poor out of the dust* (1Sam. 2:8). R. Abba heard that and came out towards him, saying: Now, I must come forth to appease you, as it is written: 'Go, humble thyself and urge thy neighbour'. When R. Zera had any complaint against any man, he would repeatedly pass by him, showing himself to him, so that he may come forth to [pacify] him. Rab once had a complaint against a certain butcher, and when on the eve of the Day of Atonement he [the butcher] did not come to him, he said: I shall go to him to pacify him. R. Huna met him and asked: Whither are you going, Sir? He said, To pacify So-and-so. He thought: Abba is about to cause one's death. He went there and remained standing before him [the butcher], who was sitting and chopping an [animal's] head. He raised his eyes and saw him [Rab], then said: You are Abba, go away. I will have nothing to do with you. Whilst he was chopping the head, a bone flew off, struck his throat, and killed him.

⇨ N. 52

1 CHR 29:10-11

10 Therefore David blessed the Lord in the presence of all the assembly; and David said: "Blessed art thou, O Lord, the God of Israel our father, for ever and ever. 11 Thine, O Lord, is the greatness, and the power, and the glory, and the victory, and the majesty; for all that is in the heavens and in the earth is thine; thine is the kingdom, O Lord, and thou art exalted as head above all."

Targum of Chronicles to 1Chr 29:10-11 (McIvor, p. 138)

10 Then David blessed the Lord in the *sight* of the whole assembly and David said: "Blessed are you, O Lord, the God of Israel, our father, from *this* age and to the age *to come.* 11 Yours, O Lord, is the greatness, *for with great power you created the world,* and the might, *for you brought our fathers out of Egypt with many mighty acts and brought them across the sea, and you were revealed in* splendor *upon the mountain of Sinai, with bands of angels, to give the law to your people.* You gave victories over Amalek, Sihon, Og, and the kings of the Canaanites; *in* the majesty *of your glory you caused the sun to stand still in Gibeon and the moon in the plain of Ajalon, until your people, the house of Israel, were avenged on those who hated them.* For all *these things are the works of your hand,* in heaven and on earth, *and you have authority over them and sustain everything which is in heaven an everything which is on earth.* Yours, O Lord, is the dominion *in the firmament,* and you are exalted above all *the angels that are in heaven and above all* those *who are appointed* as leaders *on earth.*

t. Berakhot 3:7

See above, n. 30.

b. Berakhot 29b

Our Rabbis taught: One who passes through a place infested with beasts or bands of robbers says a short Tefillah. What is a short Tefillah? – R. Eliezer says: Do Thy will in heaven above, and grant relief to them that fear Thee below and do that which is good in Thine eyes. Blessed art Thou, O Lord, who hearest prayer.

⇨ **N. 55**

11QPsalms^a XXIV 3-14 [11Q5] (García Martínez–Tigchelaar, v. 2, p. 1177)

3 YHWH, I call to you, listen to me; I extend my hands 4 to your holy dwelling; bend your ear and grant my plea, and what I ask, 5 do not deny me; build up my soul and do not demolish it; and do not forsake it in the presence of 6 wicked people. May the judge of truth turn away from me the recompenses of evil. O YHWH, 7 do not judge me by my sin because

no-one living is just in your presence. 8 Instruct me, YHWH, in your law, and teach me your precepts 9 so that many hear your deeds and nations may honour your glory. 10 Remember me and do not forget me or lead me into difficulties too great for me. 11 Remove the sin of my childhood from me and may my offences not be remembered against me. 12 Purify me, O YHWH, from evil plague, and may it stop coming back to /me/; dry up 13 its roots from me, may its lea[ve]s not become green in me. Glory are you, YHWH, 14 therefore my plea is achieved in your presence.

11QPs^a Plea XIX [11Q5] (García Martínez–Tigchelaar, v. 2, p. 1175)

1 For a maggot can not give you thanks, and a worm can not tell of your kindness. 2 The living, the living *Blank* can praise you, even can praise you all those who stumble when you make known 3 your kindness to them, and your justice you instruct to them. For in your hand is the soul of every 4 living being, the breath of all *Blank* flesh you have given. Deal with us, YHWH, 5 according to your goodness, according to the abundance of your compassion and the abundance of your just acts. YHWH has heard 6 the voice of those loving his Name and has not denied them his kindness. 7 Blessed be YHWH who performs just deeds, who crowns his devout 8 with kindness and compassion. My soul cried out to extol your Name, to give thanks with shouts 9 for your kind deeds, to proclaim your faithfulness; to the praise of you there is no end. I was near to death 10 because of my sins, and my iniquities have sold me to Sheol, but you, 11 YHWH, saved me, according to the abundance of your compassion and the abundance of your just acts. I, too, 12 have loved your Name and I have found refuge in your shelter. When I recall your power my heart is strengthened, 13 and I rely on your kind deeds. Forgive my sins, YHWH, 14 and cleanse me from my iniquity. Bestow on me a spirit of faith and knowledge. Let me not stumble 15 in transgression. Let not Satan rule over me, nor an evil spirit; let neither pain nor evil purpose 16 take possession of my bones. Because you, YHWH, are my praise and in you I hope 17 all day. May my brothers be happy with me and my father's house, who are baffled by your favour 18 ... [... for e]ver I shall rejoice in you.

b. Berakhot 60b

On going to bed one says from 'Hear, oh Israel' to 'And it shall come to pass if ye hearken diligently'. Then he says: 'Blessed is He who causes the bands of sleep to fall upon my eyes and slumber on my eyelids, and gives light to the apple of the eye. May it be Thy will, O Lord, my God, to make me lie down in peace, and set my portion in Thy law and accustom me to the performance of religious duties, but do not accustom me to transgression, and bring me not into sin, or into iniquity, or into temptation, or into contempt. And may the good inclination have sway over me and let not the evil inclination have sway over me. And deliver me from evil hap and sore diseases, and let not evil dreams and evil thoughts disturb me, and may my couch be flawless before Thee, and enlighten mine eyes lest I sleep the sleep of death. Blessed art Thou, oh Lord, who givest light to the whole world in Thy glory.'

⇨ N. 56

4QBer^a 7 II [4Q286] (García Martínez–Tigchelaar, v. 2, pp. 647-649)

1 (of) the Community Council shall say, all together: "Amen. Amen." *Blank* And afterwards [t]he[y] shall damn Belial 2 and all his guilty lot. Starting to speak, they shall say: "Accursed be [Be]lial in his hostile [pl]an, 3 and may he be damned in his guilty service. And cursed be all the spir[its of] his [l]ot in their wicked plan, 4 and may they be damned in their plans of [f]oul impurity. For [they are the lo]t of darkness, and their visitation (will lead) 5 for the everlasting pit. Amen. Amen. *Blank* And cursed be the wick[ed ...] (of) his rule, and damned be 6 all the sons of Beli[al] in all the iniquities of their office until their annihilation [... Amen. Amen.] *Blank* 7 And [cursed be ... the ange]l of the pit and the sp[irits of des]truction in al[l] the designs of [your] g[uilty] inclination 8 [...] and [your] wicked counsel. [And da]mned be you in the r[u]l[e of] 9 [... and in the dominion ...] with all [...] 10 [and with the dis]grace of destruction w[ithout remnant, without forgive]ness, by the destructive wrath of [God ...] Amen. Amen. 11 [And cursed be a]ll who carry out [their ev]il [designs,] and those who implant wickedness [in their hearts, to plot] 12 [against the covenant of Go]d and to [...] and to alter the prece[pts of the law] 13 [...] ... [...]

4QVisions of Amram^b ar [4Q544] (García Martínez–Tigchelaar, v. 2, pp. 1087-1089)

Frag. 1. <...> 10 in my vision, the vision of the dream. *Blank* And behold, two were quarrelling over me and they said: [...] 11 and they entered into a great debate over me. And I asked them: "Who are you, that have recei[ved control and rule over me?" And they replied to me: "We] 12 [have received] control and we rule over all the sons of Adam." And they said to me: "Which of us do you [choose to be ruled?" I raised my eyes and saw] 13 [that one] of them had a dre[ad]ful appearance [like the pesti]lence and his [cl]o[th]ing was coloured and obscured by darkness [...] 14 [And I looked at the other,] and behold [...] in his appearance and his face was smiling and [he was covered with ...]

Frag. 2. 1 [... I] rule over you [...] 2 [...] this [Wathcer,] who is he? And he said to me: "This one is ca[lled ...] 3 [...] and Melki-resha'. *Blank* And I said: "My Lord: What is the ru[ling ...] 4 [... da]rk and all his work is d[a]rk, and in darkness he [...] 5 [... yo]u see. And he rules over all darkness, and I [...] 6 [... from the] upper up to the lower regions, I rule over all that is bright and al[l ...]

Frag. 3. 1 [... and I] have been made ruler [over all the sons of lig]ht. And I asked him [and said to him: "What ...] 2 [..." He replied and sa]id to me: three names [...]

4QCurses [=4Q280] (García Martínez–Tigchelaar, v. 2, p. 637)

1 [... May God separate him] for evil from the amongst the sons of li[ght, because of his straying from following him. *Blank*?] 2 [And they will say: Accur]sed are you, Melki-resha', in all the pla[ns of your blameworthy inclination. May] 3 God [hand you over] to terror by the hand of those carrying out acts of vengeance. May God not be merciful [when] you entreat him. [May he lift the countenance of his anger] 4 upon you for a curse. May there be no peace for you by the mouth of those who intercede. [Be cursed,] 5 without a remnant; and be damned, without a survivor. And accursed be those who act [...] 6 and those who fulfil your plan in their hearts to plot against the covenant of God [... and against] 7 [the word]s of those seeing [his] tru[th. And any]one who declines to enter [the covenant of God ...]

11QPs^a Plea XIX 15-16

See above, n. 55.

Apocryphon of James 4:28-31 (Elliott, p. 676)

And I answered and said to him, 'Lord, we can obey you if you wish, for we have forsaken our fathers and our mothers and our villages and have followed you. Give us the means, [then], not to be tempted by the evil devil.'

b. Berakhot 16b

Rabbi on concluding his prayer added the following: May it be Thy will, O Lord our God, and God of our fathers, to deliver us from the impudent and from impudence, from an evil man, from evil hap, from the evil impulse, from an evil companion, from an evil neighbour, and from the destructive Accuser, from a hard lawsuit and from a hard opponent, whether he is a son of the covenant or not a son of the covenant! [Thus did he pray] although guards were appointed to protect Rabbi.

⇨ N. 57

Didache 8:2

See above, n. 8.

Didache 10:5 (Lake, p. 325)

Remember, Lord, thy Church, to deliever it from all evil and to make it perfect in thy love, and gather it together in its holiness from the four winds to thy kingdom which thou hast prepared for it. For thine is the power and the glory for ever.

Seventh Benediction of *Amida* (Birnbaum, p. 164)

Look upon out affliction and champion our cause; redeem us speedily for thy name's sake, for thou art a mighty Redeemer. Blessed art thou, Redeemer of Israel.

b. Berakhot 60b

On going to bed one says from 'Hear, oh Israel' to 'And it shall come to pass if ye hearken diligently'. Then he says: 'Blessed is He who causes the bands of sleep to fall upon my eyes and slumber on my eyelids, and gives light to the apple of the eye. May it be Thy will, O Lord, my God, to make me lie down in peace, and set my portion in Thy law and accustom me to the performance of religious duties, but do not accustom me to transgression; and bring me not into sin, or into iniquity, or into temptation, or into contempt. And may the good inclination have sway over me and let not the evil inclination have sway over me. And deliver me from evil hap and sore diseases, and let not evil dreams and evil thoughts disturb me, and may my couch be flawless before Thee, and enlighten mine eyes lest I sleep the sleep of death. Blessed art Thou, oh Lord, who givest light to the whole world in Thy glory.'

<...> When he washes his face he should say: 'Blessed is He who has removed the bands of sleep from mine eyes and slumber from mine eyes. And may it be Thy will O Lord, my God, to habituate me to Thy law and make me cleave to Thy commandments, and do not bring me into sin, or into iniquity, or into temptation, or into contempt, and bend my inclination to be subservient unto Thee, and remove me far from a bad man and a bad companion, and make me cleave to the good inclination and to a good companion in Thy world, and let me obtain this day and every day grace, favour, and mercy in Thine eyes, and in the eyes of all that see me, and show lovingkindness unto me. Blessed art Thou, O Lord, who bestowest lovingkindness upon Thy people Israel'.

b. Berakhot 16b

See above, n. 56.

Testament of Asher 1:3, 5 (Charlesworth, v. 1, pp. 816-817)

3 God has granted two ways to the sons of men, two mind-sets, two lines of action, two models, and two goals. <...> 5 The two ways are good and evil; concerning them are two dispositions within our breasts that choose between them.

⇨ N. **60**

EZEK 36:23

And I will vindicate the holiness of my great name, which has been profaned among the nations, and which you have profaned among them; and the nations will know that I am the Lord, says the Lord God, when through you I vindicate my holiness before their eyes.

Targum of Isaiah 24:23 (Chilton, p. 49)

Then *those who serve* the moon will be *ashamed* and *those who worship* the sun will be *humiliated*; for the *kingdom* of the Lord of hosts *will be revealed* on *the* Mount *of* Zion an in Jerusalem and before the elders *of* his *people in* glory.

Targum of Isaiah 31:4-5 (Chilton, p. 62)

4 For thus the Lord said to me, As *a* lion or *a* young lion *roars over its* prey, and, when a band of shepherds *are appointed* against it, it is not *broken* up at their shouting or *checked* at their *tumult*, so *the kingdom of* the Lord of hosts will *be revealed* to *settle* upon *the* Mount *of* Zion and upon its hill. 5 Like *the* bird *soars*, so the *might of* the Lord *of hosts* will *be revealed* over Jerusalem; he will protect and deliver, *rescue* and *remove*.

Targum of Isaiah 40:9 (Chilton, p. 77)

Get you up to a high mountain, *prophets who* herald good tidings *to* Zion; lift up your voice with *force, you who* herald good tidings to Jerusalem, lift up, fear not; say to the cities *of the house* of Judah, "*The kingdom of* your *God is revealed!*"

Targum of Isaiah 52:7 (Chilton, p. 102)

How beautiful upon the mountains *of the land of Israel* are the feet of him who announces, who publishes peace, who announces good tidings, who publishes salvation, who says to *the congregation of* Zion, "*The* king*dom of* your God *is revealed.*"

MICAH 4:7

And the lame I will make the remnant; and those who were cast off, a strong nation; and the Lord will reign over them in Mount Zion from this time forth and for evermore.

⇨ N. **61**

m. Berakhot 2:2 (Danby, p. 3)

R. Joshua b. Karha said: Why does the section *Hear, O Israel* precede *And it shall come to pass if ye shall hearken*? – so that a man may first take upon him the yoke of the kingdom of heaven and afterward take upon him the yoke of the commandments. [And why does the section]

And it shall come to pass if ye shall hearken precede *And the Lord spake unto Moses?* Because *And it shall come to pass if ye shall hearken* applies both day and by night, but *And the Lord spake unto Moses* applies by day only.

m. Berakhot 2:5 (Danby, pp. 3-4)

A bridegroom is exempt from reciting the *Shema'* on the first night, or until the close of the [next] Sabbath if he has not consummated the marriage. Once when Rabban Gamliel married he recited the *Shema'* on the first night. His disciples said to him, 'Master, didst thou not teach us that a bridegroom is exempt from reciting the *Shema'* on the first night?' He said to them: 'I will not hearken to you to cast off from myself the yoke of the kingdom of heaven even for a moment.'

b. Berakhot 14b–15a

R. Johanan also said: If one desires to accept upon himself the yoke of the kingdom of heaven in the most complete manner, he should consult nature and wash his hands and put on tefillin and recite the Shema' and say the tefillah: this is the complete acknowledgment of the kingdom of heaven.

m. Avot 2:4 (Danby, p. 448)

He (i.e. Rabban Gamaliel) used to say: Do his will as if it was thy will that he may do thy will as if it was his will. Make thy will of none effect before his will that he may make the will of others of none effect before thy will.

Mekhilta de-Rabbi Ishmael, Shira 10 [on Exod. 15:18] (Lauterbach, v. 2, pp. 79-80)

The Lord shall reign for ever and ever. R. Jose the Galilean says: Had the Israelites at the sea said: "The lord is king for ever and ever," no nation or kingdom would ever have ruled over them. But they said: "The Lord shall reign for ever and ever" – in the future – surely, over Thy people, Thy herd, Thy flock, the flock of Thy pasture, the seed of Abraham Thy friend, the children of Isaac Thine only one, the congregation of Jacob, Thy first-born son, the vine which thou didst pluck up out of Egypt and the stock which Thy right hand hath planted.

b. Berakhot **29b**

See above, n. 30.

⇨ N. 63

SIRACH **27:30–28:7**

See above, n. 43.

⇨ N. 67

Gospel of Thomas **6, 14**

See above, n. 7.

b. Rosh Hashanah **18a–18b**

Why should they not also go forth to report Tammuz and Tebeth seeing that R. Hanah b. Bizna has said in the name of R. Simeon the Saint: 'What is the meaning of the verse, *Thus had said the Lord of Hosts: The fast of the fourth month and the fast of the fifth and the fast of the seventh and the fast of the tenth shall be to the house of Judah joy and gladness* (Zech. 8:19)? The prophet calls these days both days of fasting and days of joy, signifying that when there is peace they shall be for joy and gladness, but if there is not peace they shall be fast days'! – R. Papa replied: What it means is this: When there is peace they shall be for joy and gladness; if there is persecution, they shall be fast days; if there is no persecution but yet not peace, then those who desire may fast and those who desire need not fast. If that is the case, the ninth of Ab also [should be optional]? – R. Papa replied: The ninth of Ab is in a different category, because several misfortunes happened on it, as a Master has said: On the ninth of Ab the Temple was destroyed both the first time and the second time, and Bethar was captured and the city [Jerusalem] was ploughed.

Testament of Joseph **4:7-8** (Charlesworth, v. 1, p. 820)

7 She was consumed with jealousy, wanting to fulfill her desire. 8 But I devoted myself the more to fasting and prayer that the Lord might rescue me from her.

***Testament of Benjamin* 1:2-6** (Charlesworth, v. 1, p. 820)

2 Just as Isaac was born of Abraham in his old age, so I was born to Jacob. 3 Since Rachel, my mother, died as she was bearing me, I had no milk from her, but was nursed instead by Bilhah, her maid servant. 4 For after Rachel bore Joseph she was sterile for twelve years; she prayed to the Lord, with fasting, 5 and conceived and gave birth to me. My father loved Rachel exceedingly, and prayed that he might see two sons born from her. 6 For this reason I was called Benjamin, that is 'son of days'.

1 Sam 31:11-13

11 But when the inhabitants of Jabeshgilead heard what the Philistines had done to Saul, 12 all the valiant men arose, and went all night, and took the body of Saul and the bodies of his sons from the wall of Bethshan; and they came to Jabesh and burnt them there. 13 And they took their bones and buried them under the tamarisk tree in Jabesh, and fasted seven days.

2 Sam 3:30-35

30 So Joab and Abishai his brother slew Abner, because he had killed their brother Asahel in the battle at Gibeon. 31 Then David said to Joab and to all the people who were with him, "Rend your clothes, and gird on sackcloth, and mourn before Abner." And King David followed the bier. 32 They buried Abner at Hebron; and the king lifted up his voice and wept at the grave of Abner; and all the people wept. 33 And the king lamented for Abner, saying, "Should Abner die as a fool dies? 34 Your hands were not bound, your feet were not fettered; as one falls before the wicked you have fallen." And all the people wept again over him. 35 Then all the people came to persuade David to eat bread while it was yet day; but David swore, saying, "God do so to me and more also, if I taste bread or anything else till the sun goes down!"

1 Sam 14:24

And the men of Israel were distressed that day; for Saul laid an oath on the people, saying, "Cursed be the man who eats food until it is evening and I am avenged on my enemies." So none of the people tasted food.

2 Sam 12:16-17

16 David therefore besought God for the child; and David fasted, and went in and lay all night upon the ground. 17 And the elders of his house stood beside him, to raise him from the ground; but he would not, nor did he eat food with them.

Jonah 3:5-10

5 And the people of Nineveh believed God; they proclaimed a fast, and put on sackcloth, from the greatest of them to the least of them. 6 Then tidings reached the king of Nineveh, and he arose from his throne, removed his robe, and covered himself with sackcloth, and sat in ashes. 7 And he made proclamation and published through Nineveh, "By the decree of the king and his nobles: Let neither man nor beast, herd nor flock, taste anything; let them not feed, or drink water, 8 but let man and beast be covered with sackcloth, and let them cry mightily to God; yea, let every one turn from his evil way and from the violence which is in his hands. 9 Who knows, God may yet repent and turn from his fierce anger, so that we perish not?" 10 When God saw what they did, how they turned from their evil way, God repented of the evil which he had said he would do to them; and he did not do it.

Isa 58:3-7

3 'Why have we fasted, and thou seest it not? Why have we humbled ourselves, and thou takest no knowledge of it?' Behold, in the day of your fast you seek your own pleasure, and oppress all your workers. 4 Behold, you fast only to quarrel and to fight and to hit with wicked fist. Fasting like yours this day will not make your voice to be heard on high. 5 Is such the fast that I choose, a day for a man to humble himself? Is it to bow down his head like a rush, and to spread sackcloth and ashes under him? Will you call this a fast, and a day acceptable to the Lord? 6 "Is not this the fast that I choose: to loose the bonds of wickedness, to undo the thongs of the yoke, to let the oppressed go free, and to break every yoke? 7 Is it not to share your bread with the hungry, and bring the homeless poor into your house; when you see the naked, to cover him, and not to hide yourself from your own flesh?"

Jer 14:10-12

10 Thus says the Lord concerning this people: "They have loved to wander thus, they have not restrained their feet; therefore the Lord does not accept them, now he will remember their iniquity and punish their sins." 11 The Lord said to me: "Do not pray for the welfare of this people. 12 Though they fast, I will not hear their cry, and though they offer burnt offering and cereal offering, I will not accept them; but I will consume them by the sword, by famine, and by pestilence."

Zech 7:5-7

5 "Say to all the people of the land and the priests, When you fasted and mourned in the fifth month and in the seventh, for these seventy years, was it for me that you fasted? 6 And when you eat and when you drink, do you not eat for yourselves and drink for yourselves? 7 When Jerusalem was inhabited and in prosperity, with her cities round about her, and the South and the lowland were inhabited, were not these the words which the Lord proclaimed by the former prophets?"

Sirach 34:25-26

See above, n. 7.

Testament of Asher 2:8 (Charlesworth, v. 1, p. 817)

Someone else commits adultery and is sexually promiscuous, yet is abstemious in his eating. While fasting, he is committing evil deeds. Through the power of his wealth he ravages many, and yet in spite of his excessive evil, he performs the commandments.

Apocalypse of Elijah 1:18-19 (Charlesworth, v. 1, p. 738)

18 Let the pure one fast, but whenever the one who fasts is not pure he has angered the Lord and also the angels. 19 And he has grieved his soul, gathering up wrath for himself for the day of wrath.

m. Ta'anit 2:1 (Danby, p. 195)

How did they order the matter on the [last seven] days of fasting? They used to bring out the Ark into the open space in the town and put wood-ashes on the Ark and on the heads of the President and the Father of the court; and every one took [of the ashes] and put them on his head. The eldest among them uttered before them words of admonition: Brethren, it is not written of the men of Nineveh that 'God saw their sackcloth and their fasting,' but *And God saw their works that they turned from their evil way* (Jonah 3.10); and in [his] protest [the Prophet] says, *Rend your heart and not your garments* (Joel 2:13).

t. Ta'anit 1:8 (Neusner 2002, v. 1, pp. 621-622)

The manner of fasting: How [was it done]? They bring forth the ark into the street of the town and put wood-ashes on the ark. And they did not change guards for it. One person sits and watches it all day long.
The eldest among them makes a speech of admonition. "My children, let a person be ashamed before his fellow, but let a person not be ashamed on account of what he has done. It is better for a person to be ashamed before his fellow, but let him and his children not suffer from famine. And so it says, *Why have we fasted, and you see it not? Why have we humbled ourselves, and you take no knowledge of it* (Isa 58:3)? What does [Scripture] answer them? *Behold, you fast only to quarrel and to fight and to hit with wicked fist. Fasting like yours this day will not make your voice to be heard on high. Is such the fast that I choose, a day for a man to humble himself? Is it to bow down his head like a rush, and to spread sackcloth and ashes under him? Will you call this a fast, and a day acceptable to the Lord?* (Isa 58:4-5). But what is the fast which I want? *Is not this the fast that I choose: to loose the bonds of wickedness, to undo the thongs of the yoke, to let the oppressed go free, and to break every yoke* (Isa 58:6). Now if there was a dead creeping thing in someone's hand, even if he immersed himself in a fountain or in all of the waters of creation, he will never, ever be clean. [But if] he tossed the dead creeping thing from his hand, then he gains the benefit of immersion in [only] forty *seahs* of water."

b. Ta'anit 16a

[And this is what he says], 'Our brethren, neither sackcloth nor fastings are effective but only penitence and good deeds, for we find that of the men of Nineveh Scripture does not say, And God saw their sackcloth and their fasting, but, *God saw their works that they turned from their evil way* (Jonah 3:10).'

b. Ta'anit 22b

THE ALARM IS SOUNDED ON THE SABBATH etc. Our Rabbis have taught: When a city is surrounded by hostile Gentiles, or threatened with inundation by the river, or when a ship is foundering in the sea, or when an individual is being pursued by Gentiles or robbers or by an evil spirit, the alarm is sounded [even] on the Sabbath; and on account of all these an individual may afflict himself by fasting. R. Jose says: An individual may not afflict himself by fasting lest thereby he come to need the help of his fellow men and it may be that they will not have mercy upon him. Rab Judah said in the name of Rab: R. Jose's reason is because it is written, *And became a living soul* (Gen. 2:7); Scripture thereby implies, [God says], Keep alive the soul which I gave you.

b. Baba Bathra 60b

Our Rabbis taught: When the Temple was destroyed for the second time, large numbers in Israel became ascetics, binding themselves neither to eat meat nor to drink wine. R. Joshua got into conversation with them and said to them: My sons, why do you not eat meat nor drink wine? They replied: Shall we eat flesh which used to be brought as an offering on the altar, now that this altar is in abeyance? Shall we drink wine which used to be poured as a libation on the altar, but now no longer? He said to them: If that is so, we should not eat bread either, because the meal offerings have ceased. They said: [That is so, and] we can manage with fruit. We should not eat fruit either, [he said,] because there is no longer an offering of firstfruits. Then we can manage with other fruits [they said]. But, [he said,] we should not drink water, because there is no longer any ceremony of the pouring of water. To this they could find no answer, so he said to them: My sons, come and listen to me. Not to mourn at all is impossible, because the blow has fallen. To mourn overmuch is also impossible, because we do not impose on the community a hardship which the majority cannot endure, as it is written, *Ye are cursed with a curse, yet ye rob me [of the tithe], even this whole nation* (Malachi 3:9). The Sages therefore have ordained thus. A man may stucco his house, but he should leave a little bare. (How much should this be? R. Joseph says, A cubit square; to which R. Hisda adds that it must be by the door.) A man can prepare a full-course banquet, but he should leave out an item or two. (What should this be? R. Papa says: The hors d'oeuvre of salted fish.) A woman can put on all her ornaments, but leave off one or two. (What should this be? Rab said: [Not to remove] the hair on the temple.) For so it says, *If I forget thee, O Jerusalem, let my right hand forget, let my tongue cleave to the roof of my mouth if I remember thee not, if I prefer not Jerusalem above my chief joy* (Ps. 137:5-6).

⇨ N. **68**

Gospel of Thomas **6, 14**

See above, n. 7.

m. Berakhot **9:5** (Danby, p. 10)

Man is bound to bless [God] for the evil even as he blesses [God] for the good, for it is written, *And thou shalt love the Lord thy God with all thy heart and with all thy soul and with all thy might* (Deut. 6:5). *With all thy heart* (*lebab*) – with both thine impulses, thy good impulse and thine evil impulse; *and with all thy soul* – even if he take away thy soul; *and with all thy might* (*meodeka*) – for whichever measure (*middah o middah*) he measures out to thee, do thou give him thanks (*modeh*) exceedingly (*bimeod meod*).

Sifre on Deuteronomy **41** [on Deut 11:13]

See above, n. 24.

b. Sukkah **49b**

The School of R. Anan taught: It is written, *The roundings of thy thighs* (Cant. 7:1). Why are the words of the Torah compared to the thigh? To teach you that just as the thigh is hidden, so should the words of the Torah be hidden, and this is the import of what R. Eleazar said, What is the implication of the text, *It hath been told thee, O man, what is good, and what the Lord doth require of thee: Only to do justly, and to love mercy, and to walk humbly with thy God* (Mic. 6:8)? 'To do justly' means [to act in accordance with] justice; 'to love mercy' refers to acts of loving kindness' 'and to walk humbly with thy God' refers to attending to funerals and dowering a bride for her wedding. Now can we not make a deduction a fortiori: If in matters which are normally performed publicly the Torah enjoins 'to walk humbly', how much more so in matters that are normally done privately?

R. Eleazar stated, Greater is he who performs charity than [he who offers] all the sacrifices, for it is said, *To do charity and justice is more acceptable to the Lord than sacrifice* (Prov. 21:3).

R. Eleazar further stated, *Gemiluth Hasadim* is greater than charity, for it is said, *Sow to yourselves according to your charity, but reap according to your hesed* (Hos. 10:12); if a man sows, it is doubtful whether he will eat [the harvest] or not, but when a man reaps, he will certainly eat. R. Eleazar further stated, The reward of charity depends entirely upon the extent of the kindness in it, for it is said, '*Sow to yourselves according to charity, but reap according to the kindness*'.

Our Rabbis taught, In three respects is *Gemiluth Hasadim* superior to charity: charity can be done only with one's money, but *Gemiluth Hasadim* can be done with one's person and one's money. Charity can be given only to the poor, *Gemiluth Hasadim* both to the rich and the poor. Charity can be given to the living only, *Gemiluth Hasadim* can be done both to the living and to the dead.

R. Eleazar further stated, He who executes charity and justice is regarded as though he had filled all the world with kindness, for it is said, *He loveth charity and justice, the earth is full of the lovingkindness of the Lord* (Ps. 33:5). But lest you say that whoever wishes to do good succeeds without difficulty, Scripture expressly says, *How precious is Thy lovingkindness, O God* etc. (Ps. 36:8). As one might say that this applies also to a man who fears God, Scripture expressly says, *But the lovingkindness of the Lord is from everlasting to everlasting upon them that fear Him* (Ps. 103:17).

R. Hama b. Papa stated, Every man who is endowed with grace is without doubt a God-fearing man, for it is said, '*But the lovingkindness of the Lord is from everlasting to everlasting to them that fear Him.*' R. Eleazar further stated, What is the purport of what was written, *She openeth her mouth with wisdom, and the Torah of lovingkindness is on her tongue* (Prov. 31:26)? Is there then a Torah of lovingkindness and a Torah which is not of lovingkindness? But the fact is that Torah [which is studied] for its own sake is a 'Torah of lovingkindness', whereas Torah [which is studied] for an ulterior motive is a Torah which is not of lovingkindness.

Some there are who say, Torah [which is studied] in order [subsequently] to teach it is a 'Torah of lovingkindness', but Torah [which is] not [studied subsequently] to teach it is a Torah which is not of lovingkindness.

⇨ N. 69

***t. Peah* 4:19** (Neusner 2002, v. 1, p. 75)

Charity and righteous deeds outweigh all other commandments in the Torah. Nevertheless, charity [can be given only to the] living, but righteous deeds [can be performed for the] living and the dead. Charity [is given only] to the poor people, but righteous deeds [are done for both] poor and rich people. Charity [is given as an aid for a poor person's] finances, but righteous deeds [aid both a poor person's] finances and his physical needs.

***Mekhilta de-Rabbi Ishmael*, Amalek 4** [on Exod 18:27] (Lauterbach, v. 2, p. 190)

It is said: "The poor man and the man of means meet together; the Lord giveth light to the eyes of both" (Prov. 29:13). And it also says: "The rich and the poor meet together – the Lord is the maker of them all" (ib. 22:2). <...> How so? If the poor man stretches out his hand towards the householder, and the householder gives willingly, then "the Lord giveth light to the eyes of both." If, however, the poor man stretches out his hand towards the householder, and the latter is unwilling to give, then "the Lord is the maker of them all" – He who had made the one poor will in the end make him rich, and He who had made the other rich will in the end make him poor.

***b. Baba Bathra* 9a–11a**

R. Eleazar said: He who causes others to do good is greater than the doer, as it says, *And the work of righteousness [zedakah] shall be peace, and the effect of righteousness quiet and confidence for ever* (Isa. 32:17). If a man is deserving, then *shalt thou not deal thy bread to the hungry* (Isa. 58:7), but if he is not deserving, then *thou shalt bring the poor that are cast out to thy house* (Ibid.). Raba said to the townsfolk of Mahuza: I beg of you, hasten [to the assistance of] one another, so that you may be on good terms with the Government. R. Eleazar further said: When the Temple stood, a man used to bring his shekel and so make atonement. Now that the Temple no longer stands, if they give for charity, well and good, and if not, the heathens will come and take from them forcibly. And even so it will be reckoned to them as if they had given charity, as it is written, *[I will make] thine exactors righteousness [zedakah]* (Isa. 60:17). <...> [9b]

R. Eleazar said: A man who gives charity in secret is greater than Moses our Teacher, for of Moses it is written, *For I was afraid because of the anger aid the wrath* (Deut. 9:19), and of one who gives charity [secretly] it is written, *A gift in secret subdues anger* (Prov. 21:14). In this he [R. Eleazar] differs from R. Isaac, for R. Isaac said that it subdues 'anger' but not 'wrath', since the verse continues, *And a present in the bosom fierce wrath*, [which we can interpret to mean], 'Though a present is placed in the bosom, yet wrath is still fierce.' According to others, R. Isaac said: A judge who takes a bribe brings fierce wrath upon the world; as it says, *And a present* etc. R. Isaac also said: He who gives a small coin to a poor man obtains six blessings, and he who addresses to him words of comfort obtains eleven blessings. 'He who gives a small coin to a poor man obtains six blessings' – as it is written, *Is it not to deal thy bread to the hungry and bring the poor to thy house* etc., *when thou seest the naked* etc. (Isa. 58:7). 'He who addresses to him comforting words obtains eleven blessings', as it is written, *If thou draw out thy soul to the hungry and satisfy the afflicted soul, they shall thy light rise in the darkness and thine obscurity be as the noonday, and the Lord shall guide thee continually and satisfy thy soul in drought ... and they shall build from thee the old waste places and thou shalt raise up the foundations of many generations*, etc. (Isa. 58:10-11). <...>

It has been taught: R. Meir used to say: The critic [of Judaism] may bring against you the argument, 'If your God loves the poor, why does he not support them?' If so, answer him, 'So that through them we may be saved from the punishment of Gehinnom.' This question was actually put by Turnus Rufus to R. Akiba: 'If your God loves the poor, why does He not support them?' He replied, 'So that we may be saved through them from the punishment of Gehinnom.' 'On the contrary,' said the other, 'it is this which condemns you to Gehinnom. I will illustrate by a parable. Suppose an earthly king was angry with his servant and put him in prison and ordered that he should be given no food or drink, and a man went and gave him food and drink. If the king heard, would he not be angry with him? And you are called "servants", as it is written, *For unto me the children of Israel are servants* (Lev. 25:55).' R. Akiba answered him: 'I will illustrate by another parable. Suppose an earthly king was angry with his son, and put him in prison and ordered that no food or drink should be given to him, and someone went and gave him food and drink. If the king heard of it, would he not send him a present? And we are called "sons", as it is written, *Sons are ye to the Lord your God* (Deut. 14:1).' He said to him: 'You are called both sons and servants. When you carry out the desires of the Omnipresent you are called "sons", and when you do not carry out the desires of the Omnipresent, you are called "servants". At the present time you are not carrying out the desires of the Omnipresent. R. Akiba replied: 'The Scripture says, *Is it not to deal thy bread to the hungry and bring the poor that are cast out to thy house.* When "dost thou bring the poor who are cast out to thy house"? Now; and it says [at the same time], Is it not to deal thy bread to the hungry?' <...>

It has been taught: R. Judah says: Great is charity, in that it brings the redemption nearer, as it says, *Thus saith the Lord, Keep ye judgment and do righteousness [zedakah], for my salvation is near to come and my righteousness to be revealed* (Isa. 56:1). He also used to say: Ten strong things have been created in the world. The rock is hard, but the iron cleaves it. The iron is hard, but the fire softens it. The fire is hard, but the water quenches it. The water is strong, but the clouds bear it. The clouds are strong, but the wind scatters them. The wind is strong, but the body bears it. The body is strong, but fright crushes it. Fright is strong, but wine banishes it. Wine is strong, but sleep works it off. Death is stronger than all, and charity saves from death, as it is written, *Righteousness [zedakah] delivereth from death* (Prov. 10:2).

⇨ N. 71

y. Sanhedrin **10,2 [28b-c]**

See above, n. 18.

***Testament of Joseph* 10:1-2**

See above, n. 18.

***m. Avot* 1:2** (Danby, p. 446)

Simeon the Just was of the remnants of the Great Synagogue. He used to say: By three things is the world sustained: by the Law, by the [Temple-] service, and by deeds of loving-kindness.

***m. Avot* 1:18** (Danby, p. 447)

Rabban Simeon b. Gamaliel said: By three things is the world sustained: by truth, by judgement, and by peace, as it is written, *Execute the judgement of truth and peace* (Zech. 8:16).

⇨ N. 72

***b. Berakhot* 32b**

R. Eleazar also said: Fasting is more efficacious than charity. What is the reason? One is performed with a man's money, the other with his body.

***b. Berakhot* 6b**

Mar Zutra says: The merit of a fast day lies in the charity dispensed.

⇨ N. 73

***4QDamascus Document*^{a}** [4Q266] **Frag. 11, 4-8** (García Martínez–Tigchelaar, v. 1, p. 597)

4 <...> And in another place 5 it is written: "to returnt to God in tears and in fasting" (Joel 2:12 ?). /And in [anoth]er pla[ce] it is written: "Tear your heart and not your clothes" (Joel 2:13)/. And anyone who despises these regulations 6 according to all the precepts which are found in the law of Moses, shall not be considered 7 among all the sons of his truth, for his soul has loathed the disciplines of justice. In rebellion he will be expelled from the presence of 8 the Many.

⇨ N. 74

***m. Sheqalim* 5:6** (Danby, p. 158)

There were two chambers in the Temple: one the Chamber of Secrets and the other the Chamber of Utensils. Into the Chamber of Secrets the devout used to put their gifts in secret and the poor of good family received support therefrom in secret. The Chamber of Utensils – whosoever made a gift of any article used to cast it therein, and every thirty days the treasurer opened it; and any article which they found of use for the Temple fund they left there; and the rest were sold and their price fell to the Chamber of the Temple fund.

⇨ N. 75

***b. Baba Bathra* 9b**

See above, n. 69.

⇨ N. 76

y. Berakhot 4,4 [8c] (Neusner 1982-91, v. 1, p. 77, tr. T. Zahavy)

R. Abba, R. Hiyya in the name of R. Yohanan, "A person must pray in a place designated for Prayer [i.e. a synagogue]. And what is the basis [in Scripture for this rule]? 'In every place where I cause my name to be remembered I will come to you and bless you' (Exod. 20:24). It is not written, 'Where you shall [happen to] remember my name.' But rather, 'In every place where I cause my name to be remembered' [i.e., where there is regular service or Prayer – the Temple, and, after its destruction, the synagogue]." Said R. Tanhum bar Hanina, "A person must designate for himself a place to pray in the synagogue. And what is the basis [in Scripture for this rule]? 'When David came to the summit where he worshipped God' (2Sam. 15:32). It is not written, 'Where he shall worship God.' [The verse implies that he regularly worshipped in that place.]"

y. Berakhot 5,1 [8d–9a] (Neusner 1982-91, v. 1, pp. 195-197, tr. T. Zahavy)

Huna said, "One who prays behind a synagogue is called a wicked person, as it says, 'On every side the wicked prowl' (Ps. 12:8)". R. Huna said, "Anyone who does not enter the synagogue [during his lifetime] in this world will not enter the synagogue in the afterlife. What is the basis [in Scripture for this view]? 'On every side [shall] the wicked prowl [*ythlkwn*. In the future, in the world to come, they will prowl. They will not enter paradise.]" Said R. Yohanan, "It is as if an iron wall surrounds one who prays at home." [He will be protected and his prayers will be heard.] But another contradictory tradition is ascribed to R. Yohanan: Elsewhere said R. Abba, said R. Hiyya in the name of R. Yohanan, "A person must pray in a place designated for prayer [i.e. a synagogue]." And here you say this [in his name]! [You may reconcile the discrepancy between them as follows: He said to them both, and] the first [teaching] refers to [the prayer of] an individual. [It is better that one pray at home if there is no communal prayer.] The second [teaching] refers to [the prayer of] a congregation. [when there is communal prayer, one must pray in a synagogue.] R. Pinhas in the name of R. Yohanan Hoshaia, "It is as if one who prays in the synagogue offered a pure meal offering [at the Temple]. What is the basis [in Scripture for this view]? '[They shall declare my glory... to my holy mountain Jerusalem, says the Lord,] just as the Israelites bring their cereal offerings in a clean vessel to the house of the Lord' (Is. 66:19-20)." R. Jeremiah in the name of R. Abahu, "'Seek the Lord while he may be found' (Is. 55:6). Where may he be found? In the synagogues and study halls. 'Call upon him while he is near' (ibid.). Where is he near? [In the synagogues and study halls.]" Said R. Yitzhak b. R. Eleazar, "Moreover, it is as if God stands next to those [who are in synagogues and study halls]. What is the basis [in Scripture for this view]? 'God has taken his place in the divine congregation; in the midst of the gods he holds judgment' (Ps. 82:1)."

b. Berakhot 7b–8a

R. Isaac said to R. Nahman: Why does the Master not come to the Synagogue in order to pray? – He said to him: I cannot. He asked him: Let the Master gather ten people and pray with them [in his house]? – He answered: It is too much of a trouble for me. [He then said]: Let the Master ask the messenger of the congregation to inform him of the time when the congregation prays? He answered: Why all this [trouble]? – He said to him: For R. Johanan said in the name of R. Simeon b. Yohai: What is the meaning of the verse: *But as for me, let my prayer be made unto Thee, O Lord, in an acceptable time* (Ps. 69:14)? When is the time acceptable? When the congregation prays. R. Jose b. R. Hanina says: [You learn it] from here: *Thus saith the Lord, In an acceptable time have I answered thee* (Isa. 49:8). R. Aha son of R. Hanina says: [You learn it] from here: *Behold, God despiseth not the mighty* (Job 36:5). And it is further written: *He hath redeemed my soul in peace so that none came nigh me; for they were many with me* (Ps. 55:19). It has been taught also to the same effect; R. Nathan says: How do we know that the Holy One, blessed be He, does not despise the prayer of the congregation? For it is said: '*Behold, God despiseth not the mighty*'. And it is further written: '*He hath redeemed my soul in peace so that none came nigh me, etc.*'. The Holy One, blessed be He, says: If a man occupies himself with the study of the Torah and with works of charity and prays with the congregation, I account it to him as if he had redeemed Me and My children from among the nations of the world.

Isa 26:20

Come, my people, enter your chambers, and shut your doors behind you; hide yourselves for a little while until the wrath is past.

***Sifre on Deuteronomy* 41** [on Deut 11:13]

See above, n. 24.

***m. Berakhot* 5:1** (Danby, p. 5)

None must stand up to say the *Tefillah* save in sober mood. The pious men of old used to wait an hour before they said the *Tefillah*, that they might direct their heart toward God. Even if the king salutes a man he may not return the greeting; and even if a snake was twisted around his heel he may not interrupt his prayer.

***t. Berakhot* 3:18** (Neusner 2002, v. 1, p. 19; tr. T. Zahavy)

One who was riding on an ass [*m.Ber.* 4:5], *if there is someone who can hold the ass* [*so that it will not run away*], *he should dismount and pray, and if not, then he prays where he is* [i.e., mounted on the ass]. *Rabbi says, "In either case he prays where he is, as long as he concentrates* [properly]."

***b. Ta'anit* 8a**

R. Ammi said: A man's prayer is only answered if he takes his heart into his hand, as it is said, *Let us lift up our heart with our hands* (Lam. 3:41). [But it is not so. Surely] Samuel appointed an amora to act for him and his exposition ran thus: *But they beguiled Him with their mouth, and lied unto Him with their tongue. For their heart was not steadfast with Him, neither were they faithful in His covenant*; and yet, *But He being full of compassion, forgiveth iniquity* etc. (Ps. 78:36-38)? – This is no contradiction. The one refers to the individual, and the other to the community.

***b. Berakhot* 30b**

It has been stated: R. Isaac b. Abdimi said in the name of our Master: The halachah is as stated by R. Judah in the name of R. Eleazar b. Azariah. R. Hiyya b. Abba prayed once and then prayed again. Said R. Zera to him: Why does the Master act thus? Shall I say it is because the Master was not attending? Has not R. Eleazar said: A man should always take stock of himself: if he can concentrate his attention he should say the Tefillah, but if not he should not say it? Or is it that the Master did not remember that it is New Moon? But has it not been taught: If a man forgot and did not mention the New Moon in the evening Tefillah, he is not made to repeat, because he can say it in the morning prayer; if he forgot in the morning prayer, he is not made to repeat, because he can say it in the musaf if he forgot in musaf, he is not made to repeat, because he can say it in minhah? – He said to him: Has not a gloss been added to this: R. Johanan says: This applies only to prayer said in a congregation?

Midrash on Psalms on Psalm 108:1 (Braude 1959, v. 2, pp. 199-201)

A song, a Psalm of David. My heart is prepared, O God; I will sing, yea, I will sing praises (Ps. 108:1-2). Elsewhere, this is what Scripture says: *And I set my face unto the Lord God, to seek by prayer and supplications* (Dan. 9:3). But is not *prayer* the same as *supplication*? The distinction between them is this. Righteous men first incline themselves toward the Holy One, blessed be He, so that He will listen to their prayers. And so our Rabbis taught: A man must begin to pray only in a mood of humility – not in mood frivolity, nor in a mood of lightness, nor in a mood of banter – so that the Holy One, blessed be He, will listen to his prayer. For in saying, *Then David the king went in, and sat before the Lord* (2Sam. 7:18), does Scripture mean that sitting is permitted in the presence of the Holy One, blessed be He? Does not a man pray only in a standing position, as it is said *Then stood up Phineas, and prayed* (Ps. 106:30)? How, then, can it be said *Then David... sat before the Lord*? What the verse implies, however, is not that he sat, but that he had his heart set to pray. Indeed, since he asked at once: *Who am I, O Lord God, and what is my house?* (2Sam. 7:18), his humility means that he had prepared his heart for prayer, as is said *Thou wilt prepare their heart, Thou wilt cause Thine ear to attend* (Ps. 10:17).

R. Samuel bar Nahmani taught: When you prepare your heart for prayer, you may be assured that your prayer will be heard by the Holy One, blessed be He, for it is said, *Thou wilt prepare their heart, Thou wilt cause Thine ear to attend*, and again, *If the people... shall pray unto the Lord... Thou in heaven wilt hear their prayer* (1Kings 8:45). Scripture also says, *For Ezra had prepared his heart* (Ezra 7:10) and *The king granted him all his request, according to the hand of the Lord his God upon him* (ibid. 7:6). So, too, you find that of Hezekiah who prayed for

Israel it is said *Hezekiah had prayed for them, saying: The good Lord pardon* (2Chr. 30:18), but before he prayed, he had prepared his heart, as is said *He prepared his whole heart to seek God, the Lord, the God of his fathers* (ibid. 30:19). And because he prepared his heart, the Holy One, blessed be He, hearkened to his prayer, *and healed the people* (ibid. 30:20). Scripture also says, *Then the priests, the Levites, arose and blessed the people; and their voice was heard of the Lord, and their prayer came up to His holy habitation, even unto heaven* (ibid. 30:27). David said: accordingly, behold, I shall prepare my heart so that the Holy One, blessed be He, will hear my prayer. Hence it is said *My heart is prepared, O God; I will sing, yea, I will sing praises* (Ps. 108:2).

2. Another interpretation of *My heart is prepared, O God*. David said: "I shall prepare my heart as incense." Therefore it is written *Let my prayer be prepared as incense before Thee* (Ps. 141:2). The Holy One, blessed be He, answered David: "Thou hast prepared for thy prayer. Therefore I shall prepare thy throne, as is said *And thy house and thy kingdom shall be made sure for ever before thee; thy throne shall be prepared for ever* (2 Sam. 7:16).

⇨ N. 77

y. Berakhot 5,1 [8d–9a]

See above, n. 76.

b. Berakhot 6b

R. Johanan says: Whenever the Holy One, blessed be He, comes into a Synagogue and does not find ten persons there, He becomes angry at once. For it is said: *Wherefore, when I came, was there no man? When I called, was there no answer* (Isa. 50:2)?

⇨ N. 78

2 KGS 4:32-35

32 When Elisha came into the house, he saw the child lying dead on his bed. 33 So he went in and shut the door upon the two of them, and prayed to the LORD. 34 Then he went up and lay upon the child, putting his mouth upon his mouth, his eyes upon his eyes, and his hands upon his hands; and as he stretched himself upon him, the flesh of the child

became warm. 35 Then he got up again, and walked once to and fro in the house, and went up, and stretched himself upon him; the child sneezed seven times, and the child opened his eyes.

Testament of Joseph 3:3 (Charlesworth, v. 1, p. 820)

But I recalled my father's words, went weeping into my quarters, and prayed to the Lord.

Testament of Jacob 1:9 (Charlesworth, v. 1, p. 914)

Jacob had a secluded place which he would enter to offer his prayers before the lord in the night and in the day.

b. Ta'anit 23b

R. Zerika said to R. Safra: Come and see the difference between the [so called] hard men of Palestine and the pious men of Babylonia. When the world was in need of rain the pious men of Babylonia, R. Huna and R. Hisda said: Let us assemble and pray, Perhaps the Holy One, Blessed be He, may be reconciled and send rain. But the great men of Palestine, as for example, R. Jonah the father of R. Mani, would go into his house when the world was in need of rain and say to his [family]: Get my haversack and I shall go and buy grain for a *zuz*. When he left his house he would go and stand in some low-lying spot, and then standing in this hidden spot, as it is written, *Out of the depths have I called thee O Lord* (Ps. 130:1), dressed in sackcloth he prayed and rain came. When he returned home [his family] asked him, Have you brought the grain? He replied: Now that rain has come the world will feel relieved.

BIBLIOGRAPHY

BIRNBAUM, P., trans. *Daily Prayer Book*. New York: Hebrew Publishing Company, 1949

BRAUDE, W.G., trans. *The Midrash on Psalms*. New Haven: Yale University Press, 1959.

——., trans. *Pesikta Rabbati*. New Haven: Yale University Press, 1968.

CHILTON, B.D., trans. *The Isaiah Targum*. Wilmington, Det.: M. Glazier, 1987.

DANBY, H., trans. *The Mishna*. London: Oxford University Press, 1933.

ELLIOTT, J.K., ed. *The Apocryphal New Testament*. Oxford: Clarendon Press, 1993.

FREEDMAN, H. and M. SIMON, eds., J. ISRAELSTAM, trans. *Midrash Rabbah*, vol. 4 (Leviticus). London / New York: Soncino Press, 1983.

GARCÍA MARTÍNEZ, F. and E. J. C. TIGCHELAAR, eds. *The Dead Sea Scrolls: Study Edition*, 2 vols. Leiden: Brill, 1997–98.

HAMMER, R., trans. *Sifre on Deuteronomy*. New Haven: Yale University Press, 1986.

HOLMES, M.W., ed. *The Apostolic Fathers: Greek Texts and English Translations*. Grand Rapids, Mich.: Baker Books, 1999.

LAKE, K., ed. and trans. *The Apostolic Fathers*, vol. 1. The Loeb Classical Library; London: William Heinemann / Cambridge: Harvard University Press, 1952.

LAUTERBACH, J.Z., ed. and trans. *Mekilta de-Rabbi Ishmael*, 3 vols. Philadelphia: Jewish Publication Society, 1949.

LAYTON, B., ed. *Nag Hammadi Codex II, 2–7*, vol. 1. Nag Hammadi Studies 20; Leiden / New York / København / Köln: E.J. Brill, 1989.

MANGEY, Th., ed. *Philo of Alexandria. Works – Latin and Greek*. London: Typis Gulielmi Bowyer. Prostant venales apud Gulielmum Innys, in area occidentali Divi Pauli; & Carolum Bathurst, 1742.

McIVOR, J.S., trans. *The Targum of Chronicles*. Collegeville, Minn.: Liturgical Press, 1994.

NEUSNER, J., trans. *Sifra: An Analytical Translation*. Atlanta, Georgia: Scholars Press, 1988.

———., ed. *The Talmud of the Land of Israel*. Chicago: University of Chicago Press, 1982–1991.[3]

———., trans. *The Tosefta – Translated from the Hebrew with a New Introduction*, 2 vols. Peabody, Mass.: Hendrickson Publishers, 2002.

PETUCHOWSKI, J. J., ed. and trans. "Jewish Prayer Texts of the Rabbinic Period." In J. J. PETUCHOWSKI and M. BROCKE, eds. *The Lord's Prayer*, pp. 21-44. London: Burns & Oates, 1978.

---

[3] Trans. by J. Neusner unless otherwise indicated.

INDEX OF ANCIENT SOURCES

◆

CONTRIBUTORS

◆

INDEX OF ANCIENT SOURCES*

Hebrew Bible

Genesis

1	112, 114
1:27	110-2
1:28	110
2	112, 114
2:24	110
5:2	111
9:6	91n7, 92-6
9:6 (LXX)	91n7
9:6 (Targum)	91-2, 94
21:9	77n19
34:21	133
42:21 (Targum)	119n10
49:25 (Targum)	135, 136

Exodus

15:18	64
15:18 (Targum)	64-65
17:14	64
20	90
20:2	63
20:7	81n32, 98, 100, 100n33, 101
20:7 (Targum)	98
20:7 (Pesh)	98n28
20:13	91-4, 96
20:14	103-5, 105n45, 106
20:15	9
20:17	103, 105
21	84
21:23-25	83
22:26	133, 134

Leviticus

15:29	97n25
15:33	97
18:10-16	104
19	86 8, 90
19:1	86
19:2	133
19:12	81n32, 98, 100, 100n33, 101
19:17	86, 87
19:17 (LXX)	86
19:18	86, 87n47, 128, 129n50, 133-4, 161, 161n45
19:18 (LXX)	128
19:18 (Targum)	128
19:34	88, 129n47
20:10	103-6
24:19	83
24:20	83
25	32
25:26	32
25:26-28	32
25:29	32
25:31	32
25:35-37	32
25:35-55	32
25:39	32
25:44-46	32n104
25:47	32

Numbers

11:21	77n19
15:24	145n102
35:16	92

---

* Prepared by Gaukhar Dyusembaeva and Sergey Minov.
References in bold type designate the sources quoted in full in Appendix (pp. 178-242).

Deuteronomy
4:6	52
5	90
5:18	9, 91, 103
5:21	103
6:4	77n19
6:4f	167n62
6:4-5	169n68
6:4-9	63
6:5	51
11:13-21	63
15:2	32
15:3	32n103
19:16	84
19:16 (LXX)	84
19:18	84
19:18 (LXX)	84
19:19	84
19:19 (LXX)	84
19:20	84
19:20 (LXX)	84
19:21	84
23:22	101
24:1	103, 106-9, 113, 115, 116

Joshua
6:5	118n7

1 Samuel
14:24	168n67, **224**
31:11-13	168n67, **224**

2 Samuel
1:24	141n87
3:30-35	168n67, **224**
12:16-17	168n67, **225**

2 Kings
4:32-35	171n78, **239-240**

Isaiah
1:15	160n36, **198**
24:23 (Targum)	167n60, **220-1**
26:20	170n76, **237**
28:16	122
31:4-5 (Targum)	167n60, **221**
40:6-8	52
40:9 (Targum)	167n60, **221**
50:6	85
52:7 (Targum)	167n60, **221**
55:12 (Targum)	121, 121n12, 122, 122n14
58:3-7	169n67, **225**
61:10 (Targum)	121n12, 122n14
65:24	160n36, **198**

Jeremiah
14:10-12	169n67, **226**
15:5	130n53

Ezekiel
36:23	167n60, **220**
36:25-27	155n15, **183**

Joel
4:6	33

Jonah
3:5-10	168n67, **225**

Micah
4:7	167n60, **221**

Nahum
1	52

Zechariah
7:5-7	169n67, **226**
14:3	64
14:9	64

Malachi		3:19	131n54
2:16	109n58	5:1-2	160n36, **198**
3	52	5:15	131n55
		10:11	131n54
Psalms 43		10:16f	47
2:12	44		
32:2	44	*Lamentations*	
51:9-11	155n15, **183**	3:66	64
55:21	133n58		
83:12	45n13	*Nehemiah*	
90:5-6	52	5:1-5	31
103:15-16	52	5:6-13	32
104:35	162n47	5:7-8	32
132:4	29	10:31-32	32
141:1	157n25, **193**		
		1 Chronicles	
Job		29:10-11	164n52, **214**
14:1	52	29:10-11 (Targum)	164n52, **215**
31:29-30	162n46, **204**		
Proverbs		**QUMRAN**	
6:1-5	21		
6:2	21	*1Q26*	25n73
6:4	29, 37		
6:17-18	21	*1Q27* II 6	118n4
6:22-27	21		
11:15	21n60	*1QS* (Rule of the Community)	
11:27	26n80		54
17:18	21n60	I 9-11	162n46, **205**
20:16	21n60	II 1f	54-5
22:26f	21n60	IX 3-6	157n25, **194**
24:17-18	162n46, **204**	IX 10-11	97, 97n26
25:21-22	162n46, **204**	X 5-8	157n25, **194-5**
27:13	21n60	X 17-20	162n46, **205**
		XI	6n7
Ecclesiastes		XI 4	122-3
1:3	131n54		
2:11	131n54	*1QM* (War Scroll)	54
2:13	131n54	XIII 2f	47-48, 54
3:9	131n54		

1QH^a (Hodayot)	6n7, 54
IV 17-28	155n15, **182-3**
VI	54
VI 13-15	41
VI 13-16	53
XII 28-33	155n15, **183**
XIV 24	123
XIV 25-26	122
1Q/4QInstruction	23-31, 35, 37, 39
4Q185	51, 52n29, 53, 54
1-2 I 8	53
1-2 I 9-13	52
1-2 I 14	53
1-2 II 1-4	53
1-2 II 3	53
1-2 II 9-11	53
1-2 II 13	53
4Q213 1 II 4	118
4Q242 (4QPrNab)	163n49, **212**
4Q266 11	170n73, **234**
4Q280	55
1	165n56, **218**
4Q286 7 II	165n56, **217**
4Q325 1	118n7
4Q372 (4QApocryphon of Joseph)	
1 16	167n62
4Q396 II (4QMMT B)	
55, 64f, 73 (II 6-7, III 4-5)	
	80n28
4Q415	25n73
4Q416	25n73, 25n75
1 II 4-6	30n92
1 II 17-18	28n85
2 II 3	26n81
2 II 6	28n85
2 II 18-20	27n83
2 II 20-21	27
2 III 2	27n82
2 III 5-6	28n86, 35n117
2 III 8	27n82, 27n83
2 III 9	26n81
2 III 9-12	26
2 III 12	26n80, 27n82
2 III 12-13	27
2 III 19	27n82
4Q417	25n73, 25n75
2 I 17	27n83
2 I 19	27n84
2 I 21-23	29n88
2 I 24	29n90
2 I 24f	28n87
4Q418	25n73, 25n75, 27n82, 25n73, 25n73
4Q420-421	24n68
4Q423	25n73
4Q429 4 2:7	122
4Q460 9 I 6	167n62
4Q509	55

4Q525	40-3, 53, 54	92-106	30
2 II 1-10	40-1	94:8	30n92
4Q544 (Amram[b]) 1-3	165n56, **217-8**	*2 Enoch*	
		42:6f	46
		42.11	45
5Q14	55	42:14	42
		52	47
11Q5 (11QPs[a])			
XIX 13-16	165n55, **216**	*4 Ezra*	5
XIX 15-16	165n56, **216**		
XXIV 3-14	165n55, **215-6**	*Joseph and Aseneth*	
XXIV 4-7	158	28:5	83n35
XXIV 10-11	165n55	28:10	83n35
XXIV 10-13	165n55	28:14	83n35
		29:3	83
11Q11 (11QApPs[a])	55		
		Jubilees	5
11QTemple 57:15-19	111		
		Judith	
CD (Damascus Document)		15:12-13	121
	5, 54, 112		
CD-A IV 15-18	102n37, 111	*1 Maccabees*	
CD-A V 1-8	110n60	13:51	121
CD-A VII 6-9	102n38		
CD-A XI 17-21	157n25, **195**	*2 Maccabees*	
CD-A XVI 10-12	102n38	7:18	157n21, **187**
		7:30-38	157n21, **187-8**
		7:32	157n21
APOCRYPHA AND			
PSEUDEPIGRAPHA		*4 Maccabees*	
		7	45
Ahiqar	30, 39		
43	29n91	*Pseudo-Phocylides*	
		16	81n32
Apocalypse of Elijah			
1:18-19	169n67, **226**	*Sirach*	25, 25n75, 27, 30, 38, 39, 172
1 Enoch		3:1-4:14	156n20, **186-7**
58:2	45, 50	3:30	157n25, **193**

5:5-7	157n22, **191**	*Testament of Asher*	
6:5	130n53	1:3,5	166n57, **220**
7:8-10	156n18, 157n25, **184**	2:8	169n67, **226**
7:14	160n36, **198**		
8:1-2	23	*Testament of Benjamin*	
8:5	161n43, **202**	1:2-6	168n67, **224**
8:12	23	3:1-6	162n48, **209-210**
12:3	157n25, **195**	4	162n48, **210**
14:11	22	5	162n48, **210**
14:13	22		
14:15	22	*Testament of Gad*	
14:20-27	42	6:1-7	161n44, **203**
16:14	157n25, **195**		
17:22	157n25	*Testament of Jacob*	
17:22-29	157n22, **191**	1:9	171n78, **240**
19:18	22		
25:7-11	45	*Testament of Joseph*	
27:1	23	3:3	171n78, **240**
27:30-28:7	161n43, 168n63, **201-2**	4:3-6	157n22, **191**
		4:7-8	168n67, **223**
28:1-7	129n50	10:1-2	156n18, 169n71, **185**
29:1	22	17	162n48, **209**
29:2	23	18	162n48, **209**
29:4f	22n63	18:2	161n44, **203**
29:5	22		
29:6	22	*Testament of Levi*	
29:8-13	157n25, **195-6**	14:3-4	143, 144
29:14	22		
29:16f	23, 29n89	*Testament of Zebulun*	
29:20	22	5:3	161n44, **203**
34:11	157n25, **196**	8:1	161n44, **203**
34:25-26	157n22, 169n67	8:2	161n44, **203**
34:25-35:3	153n7, **178**		
35:1-7	157n25, **193-4**	*Tobit*	
35:11-36:8	153n7, **178-9**	4:7-11	157n25, **194**
38:9-15	163n49, **211-2**	12:8	156n18
40:17	157n25, **196**	12:8-10	153n7, 154, 169, **179**
40:18	131	12:9	157n25
40:24	157n25, **196**	14:11	157n25, **194**
45:15-16	156n20, **187**		

INDEX

HELLENISTIC JEWISH AUTHORS

Josephus

Antiquities
14.235   37n123

War
2.273   35n118, 36n119
2.425-29   34n111
7.60-61   34n111

Philo

Decal.
132   94n16
164   104n43
170   93n15

Ex Antonio   161n43, **202**

Mos. II,188-91   109n57

Quaest. in Gn. 61   91n7

Spec. Leg. 7   104n43

NEW TESTAMENT

Matthew
1:22	73n6
2:17	73n6
2:23	73n6
3:1-2	157n23
3:5-9	157n22
3:8	157n23
4:13	157n23
4:17	60
5	72-4, 74n9, 75-6, 78-9, 79n26, 80-2, 85-6, 89, 97, 113-4, 151, 156-7, 162n46, 167n60
5:3	68
5:3f	40
5:3-12	41, 70
5:9	132, 133n58
5:10	68
5:11f	42
5:11-12	68
5:13	144
5:13-14	144-5
5:13-16	70
5:14	145
5:15-16	146
5:16	146
5:17	97, 115
5:17-20	70, 72, 75
5:17-48	156n19
5:18	109n56
5:19	102n39
5:20	68
5:21	75, 91-2, 94, 115
5:21 (OS)	91n8
5:21f	71n1, 74n9, 78n20, 81
5:21-22	8-10, 95-6, 96n20, 102
5:21-26	6, 8
5:21-33	70
5:21-37	115
5:21-48	70-2, 74n9, 75-6, 78, 79n26
5:22	8, 70
5:22-23	165n54
5:23-24	7-10
5:23-26	163
5:25	18n46
5:25f	12n26, 17
5:25-26	6, 7-12, 14, 34, 36, 38, 39, 168n65

5:26	18, 165n54	6:9-10	159n32, 166
5:27	70, 103	6:9-13	151, 159
5:27f	81	6:11	155n15, 163
5:27-30	105	6:12	155n16, 158, 160, 160n39, 162-5, 167, 168
5:27-32	102-3, 105, 106		
5:28	103	6:13	163-5, 165n54-5, 166, 166n57
5:31	70, 103, 108		
5:31f	81	6:14-15	152n3, 155, 155n15, 158, 160, 160n39, 162-4
5:31-32	106, 108, 116		
5:33	101, 115	6:15	161n42
5:33-37	71n1, 81, 98, 101-2	6:16-18	151, 152n3, 154, 158, 168
5:34-35	101		
5:36	101	6:18	152n3, 154
5:37	99, 101	6:19	167n60
5:38	70, 86	6:22	145
5:38-42	82	6:22-23	144, 145n102
5:39	85, 85n39, 86, 166n57	6:23	144
5:43	70, 86, 87	6:24-25	167n60
5:43-48	82, 127-8, 132, 162	7:1-5	160n40
5:45-48	132	7:7-11	158
5:47	131n55	8:11	68
6	151, 156, 157, 159n31, 162n46, 163, 168n67, 169n68, 170-2	8:17	73n6
		9:2-7	163n49
		9:13	157n23
6:1	152n3, 154, 156n18	9:14-15	158n27, 168n67
6:1-4	158, 169	10:24	125
6:1-6	151, 152n3	11:5	67
6:1-8	170n75	11:10-11	157n23
6:1-18	151-2, 152n3, 153, 155-6, 156n18-19, 157, 157n21, 158, 166, 168, 171-2	11:21	56
		11:22-26	158n26
		11:25	160n39
		11:27	139-140
6:2-6	152n3	12:17	73n6
6:2-4	154	12:28	66
6:4	154	12:32	66
6:5-6	154, 171, 171n78	12:41	157n23
6:5-13	158, 168	12:42	18
6:6	154	13:35	73n6
6:7-8	152n3, 160	13:52	67
6:7-13	152n3		

14:23	171n78	26:42	171n78
16:3	16n40	26:44	171n78
16:28	119n8	27:9	73n6
16:18	122, 123		
17:15	124	*Mark*	
18:3	68	2:3-11	163n49
18:7	56	2:17	157n23
18:9	9	2:18-20	158n27, 168n67
18:15-18	162n47	2:18-22	168n67
18:21	162n47	3:31-35	137, 137n74
18:23-35	34, 36n122, 160n39, 161n42	4:24	160n40
		6:12	157n23
18:30	36	9:1	119n8
19:3	107, 108, 108n55	9:17	124
19:3-9	89n1, 108n55, 111, 113-6	10:2-12	89n1, 112n64
		11:8-10	120
19:4-6	110, 113-4	11:21	56
19:7-8	108, 110	11:24	161
19:9	112	11:24-25	161
19:16-20	116	11:24-26	171n80
21:4	73n6	11:25	8n10, 159n34, 160n39, 161, 161n41
21:8-9	120		
22:16-22	90n3	11:25-26	160n40
22:23-33	90n3	11:26	161n42
22:31	73n6	12:28-34	89n1
22:34-40	89n1, 90n3	12:41-44	34
22:40	67	12:42	19
22:41-46	90n3	14:21	56
23	56	14:38	166n57
23:8	123-4, 127		
23:9	127n37	*Luke*	
23:10	127	4:7	138-9
23:11	127	5:20-24	163n49
23:13	68	5:32	157n23
23:16-22	71n1	5:33-35	158n27, 168n67
24:15	73n6	6:17-49	151n1
25:14-30	34	6:23f	42
26:24	56	6:27-36	133n59
26:39	171n78	6:28	56

6:36-42	160n40	13:1	14
6:40	125n31	13:1-5	14
6:45	166n57	13:3-5	157n23
7:41-42	34, 160n39	13:6-9	14
9:27	119n8	15:7-10	157n23
10:13	157n23	16:1-8	34
10:22	140	16:14-18	102n37
10:25-37	89n1	16:30	157n23
11	159n31	17:3-4	157n23
11:1	159n30	18:12	158n27, 168n67
11:1-3	168	19:12-27	34
11:1-4	153n8, 158	21:2	19
11:1-10	171n80	22:22	56
11:2	155n15	23:28-30	141
11:4	160n39, 166n57	23:31	141
11:5-10	160n38	24:47	157n23
11:5-12	155n15		
11:9-13	158	*John*	
11:13	155n15	1:38	123n19
11:27	137	15:20	126n33
11:27-28	134	20:16	123n19
11:28	137		
11:32	157n23	*Acts*	
11:33	146	2:16	73n6
11:34	145n102	2:37-38	157n23
12:35-48	12-3	3:19	157n23
12:49-50	13	13:2-3	158n27, 168n67
12:49-59	15	13:40	73n6
12:50	16	16:16	20n54
12:51-53	12-3	16:19	20n54
12:52	16	19:24-25	20n54
12:54-56	12-3, 16, 16n40	23:14	56
12:54-59	16n40		
12:56	14	*Romans*	
12:57	13-4, 15n36, 16, 16n40, 20, 20n55, 37	7	102n39
		9:3	56
12:57-59	8n10, 11n18, 12n23	9:12	73n6
12:58f	17	12:9	166n57
12:58-59	11, 13-6, 34, 36	12:14	56
		12:20	162n46

1 Corinthians	
6	102n39
6:1f	37n124
12:13	56
16:22	56, 125n22
2 Corinthians	
1:17	99n30
Galatians	
1:4f	166n57
1:8f	56
3:16	73n6
1 Thessalonians	
4	102n39
5:22	166n57
2 Timothy	
4:18	164n52, 166n57
James	
5:12	99n30
Revelation	
9:12	56
18:10	56
18:16	56
18:19	56
Q 12:49-59	15

RABBINIC LITERATURE

Mishnah

m. Ber. 2:2	63, 64, 167n61, **221-2**
m. Ber. 2:5	62, 167n61, **222**
m. Ber. 4:2	159n30, **197**
m. Ber. 5:1	170n76, **237**
m. Ber. 9:5	169n68, **229**
m. Peah 1:1	154n13, 156n18, **180**
m. Ma'aser Sheni 2:9	118n5
m. Sheq. 5:6	170n74, **234**
m. Yoma 8:8	157n22, **192**
m. Yoma 8:9	163n50, **212-3**
m. Ta'an. 2:1	169n67, **226-7**
m. Sotah 9:15	155n15, **183-4**
m. Git. 4:5	108, 110
m. Git. 8:4-5	108
m. Git. 8:8	108
m. Git. 9:9	109
m. Git. 9:10	107
m. Qid. 1:1	19n48
m. B. Qama 8:7	162n47, 163n49-50, **205**
m. B. Metz. 4:7	163n50, **213**
m. Avot 1:1	58
m. Avot 1:2	169n71, **233**
m. Avot 1:3	123n18, 156n17, **184**
m. Avot 1:6	123n18
m. Avot 1:18	169n71, **234**
m. Avot 2:4	167n61, **222**
m. Avot 2:8	135n65
m. Avot 2:11	156n18, **186**
m. Avot 2:16	154n13, **180**
m. Avot 4:19	162n46, **204**
m. Nid. 2:1	105n46

Tosephta

t. Ber. 3:7	159n30, 164n52, **196-7**
t. Ber. 3:18	170n76, **237**
t. Peah 4:19	169n69, **231**
t. Bik. 1:2	77n19

t. Pes. 1:6	77n19	**Talmud Bavli**	
t. Yoma 5:9	157n22, **192**	b. Ber. 5b	160n37, **199-200**
t. Ta'an. 1:8	169n67, **227**	b. Ber. 6b	169n72, 171n77, **234, 239**
t. Hag. 2:1	135n66, 138	b. Ber. 7b-8a	170n76, **236**
t. Sotah 4:6	77n19	b. Ber. 10a	162n47, **208**
t. Sotah 4:7	77n19	b. Ber. 14b-15a	167n61, **222**
t. Sotah 4:9	77n19	b. Ber. 16b	165n56, 166n57, **219**
t. Sotah 4:11	77n19	b. Ber. 29b	159n30, 164n52, 167n61, **197, 215**
t. Sotah 10:1	141		
t. Sanh. 3:8	126, 126n34	b. Ber. 30b	170n76, **237-8**
t. Bekh. 2:12	77n19	b. Ber. 32b	169n72, **234**
t. Miq. 3:4	77n19	b. Ber. 38b	77n19
		b. Ber. 58b	126n32-33
Talmud Yerushalmi		b. Ber. 60b	165n55, 166n57, **216-7, 219-220**
y. Ber. 4,1 [7b-c]	160n37, **199**		
y. Ber. 4,4 [8c]	170n76, **235**	b. Ber. 61a	105n45, 160n36, **198**
y. Ber. 5,1 [8d-9a]	170n76, 171n77, **235-6**		
		b. Ber. 61b	48, 65
y. Shevi'it 9,5 [39a]	130n53	b. Shab. 25b	77n19
y. Er. 1, 1 [18d]	77n19	b. Shab. 118a	95n18
y. Er. 2,1 [20a]	77n19	b. Shab. 133b	162n48, **211**
y. Pes. 5,2 [32a]	77n19	b. Pes. 66b-67a	77n19
y. Pes 6,1 [33a]	58	b. Yoma 22b-23a	162n47, **205-6**
y. Yoma 1,1 [38d]	77n19	b. Yoma 43b	77n19
y. R. Hashan. 3,1 [58d]	77n19	b. Yoma 86a	51, 157n21, **189**
y. Ta'an. 1,3 [64b]	142n94	b. Yoma 87a	163n50, **214**
y. Ta'an. 2,1 [65a]	156n18, **184**	b. Sukk. 49b	169n68, **229-30**
y. Ta'an. 4,8 [68c]	77n19	b. R. Hashan. 17b	163n50, **213-4**
y. Hag. 3,4 [79c]	77n19		
y. Yeb. 15,1 [14d]	77n19	b. R. Hashan. 18b	168n67, **223**
y. Git. 1,2 [43c]	77n19	b. Bezah 32b	162n48, **208-9**
y. B. Qam. 1,1 [2b]	77n19	b. Ta'an. 8a	170n76, **237**
y. Sanh. 10,2 [28b-c]	156n18, 169n71, **184-5**	b. Ta'an. 16a	169n67, **227**
		b. Ta'an. 22b	169n67, **228**
y. Sanh. 11,7 [30b]	77n19	b. Ta'an. 23b	171n78, **240**
y. Mak. 2,7 [31d]	77n19	b. Ta'an. 24a	145n102
y. Sheb. 3,8 [34d]	99	b. Ta'an. 25b	162n47, **206**
y. Hor. 3,3-5 [47d]	77n19	b. Meg. 28a	162n47, **208**

b. Moʿed Qatan 25b	141n87, 142	Pisha 16 (on Exod 13:1)	135n66
b. Hag. 5a	162n48, **211**	Shira 3	162n48, **211**
b. Hag. 14b	50, 51, 135n65	Shira 10 (on Exod 15:18)	
b. Hag. 19b	77n19		167n61, **222**
b. Yeb. 52b	77n19	Vayassa 1	160n37, **200**
b. Yeb. 63a	111	Amalek 4 (on Exod 18:27)	
b. Yeb. 70a	77n19		169n69, **231**
b. Yeb. 79a	162n48, **211**	Bachodesh 5 (on Exod 20:2)	
b. Ket. 96a	124		63-64
b. Ket. 106a	77n19	Bachodesh 7 (on Exod 20:7)	
b. Gitt. 88b	37n123		157n21, **188-9**
b. Qid. 4a	77n19	Bachodesh 11 (on Exod 20:22)	
b. B. Qama 11a	77n19		133
b. B. Qama 92a	162n47, **207**	Nezikin 18 (on Exod 22:22)	
b. B. Qama 93a	162n48, **211**		157n21, **189**
b. B. Mez. 41b	77n19	Ithro 8 [ed. Horovitz]	90n2
b. B. Mez. 58b	93		
b. B. Mez. 59a	77n19	*Mekhilta de-R. Shimon b. Yohai*	
b. B. Bath. 4a	145n102	92n12, 126, 134, 146n105	
b. B. Bath. 9a-11a	169n69, **231-3**	19, 17	77n19
b. B. Bath. 9b	170n75	Ithro 20	103, 103n42, 104n44
b. B. Bath. 60b	169n67, **228-9**	(on Exod 21:1)	135n65-66
b. Sanh. 47a	157n21, **189-90**		
b. Sanh. 52a	135	*Sifra*	
b. Sanh. 58a	111n61	91a	99
b. Av. Zar. 16b	77n19	Acharei Mot 8 (on Lev 16:30)	
b. Av. Zar. 17b	125n23		163n50, **213**
b. Zev. 34a	77n19	Behar 4:8 (on Lev 25:23)	
b. Zev. 44b	125n26		126n32-3
b. Zev. 82b	77n19	Metsora 5, 12 (on Lev 15:33)	97, 97n25
b. Nid. 13b	105n46	Qedoshim 2	100n32
		Qedoshim IV,12	87n47
Minor Tractates		(on Lev 1:2)	125n25
Semahot 8:9	141	(on Lev 15:29)	97n25
		(on Lev 18:5-6)	134n62
Tannaitic Midrashim		(on Lev 19:34)	129n48
Mekhilta de-R. Ishmael		(on Lev 19:18)	129n49
92n11, 95n18, 103, 103n40-1			

Sifre Numbers
75   135n66
95 (on Num 11:21)   77n19

Sifre Deuteronomy
31 (on Deut 6:4)   77n19
41 (on Deut 11:13)   157n24,
        169n68, 170n76, **192-3**
323 (on Deut 32:29)   161n45,
                             204

Sifre Zuta
19, 3   77n19

Amoraic and Later Midrashim
Avot de-Rabbi Nathan   58
A 4   121, 122n14
A 16   87n47, 129n49
B 13   119n9, 135n66

Canticles Zuta   144
1:1   131-2
3:11   132

Ecclesiastes Rabbah
8:8   87n47

Exodus Rabbah
25:6   125n28
26:2   83n37
29:9   142n94
42:5   126n32
51:6   135n65

Genesis Rabbah
5:9   135
53 (on Gen 21:9)   77n19
91:8   119n10
98:20   135

Leqah Tov 100 (on Exod 23:2)
                             126n34

Leviticus Rabbah
10:5   160n40, **200-1**
28:2   131n55

Midrash ha-Gadol
(on Exod 23:20)   146
(on Deut 3:21)   125n30

Midrash Psalms
18:29   125n28
27:5   126n32
(on Ps 108:1)   170n76, **238-9**

Numbers Rabbah
16:27   125n27

Otiyyoth de-Rabbi Aqiva   121,
                             122, 122n14

Pesiqta de-Rav Kahana   135

Pesiqta Hadta   93

Pesiqta Rabbati
38   162n47, **206-7**
113a   99n29

Tanhuma
Hayye Sara 4   126n32
Ki Tissa 21   126n32
Ki Tese 4   135

Tanhuma [ed. Buber]
Lekh Lekha 23   126n32
Pequde 4   135n65

Tanna de-Be Eliyahu
13   125n27
14   142

Yalqut Shim'oni 2.988   145

LITURGICAL TEXTS

Amidah   155n14, **180, 219**
Avinu Malkenu   155n14, **181-2**
Havinenu   155n14, **182**
Kaddish   159, 159n32, **197**
Shma   62, 64, 169n68
Shmoneh-Esreh   159, 166n57

EARLY CHRISTIAN LITERATURE

Acts of Paul
5-6   49

Apocryphon of James
4:28-31   165n56, **218-9**

2 Clement
16   153n7, **179-80**

Didache
8   159n31
8:2   153n8, 159n33, 166n57, **180**
10:5   166n57, **219**

Gospel of Thomas
6   153n7, 168n67, 169n68, **179**
14   153n7, 168n67, 169n68, **179**
54   48
68-69   48

OTHER ANCIENT SOURCES

an Aramaic inscription
(the Negev, VI CE)   139

Aristophanes   44

Aristotle   44

Elephantine (Papyrus Cowley 10)
                           32n101

Herodotus
Hist. 3.89   31n99

Hesiod   44

Homer
Od. 5,7   44
Od. 24,19f.   44

Musaios Grammaticus
Hero et Leander, ln. 138-139
                           135-136

Petronius
Satyricon 94   136

CONTRIBUTORS

Jörg FREY (b. 1962) obtained his doctoral degree in theology from the University of Tübingen in 1996 (with a dissertation on *The Johannine Eschatology I: Reflections on the Problem in Research since Reimarus*) and his *Habilitation* from the same university in 1998 (with *The Johannine Eschatology II-III: The Notion of Time* and *The Eschatological Proclamation in the Johannine Literature*). In 1998-1999 he was Professor of the New Testament in the Theology Faculty, University of Jena; and since 1999 he has been Professor of the New Testament in the Protestant Theology Faculty, University of Munich. He has published extensively on the New Testament (esp. Johannine literature), Qumran, and Apocalypticism.

Hermann LICHTENBERGER (b. 1943) obtained a doctorate in theology from the University of Marburg in 1976 (with a dissertation on *Studies in Anthropology of the Qumran Community Texts*) and his *Habilitation* from the University of Tübingen in 1986 (with *The "I" of Adam and the "I" of Mankind*). He is Professor of the New Testament and Jewish Studies at the University of Tübingen and editor of *Jüdische Schriften aus hellenistisch-römischer Zeit*. His research of the last three decades, focusing on Qumran and related literature, has resulted in many contributions to the study of the Dead Sea Scrolls.

Hans-Jürgen BECKER (b. 1956) studied protestant theology at Göttingen University and Jewish history and literature at the Hebrew University of Jerusalem. He was awarded a Ph.D. in 1988 (with a dissertation on the Gospel of Matthew) and in 1997 obtained his *Habilitation* (with a dissertation on the Talmud Yerushalmi and Genesis Rabbah). At the Freie Universität, Berlin, he collaborated in research projects on Hekhalot literature and the Talmud Yerushalmi in the period 1985-1994; was assistant professor from 1994 to1997. Since 1997 he has been Professor of the New Testament and Ancient Judaism at Göttingen University and director of its Institute of Jewish studies.

Berndt SCHALLER (b. 1930) obtained a doctoral degree in theology from the University of Göttingen in 1961 (with a dissertation on *The Use and Interpretation of the Creation Narratives in Genesis 1-2 in Ancient Judaism*) and in 1980 attained his appointment as *Dr. habil.* (with publications on the *Testament of Job*). His main fields of teaching and research are: religion, history and literature of Ancient Judaism and Early Christianity. He retired from his position as professor at the University of Göttingen in 1995; since 1998 he is Protestant president of the Societies for Christian-Jewish Cooperation in Germany.

Serge RUZER (b. 1950) studied at Moscow State University and the Hebrew University of Jerusalem and obtained a Ph.D. from the latter in 1996 (with a dissertation on *Biblical Quotations in the Old Syriac Gospels: Peshitta Influence and Hermeneutical Constraints*). He currently teaches in the Department of Comparative Religion of the Hebrew University and is a researcher at that University's Center for the Study of Christianity (the *Jerusalem Companion to the New Testament from Jewish Sources* project). His research pertains mainly to the Jewish background to the New Testament and to early Syriac literature.

Menahem KISTER (b. 1957) studied Talmud, Semitic languages and the literature of the Second Temple period at the Hebrew University of Jerusalem. His Ph.D. dissertation, *Studies in Avot de-Rabbi Nathan: Text, Redaction and Interpretation*, was submitted to the Hebrew University in 1994. Currently a professor at the Institute of Jewish Studies and teaching in the Talmud and Bible departments and in the Literature of the Second Temple unit, his research relates to midrashic and talmudic literature, the Dead Sea Scrolls, the Apocrypha and Pseudepigrapha, the Jewish background to the New Testament, early biblical exegesis and Hebrew lexicology.

Mila GINSBURSKAYA (b. 1971) studied first in Leningrad (now St. Petersburg) then, in 1990, immigrated to Israel and continued her studies at the Hebrew University of Jerusalem. Her M.A. thesis in Comparative Religion submitted to the Hebrew University in 2003 was on *The Enigma of the Lord's Prayer Petition for Preservation (Matthew 6:13): Between This Worldly and Eschatological Woes*. She is presently pursuing research at Cambridge University for a Ph.D. on ethics and eschatology in the Synoptic Gospels and Qumran.

87350 PANAZOL
(France)

N° Imprimeur : 5057060-05
Dépôt légal : Juin 2005